PARTISANS

PARTISANS

The Conservative Revolutionaries Who
Remade American Politics in the 1990s

NICOLE HEMMER

BASIC BOOKS
New York

Basic Books

Hachette Book Group

1290 Avenue of the Americas, New York, NY 10104

www.basicbooks.com

Printed in the United States of America

First Edition: August 2022

Published by Basic Books, an imprint of Perseus Books, LLC, a subsidiary of Hachette Book Group, Inc. The Basic Books name and logo is a trademark of the Hachette Book Group.

The Hachette Speakers Bureau provides a wide range of authors for speaking events. To find out more, go to www.hachettespeakersbureau.com or call (866) 376-6591.

The publisher is not responsible for websites (or their content) that are not owned by the publisher.

Print book interior design by Linda Mark.

Library of Congress Cataloging-in-Publication Data

Names: Hemmer, Nicole, author.

Title: Partisans : the conservative revolutionaries who remade American politics in the 1990s / Nicole Hemmer.

Description: First edition. | New York : Basic Books, [2022] | Includes bliographical references and index. |

Identifiers: LCCN 2021057105 | ISBN 9781541646889 (Hardcover) | ISBN 9781541646872 (eBook)

Subjects: LCSH: Conservatism—United States—History—20th century. | Conservatism—United States—History—21st century. | Reagan, Ronald—Influence. | Buchanan, Patrick J. (Patrick Joseph), 1938-—Influence. | Political culture—United States. | United States—Politics and government—1989-

Classification: LCC E743 H38 2022 | DDC 320.520973/0904—dc23/eng/20220506

LC record available at https://lccn.loc.gov/2021057105

ISBNs: 9781541646889 (print), 9781541646872 (ebook)

LSC-C

Printing 1, 2022

For my mom

Contents

INTRODUCTION:
THE PUZZLE OF THE PARTISANS

THIS BOOK BEGAN WITH A PUZZLE.

In most accounts of twentieth-century politics, the victory of Ronald Reagan in 1980 marks a turning point, when the country shifted hard right after decades of liberal governance. His eight years in office were the crowning achievement for a group of conservative activists who had been trying to capture the presidency for decades. They had long been convinced they represented the vast majority of the American people, but election after election, the results at the polls had told a different story. Until Reagan.

Swept into office with overwhelming majorities—winning forty-four states in 1980 and forty-nine in 1984—Reagan provided proof of what the right had believed all along: if someone could advocate for conservatism cogently and charismatically, the hidden majority of conservative Americans would emerge. And so it began, the start of a new period in US history defined by the new president's conservative politics: the Reagan era.

Only . . . after a decade of studying Cold War conservatism, I saw those victories less as a beginning than as an end. Nearly as soon as Reagan left office, the conservative movement he represented began to rapidly evolve, skittering away from the policies, rhetoric, and even ideology that Reagan had brought into office. Republicans still had significant political power, and the 1990s were a conservative era, but with each passing year, conservatives looked less and less like Reagan, even as they invoked his name more and more.

Unpacking that puzzle required making sense of two things: Reagan's transformative effect on the conservative movement in the 1980s and the quick dissipation of the conditions that made the Reagan era possible.

In the 1980s, Reagan embodied a conservatism that was optimistic and popular, two things the American right had not been for most of the twentieth century. The Cold War conservatism that emerged in the 1950s had been born as a frustrated yawp from a group of activists, writers, and broadcasters convinced that the two major parties and most of the media in the United States were systematically shutting out their views. Some of their perspectives—like their belief that both the New Deal and communism represented an existential threat to the United States and should be wiped out, whatever the cost—had few adherents in the decades between the end of World War II and Reagan's election. Others— like their belief that society had a natural hierarchy, topped by white Christian men, that must be maintained—were deeply embedded in US culture and politics and would not begin to lose significant support until the 1960s and 1970s.

But when packaged together in the Cold War conservative movement, the right's blend of militant anticommunism, traditional social and racial hierarchies, and reduced government intervention in the economy had difficulty attracting a majority of voters in either party. In response, activists decided they needed to do more to unite conservatives and popularize their ideas. Activists who sought more mainstream acceptance also wrestled with how best to incorporate the more extreme elements of their movement, which provided a source of energetic foot soldiers but also made it easy to paint the right as a dangerous mix of kooks and revolutionaries, encompassing everyone from Ku Klux Klan members to wild-eyed Red hunters. Thus began a decades-long effort to build the media outlets, activist organizations, and think tanks that would become the backbone of the conservative movement.[1]

That effort to explain and expand conservatism was necessary not only because Cold War conservatives were in a distinct political minority but also because they were redefining the American right. Before the Cold War, what became known as the Old Right had distinctly different politics from what came after. It shared Cold War conservatism's antiunionism and anti–New Deal politics. But the Old Right, represented by people like Republican senator Robert Taft, newspaper publisher Robert E. Wood, and writer John T. Flynn, was also profoundly opposed to military intervention abroad, including US involvement in World War II. Nor did it embrace the idea of free markets, preferring instead a protectionist order that included extensive tariffs. A strain of the Old Right even opposed modern industrial capitalism, believing republicanism only thrived in an agrarian order. The Cold War, with its emphasis on the rhetoric of freedom and its tendency to redefine US politics in opposition to communism, fundamentally transformed the conservative movement.[2]

The Cold War right that replaced the Old Right was also obsessed with the presidency. That was in part a function of its outsider status. Movement conservatism in the early decades of the Cold War really was a distinct minority in both major parties: conservative segregationists were located in the Democratic Party, the home of New Deal liberalism, while the antiunion and economic libertarian faction of the Republican Party had to share power with moderate and liberal Republicans who had adapted to the New Deal order. Conservatives believed that if they could capture either party's presidential nomination—or, better yet, win the presidency outright—they would have lasting control of a major party and wield considerably more influence in national politics.[3]

The focus on the presidency also grew out of the specific circumstances of presidential politics in the 1950s. As the Old Right was giving way to Cold War conservatism, movement conservatives backed Robert Taft, the Ohio senator known as "Mr. Republican," for the GOP presidential nomination in 1952. When Dwight Eisenhower, a celebrity general with no previous party allegiance, won the nomination, conservatives felt cheated—and were convinced that liberal elites in the party had stolen the nomination from them. That formative experience shaped the founding of *National Review*, the conservative journal of opinion started by William F. Buckley Jr. in 1955. In its first issue, a writer blamed "a small band of Eastern financiers, international bankers and industrialists" for snatching the nomination from Taft.[4]

Again and again, right-wing activists sought alternatives to what they saw as moderate and liberal nominees: the third-party States' Rights candidacy of T. Coleman Andrews in 1956, the Republican primary boomlet for Arizona senator Barry Goldwater in 1960. In 1964, they finally succeeded, snagging the Republican nomination for Goldwater in a victory so profound that it triggered a party realignment: the Republican Party would become the home of the American right, welcoming conservative white Democrats, while the Democratic Party would grow increasingly liberal, becoming the party not just of economic liberals but of Black civil rights activists, feminists, and gay rights groups.[5]

Goldwater's dramatic loss to President Lyndon Johnson—the largest popular-vote defeat in nearly 150 years—obscured the radical change the Republican Party was undergoing. Four years later, movement conservatives and the Republican Party seemed to have struck a truce of sorts: activists like Buckley embraced Richard Nixon's candidacy as "good enough." He wasn't as conservative as they would like, but he was attentive to the movement, even bringing aboard writer Pat Buchanan, a young right-wing firebrand, as an ambassador between the administration and the movement. Still, other conservatives remained suspicious of Nixon, opting instead for George Wallace, the segregationist governor of Alabama whose third-party candidacy drew 13.5 percent of the popular vote in the general election.[6]

That split vote left Nixon with a tiny victory in 1968; he squeaked into the presidency with just five hundred thousand more votes than his Democratic rival, Vice President Hubert Humphrey. But running for reelection in 1972, Nixon showed what a consolidated center-right candidacy could do. Claiming to represent the "silent majority" of Americans who opposed antiwar activism and the late-1960s liberation movements, he won reelection over liberal icon George McGovern with over 60 percent of the popular vote and a historic 520–17 Electoral College victory. Nixon might have been a compromise candidate for the right, but for movement conservatives looking for a sign that their hidden-majority theory was correct, his win was promising.

The rest of the 1970s were a mixed bag for the movement. While wave after wave of new recruits replenished the ranks of the right thanks to the social movements of the era—the decade churned with activism against school integration, feminism, abortion, and taxation—at the presidential level, things were less promising. Nixon resigned in disgrace in 1974 during the Watergate scandal (exiting less than a year after his more conservative vice president Spiro Agnew resigned in disgrace over a scandal of his own). The new president, Gerald Ford, was more moderate and made Nelson Rockefeller, a liberal Republican, his vice president. The right hated Rockefeller, seeing him as part of the party's liberal elite leadership, which they had been trying to overthrow for decades. Reagan, who had vied for the Republican presidential nomination in 1968, was inspired by this liberal turn to try again in 1976, but he was again defeated. For many movement conservatives, his defeat was the final indignity: they began agitating for a new party to replace the GOP.

Just as the right was turning its back on the Republican Party, the media infrastructure that movement conservatives had built to support their efforts seemed to be crumbling as well. Regnery Publishing, the right-wing company that had published nearly every conservative tract of the mid-twentieth century, closed up shop. Right-wing radio programs like the *Manion Forum* and the *Smoot Report*, which had been a vital part of conservative organizing, went off air in the 1970s. *National Review* subscription rates dropped 33 percent over the course of the decade, and things had gotten so dire at the right-wing newsletter *Human Events* in 1975 that the publisher had to ask readers for donations in addition to subscription payments in order to stay afloat.[7]

At this bleak moment, Ronald Reagan launched his third presidential bid, the one that would not only bring the conservative movement into the White House but pioneer the upbeat and popular variant of Cold War conservatism that would come to be known as Reaganism. Not everyone on the right rooted for Reagan in 1980—some felt he was too old, others that he was out of touch with the cultural issues energizing the base—but their criticisms had little impact, and he handily won the nomination and then the presidency.

Reagan was a conservative hard-liner. His policy positions were well to the right of, say, Nixon's, and he was committed to the notion of sharply lowering taxes and cutting nonmilitary federal budgets. He wanted to roll back both the New Deal and Lyndon Johnson's Great Society and believed he had the mandate to do so. But as ideological as Reagan's politics were, in office, he would often sacrifice them to make the more popular choice. The administration typically tested out his most dramatic notions as trial balloons, quickly popping them if public opinion soured. That pragmatism, combined with his charismatic and avuncular image, allowed Reagan to retain his popularity with a large majority of white Americans throughout his presidency.

Why, then, did much of the right move so quickly away from Reaganism and toward a more pessimistic, angrier, and even more revolutionary conservatism not long after his presidency?

As I began rooting around in the history of the 1990s—a history that, from my vantage point in the 2010s, was *barely* history—it became clear why the conservatism of the 1990s felt so different from what came before. The context had entirely changed. Most significantly, the Cold War had come to an end. For forty years, the geopolitical struggle between the Soviet Union and the United States, between communism and democracy, had been the central organizing theme of conservatism. It not only shaped the movement's approach to foreign policy, shaking the right from its midwestern noninterventionist roots, but influenced nearly every aspect of conservative ideology and argumentation: Why did freedom matter? Communism. Why did religion matter? Communism. How could support for an enormous military and security state be reconciled with a small-government ethos? Communism. The Cold War may not have created the different threads of modern conservatism, but it conditioned every one of them.

The political philosophy Reagan carried into office was deeply rooted in the Cold War. He laced his speeches with appeals to freedom and democracy, but his conservative understanding of those ideas also shaped his policies: a preference for more-open borders and higher immigration levels, for fewer tariffs and a stingier social safety net. Anticommunism, though, mattered more to him than democracy or small government. He wanted a sharp increase in military spending, a more aggressive posture toward the Soviet Union, and more extensive aid to right-wing illiberal regimes in places like South and Central America and southern Africa. With the Cold War over, those political ideas had to be rethought.

Domestic politics and culture had also changed. In 1994, after having been confined to the minority in the House for more than forty years, Republicans won united control of Congress. Dubbed the Republican revolution, it was revolutionary not only because it gave an especially conservative party legislative power but because it reoriented the movement away from the presidency and toward Congress. That shift had profound consequences. With a Democrat in the White House, congressional Republicans adopted a politics of destruction, concerned less with legislation than with investigation and obstruction.

The post-Reagan right also existed in a rapidly evolving media environment entirely unlike the one Reagan had to navigate. The old film-and-radio star had come into office in the waning days of the network television era, before the rise of cable news (CNN went on air in 1980 but would not become a twenty-four-hour news channel until the Gulf War in 1991). Right-wing talk radio was still only a local phenomenon; the internet existed, but web browsers did not. Conservative media outlets held sway within the movement—*National Review* and *Human Events* were two of Reagan's favorite publications—but they had little real influence within the Republican Party.

Over the course of the next decade, political media would radically change. By the end of the 1990s, there were three cable news networks, including one with overtly right-wing programming. Right-wing punditry had spread to every network and cable news outlet and also found a home on shows like Comedy Central's *Politically Incorrect*. With the national debut of *The Rush Limbaugh Show* in 1988, conservative talk radio had transformed into a powerful, profitable institution—one that exerted significant influence in Washington, DC, first in the George H. W. Bush White House and then among the new Republican majority in Congress. And fax trees, internet message boards, and conservative websites created new avenues for grassroots activists to spread ideas, strategies, and conspiracies.

But what did it all add up to? When I first started sorting through these puzzle pieces in 2014, I wasn't quite sure. The new conservatism still had Reagan's DNA—most Republicans called for lower taxes, deregulation, military supremacy, and the like—but it had made an evolutionary leap in the 1990s that I still couldn't account for. And the more I dug, the more confusing it became.

That's in part because so many of the trends of the 1990s seemed to point away from increased partisanship and toward pursuit of a more popular, palatable form of conservatism. Consider, for instance, the Ross Perot phenomenon in the 1990s. During the 1992 election, an independent billionaire with no party affiliation and no political experience swooped into the presidential race. Perot's politics did not map neatly onto any defined political faction. He was opposed to free trade deals and supported abortion rights, strict gun

control, and significant government reforms. His rhetoric was re-
flexively populist, regularly bashing the elites and the establishment
in favor of "the people" (though he was himself a billionaire many
times over who, aides said, brought an authoritarian management
style to his campaign). Despite conducting an erratic campaign,
Perot walked away with 19 percent of the vote, more than any other
third-party candidate in eighty years.

Voters, it seemed, were happy to dispense with party preferences, to "throw the hypocritical rascals out," as one Perot-friendly
organization put it. Commentators began to muse about a postpartisan era. After his impressive showing in the 1992 election,
both parties looked for ways to attract the Perot voter with government reforms and a push to balance the federal budget and reduce
the deficit, efforts that drew Republicans and Democrats closer
together. That bipartisanship was made even easier by the election
of Bill Clinton, a Democrat with a decidedly conservative bent. He
worked with congressional Republicans to pass a free trade agreement with Mexico and Canada and deep cuts to welfare. He even
began working with congressional leaders on a plan to privatize
Social Security.

And yet, despite this bipartisanship, the decade was also a period of intensifying partisan warfare, when Republicans grew less
tolerant of dissension in the ranks and began to view Democrats not
as opponents but as enemies.

Those changes happened during an era when conservatives were
racking up victory after victory. A dramatically more conservative
Republican Party took control of Congress in 1994 and maintained
its majorities for most of the next twelve years. The decade gave
rise to massively successful talk-radio stars, television pundits, and
best-selling authors. They pulled the Democratic Party sharply to
the right and managed to impeach a president for the first time in

124 years. And yet, in the 1990s, the sunny optimism of the Reagan era fell away, and grievance politics took over. Conservatives were in power, and they were furious.

That fury fueled a new right-wing populist movement, one helmed by Pat Buchanan, a conservative pundit who had served as an aide to Nixon, Ford, and Reagan. Though a Reaganite in the 1980s, by the early 1990s he had begun resuscitating the politics of the Old Right and grafting them on to the era's modern media culture. Insisting that both Democratic and Republican leaders had betrayed working people, he came out against the bipartisan consensus on free trade and overseas intervention. He fashioned grievance politics into an agenda: a border wall to keep out non-white immigrants from the south; an end to affirmative action and civil rights legislation; a rollback of commitments to the North Atlantic Treaty Organization (NATO), the United Nations, and the World Trade Organization. He did not run from his more extreme views on race, feminism, and sexuality. Instead, he made them cornerstones of his presidential campaigns of 1992, 1996, and 2000, evidence that he would always say what he believed, no matter how outrageous.

Buchanan may not have won the Republican nomination in any of his three bids, but he did make serious inroads with the party's base, exposing an instability within conservatism that would only grow in the years that followed as pundits and activists pulled the party hard to the right while criticizing any Republican official who failed to follow their lead. And his style—harsh, outrageous, un-compromising—would become the primary mode of politics on the right. There were alternatives, political figures like Representative Jack Kemp and General Colin Powell who offered a more upbeat and inclusive vision of conservatism, but the party would ultimately reject that vision in favor of a Buchananite partisanship.

Those were the puzzle pieces I was still sorting through when Donald Trump appeared on the scene. His quick rise to the top of the Republican presidential primary field sent people scrambling for answers. Explanations for his rise to the leadership of the Republican Party—and the country—were typically told as a story of a swift and utterly unexpected transformation. Almost overnight, the story went, the Republican Party, long a bastion of free markets, traditional morality, anticommunism, and democracy promotion, flipped: in a wink, it became the party of tariffs, Russian autocrats, America First, and xenophobia. The party's base, once thought to be conservative free traders and Christian traditionalists, inexplicably embraced a thrice-married real estate developer with a scandalous personal history and a notable absence of Republican pedigree. The GOP, it seemed, was now hostage to the whims of a cynical demagogue.

There was evidence to back up this story of an overnight conversion. Prior to Trump's candidacy, for example, the base toed the Reagan line on free trade, with 55 percent of Republicans favoring free trade agreements and only 36 percent opposing. Once Trump won the nomination, the GOP became a protectionist party overnight, splitting 61 to 32 percent against free trade. Similarly, support for Russia doubled among Republicans in a short period, springing from 22 percent in 2014 to 40 percent by mid-2018. Early in Trump's campaign, 17 percent of Republicans wanted to withdraw from NATO, while 48 percent wanted to remain; two years later, the split was 38 to 38 percent. So it went: with tariffs, with immigration, with executive power, with democracy. On issue after issue, the GOP traded Reagan for a version of conservatism not seen since the 1940s.[8]

Like many others, I was puzzling over these changes as I headed to Cleveland for the Republican National Convention in July 2016.

I was there as both a historian of conservatism and a commentator on contemporary politics: at the time I was an assistant professor of presidential studies at the University of Virginia and a contributing editor at *U.S. News & World Report*, writing a weekly column on US politics and the right. My book on the history of conservative media would be published a month later. And as I watched Trump accept the nomination in the Quicken Loans Arena while thousands of delegates cheered with unreserved delight, the puzzle pieces snapped into place. The party's transformation, sudden though it seemed, had been underway for a quarter century: in the turn toward nativism and a more overt racism, in the criticisms of conservative elites, in the wariness about free trade and democracy, in the sharp-elbowed, fact-lite punditry. And none of it had happened behind the scenes, hidden away only to be sprung on the American people when the right candidate rolled around. It had happened in plain sight. But too many people were too attached to the idea of the party of Reagan to notice.

Even though Trump helped the picture snap into focus, this book is not a prehistory of Trumpism. Instead, it is an exploration of how and why Reaganism, which in the 1980s seemed to be the future not only of the conservative movement but of US politics more broadly, collapsed so quickly. Just as importantly, it is a history of the partisans who, in the fluidity of the post–Cold War moment, seized the uncertainty of the rapidly evolving political landscape to accumulate political power, wealth, and fame. Though they made their political homes in a variety of institutions—think tanks, cable networks, Congress, political organizations—they all worked to develop a politics that was not just conservative but antiliberal, that leaned into the coarseness of American culture and brought it into politics, that valued scoring political points above hewing to ideological principles.

In doing so, these partisans blurred the lines between the mainstream conservative movement and a violent far right that was particularly active in the 1990s and was split between acts of domestic terrorism and efforts to worm its way into mainstream politics. They courted militias and palled around with white nationalists, funneling extremism into the newly powerful Republican Party. They found that their flirtations with extremism did not end their political careers but instead earned them a reputation for outrageousness that played well in the new media environment.

The story that emerges from these different strands fundamentally shifts our understanding of the politics of the 1990s. The decade, so often described as an era of *polarization*, was actually an era of right-wing *radicalization*. Even as the Democratic Party moved right, the Republicans moved even further, adopting what were once far-right positions on issues like guns and immigration and new procedural obstructions like extended government and impeachment.

Not all Republicans and not all conservatives were partisans in the 1990s. There were some who still clung to the politics of the Reagan era and others who warned that the party was headed in the wrong direction. Political leaders like Kemp and Powell argued for a more inclusive, less radical party.

But they were the outliers. By the turn of the century, the party belonged to the partisans.

CHAPTER ONE

THE REVOLUTION

T HE REAGAN REVOLUTION HAD ARRIVED, AND IT WAS off to a shaky start.

The dais in the ballroom of the Century Plaza Hotel in Los Angeles, where Ronald Reagan was delivering his victory speech, looked like the kind of stage where students at a small-town high school might present their spring production: small and spare, with a faded blue backdrop and tired burgundy curtains. A thin white banner tacked to the backdrop read "REAGAN-BUSH VICTORY '80." Even the players missed their cues: just as the president-elect was sharing the details of Jimmy Carter's concession phone call, two staffers ambled out on stage with a giant cake shaped like a map of the United States. They commandeered the microphone to reveal which states Ronald Reagan had won—almost all of them—and tipped the board up to show the cameras, sending the massive cake sliding to the edge. After they had rescued it and scrambled off the stage, Reagan, looking flummoxed, turned back to the microphone and quipped, "When that began to slide, I thought that maybe the world was going out just as I was coming in!"[1]

For many Carter voters, that image captured exactly what they were feeling—that the country was sliding toward imminent ruin now that Reagan had claimed the presidency. And he hadn't just eked out a win. He had beaten Carter by ten points, winning forty-four states and 489 electoral votes. It was more than a landslide—it was a political earthquake. For nearly fifty years, politics in the United States had been defined by the policies and legacies of the New Deal, marked by an active federal government, expansive and popular social programs, support for the poor and elderly, and economic regulation. Reagan now threatened to dismantle it all.[2]

Ironically, Reagan had spent the first half of his life as a New Deal Democrat. While his politics had started shifting to the right by the 1950s, it took decades for him to develop the blend of policies, ideology, and rhetoric that led him to that rickety stage in 1980. The tumultuous politics of the Cold War era transformed his politics, which were shaped first by the anxious anticommunism of the 1950s, then the domestic unrest of the 1960s, and finally the economic woes of the 1970s. Each decade left its imprint on Reagan, fashioning his politics into a distinct form of Cold War conservatism, something that commentators came to call Reaganism.

First emerging while Reagan was governor of California from 1967 to 1975, the word "Reaganism" came into common usage during his presidency, slipping seamlessly into the political lexicon without any of the friction that comes from precise definition. While it was often used as shorthand for Reagan's policies or for conservatism more generally, making Reaganism a useful term requires a bit more precision. If it simply referred to his ideology and policy preferences, Reaganism would be synonymous with conservatism. After all, Reagan's conservatism was not unique. It was the same blend of ideologies that movement conservatives had woven together over the previous decades: small-government libertarianism, social conservatism, and muscular anticommunism. Conservative activists never really found a way to resolve all the contradictions in their creed—small government, except when it came to the military or Red-hunting at home; social conservatism, except when libertarians wanted to be left alone; muscular anticommunism, except when it required foreign aid or higher taxes. So it should be no surprise that Reaganism was full of contradictions as well, and rhetoric and reality parted ways plenty of times.

Still, there was a definable Reaganism, one formed when Cold War conservatism was filtered through Reagan's personality, rhetoric, and experiences. Those were not superficial influences but decisive ones. For decades, movement conservatism had been intractably linked with Arizona senator Barry Goldwater, far-right groups like the conspiratorial John Birch Society, and frothing segregationists unable to come to terms with the success of the civil rights movement. Many Americans saw it as dour, hateful, and nutty. And while some Americans certainly saw Reagan as embodying all three of those traits, he persuaded a hefty majority of voters that he was something different.

He did that by infusing his politics with flexibility and optimism, making movement conservatism genuinely popular for the first time in the Cold War era. Pieces of his agenda had found popular support before he became president—the antitax craze hit California in the late 1970s, for instance—but as a governing philosophy, movement conservatism had trouble winning national majorities. Goldwater had lost in a landslide in 1964 running against Lyndon Johnson; Richard Nixon, who secured a landslide of his own in 1972, had courted conservatives but never been one of them.

Changing conditions enabled Reagan's majority-making politics. Rising crime rates, a stagnant economy, double-digit inflation, and military failures, though they happened under presidents from both parties, suggested that the New Deal order was in a state of collapse and persuaded millions of Americans to consider an alternative political philosophy. Reagan promised fixes to all these problems, offering simple solutions rooted in invocations of a glorious past. His rhetoric brimmed with appeals to freedom and democracy. And while those appeals were often just words, his belief in a particular kind of freedom shaped his commitment to policies like liberalizing trade and lowering barriers to immigration. That was a marked departure from previous Republican presidents like Richard Nixon and Gerald Ford, who instituted tariffs and wage and price controls while raising barriers to entry for migrants from Mexico.

Popular though he was, Reagan was not without his detractors. The opposition to his left made sense: promising to shrink government, slash taxes, gut welfare, and superheat the Cold War clashed with liberal commitments to the New Deal order and to the notion of détente. Detractors from his right, on the other hand, were more surprising. But by the 1970s, the New Right, a new iteration of the conservative movement that focused on grassroots activism and social issues, had become a powerful and well-organized force—and a source of endless critique of Reagan both during the 1980 campaign and throughout his time in office. Though the force of his popularity kept the New Right from making much headway while he was in the White House, its adherents used the years of his administration to set the stage for a full-on revolt against Reaganism that began as soon as a less-beloved Republican president took over.

REAGAN'S POLITICAL EVOLUTION neatly tracks the development of Cold War conservatism. The first iteration of his conservatism was forged though Hollywood Red-hunting, labor conflicts, and pro-business economics. Those battles set him on a path toward political activism, culminating in his support for Barry Goldwater's ill-fated presidential bid in 1964.

Few people could have imagined that the Reagan of the 1940s—a Hollywood studio star and active member of the Screen Actors Guild (SAG)—would became a key player in a conservative movement defined by its staunch opposition to labor and its targeted campaigns against the movie industry for suspected communist influences. The only US president to have served as a union president, Reagan led SAG from 1947 to 1952 (and during a brief stint from 1959 to 1960). His rise to the SAG presidency occurred just as the House Un-American Activities Committee (HUAC) had begun targeting the industry for investigation. Still a liberal Democrat at the time, Reagan wrestled with communism in Hollywood for nearly a decade. He resigned from one professional organization in 1946, believing it had become a communist front, and along with his first wife, Jane Wyman, became an informant, passing names of suspected communist sympathizers to the FBI. Reagan continued to pass information to the FBI as SAG president and in 1947 testified before HUAC as a friendly witness.[3]

Those were the actions of a liberal anticommunist, however, not a conservative one. By the late 1940s, anticommunism had consumed US politics and was well represented in both major political parties. Reagan believed that communists had infiltrated the unions and provoked the wave of strikes that wracked Hollywood and other industries after the war. And his conviction that he had been tricked and targeted by communist groups in Hollywood had sharpened his anticommunism. But he also believed persuasion and exposure, not government intervention, were the best response. He opposed outlawing the Communist Party, considering such a ban itself un-American, even as he supported exposing groups with communist ties and blacklisting individuals. "We have exposed their lies when we came across them," he told HUAC, "we have opposed their propaganda, and I can certainly testify that in the case of the Screen Actors Guild we have been eminently successful in preventing them from, with their usual tactics, trying to run a majority of an organization with a well-organized minority."[4]

That view separated Reagan from the conservative anticommunists of the era like William F. Buckley Jr., founder of the magazine *National Review*, who believed that both HUAC and its Senate counterpart, headed by Joe McCarthy, were vitally necessary and unconscionably smeared. And it separated him from those on the right who believed liberalism was simply one step toward communism—a view he understandably rejected, given that at the time he considered himself a "near-hopeless hemophilic liberal" who "bled for 'causes.'" It would take a few more years for Reagan's liberal anticommunism to harden into a Buckley-style conservative anticommunism.[5]

His pro-business, antiunion politics developed during his time at General Electric (GE). Hired by GE in 1952, he hosted *General Electric Theater*, a popular prime-time television show, and crisscrossed the country to speak at GE plants and private social clubs. During that time, he worked under Lemuel Boulware, GE's vice president of labor and public relations, who exposed Reagan to the works of economic conservatives like Henry Hazlitt and Milton Friedman. Reagan also signed up for the new magazine *National Review*, which he would read for the next four decades. As Reagan absorbed these works, he began crafting for himself a business-friendly conservatism that was increasingly antiunion and antigovernment—though not particularly socially conservative, as the divorced actor, while not known as a libertine, took a libertarian stance toward people's personal lives. His speeches outlined the greatest dangers to freedom—and the market—as collectivism, government regulation, and union power. By the late 1950s, his speeches also spoke to specific government policies, denouncing deficit spending, opposing tax increases, and attacking New Deal projects like the Tennessee Valley Authority.[6]

General Electric Theater made Reagan, according to one national survey, "one of the most recognized men in the country." But he was still known primarily for his acting, not his politics. That changed as he became more openly conservative and began to drift toward the Republican Party. In 1960 he campaigned as a Democrat for Nixon in his bid against John F. Kennedy for the presidency; in 1962, while campaigning in support of Nixon's gubernatorial run in California, he formally became a Republican. He compared his party switch not to a religious conversion—no Saul on the road to Damascus here—but to a sexual awakening. He likened buying copies of *National Review* off the newsstand to purchasing porn, joking that he bought his first issue in a plain brown wrapper, and often told audiences, "I know what it's like to pull the Republican lever for the first time, because I used to be a Democrat myself, and I can tell you it only hurts for a minute and then it feels just great."[7]

But in the 1950s and early 1960s, Reagan rarely joked about his politics. Few conservatives did. Right-wing activists were fighting to make conservatism something more than a fringe, out-of-fashion political ideology, and their main emotional weapons were fear and frustration directed at an overactive government, communist infiltrators, civil rights activists, and powerful labor unions. They finally found themselves at the center of US politics with Goldwater's nomination in 1964, which marked the first time a Cold War conservative had appeared on either party's presidential ticket. It felt like they had finally broken through—only to watch as Goldwater pursued a bungling campaign that reinforced the idea that he was an out-of-control extremist.

While a number of prominent moderate and liberal Republicans publicly broke with Goldwater, Reagan became an eager supporter. When he cut a campaign ad for Goldwater in September 1964, shortly before that year's election, he mirrored Goldwater's—and the movement's—anger. As the ad opened, Reagan perched on a stool, glared into the camera, and crossed his arms. "I asked to speak to you because I'm mad," he began. "I've known Barry Goldwater for a long time. When I hear people say he's impulsive and such nonsense, I boil over." It was probably not the best way to defend Goldwater, who had struggled throughout the campaign to convince Americans he was not a hot-headed fringe candidate. Rather than reassuring viewers, Reagan's scowling face made it seem like Goldwater's anger was catching.[8]

To be fair, finding the right way to defend Goldwater was not an easy task. He had a habit of speaking his mind, which, rather than conveying authenticity, tended to terrify people, because his mind contained ideas like using "small, conventional nuclear weapons" as part of regular warfare. When the sixty-second "mad" ad didn't move the needle, a month later, Reagan tried a different tack. In a thirty-minute spot that aired nationally on NBC, drawn from the speech he gave to all those GE audiences, he repackaged the conservative ideas animating the Goldwater race in an effort to make them more appealing—and to present himself as a more appealing messenger for the right.[9]

It was that Reagan, with the enthusiasm of a convert but more profane than preachy, who made the closing argument for Goldwater in 1964. His new anticommunist conservatism came into full view in the final version of what conservatives, and Reagan himself, came to call "The Speech." Reagan had been delivering The Speech, now often referred to by its title, "A Time for Choosing," in some form since 1960. In it, he spoke of a world divided between totalitarianism and democracy, slavery and freedom, in which the United States faced an existential threat. If Reagan had once seen liberalism as the bulwark against communism, he now understood it as the first step toward authoritarianism. The choice, he told his audience, was not between left and right but between up and down, up toward "the ultimate in individual freedom consistent with law and order, or down to the ant heap of totalitarianism."[10]

Reagan seemed to sense that the enemy abroad was not as useful as the enemy at home. If communism was the implied frame of The Speech, liberalism was its target. The evidence: he mentioned "government" forty-three times in thirty minutes—and communism not once. He opened by decrying the tax burden, the deficit, and the national debt, then spent most of his time attacking government spending to support everything from farm programs and housing to health care and Social Security. Full of pointed anecdotes and pithy turns of phrase, The Speech represented the emergence of Reagan the charismatic conservative. It raised $8 million for the Goldwater campaign—not enough to save him from the impending landslide defeat but enough to prove that when the dust cleared, Reagan would have a major role to play in the post-Goldwater movement.[11]

A LITTLE OVER a year later, in January 1966, Reagan starred in another thirty-minute political ad, one announcing his run for governor of California. Aired over fifteen local stations across the state, the commercial centered on the idea of a "creative society," one that would be unleashed by downsizing government. Here he trod carefully: rather than promising to slash taxes, he suggested they be "looked at"; rather than painting government as the enemy, he suggested it might be a junior partner to the businesses and people of California. Other than one offhand reference to Marxism, the ad showed no signs of its Cold War context. Though barely a year had passed since he spoke in soaring tones about a "rendezvous with destiny," he now took aim at more domestic concerns: property taxes, crime, drugs, and campus unrest.[12]

If the Reagan of 1964 had little to say about social issues, the Reagan of 1966 could talk about almost nothing else. In the intervening months, President Lyndon Johnson had vigorously pursued his Great Society. To the landmark Civil Rights Act, he added the Voting Rights Act and wholesale immigration reform, as well as a slew of new social and economic programs meant to alleviate poverty, promote racial equality, and expand access to health care and education. But that period also saw the start of a sharp rise in violent crime, student antiwar protests, and uprisings and unrest in cities across the United States.

Which is where Reagan saw his opportunity: linking the victories of the Great Society to the turmoil of the mid-1960s. In his run for governor, his primary target was what he called the permissive society, one in which, thanks to liberal politicians, criminals went unpoliced, welfare recipients grew addicted to government aid, and college students ran wild. That, he argued in his opening campaign ad, was the cause for all the social unrest Californians saw around them. Though he assured viewers that no feeling person could withhold help from those in need, he insisted that too much welfare was going to freeloaders who could work but chose not to. And his voice never grew sharper than when he lacerated a "noisy, dissident minority" for degrading the state's universities.[13]

Perhaps the most important line that captured the evolution of Reaganism was his complaint about crime. "Our city streets are jungle paths after dark," he warned, "with more crimes of violence than New York, Pennsylvania, and Massachusetts combined." The language of "jungle paths," a coded reference to Black crime, signaled a turn to law-and-order politics and colorblind racism—a racism that relied on neutral-sounding language to sell policies that disproportionately harmed nonwhite people—that would become a core component of Reaganism. His call to "untie the hands of our local law enforcement" pointed to the belief, one that would grow throughout the 1960s, that a permissive society had hamstrung law enforcement and the judiciary by elevating "criminals' rights" above "victims' rights."

Despite his assertion that the people deserved equal rights and should live free from discrimination, Reagan did not believe that the government had any role in making that happen. He opposed the Civil Rights Act, Voting Rights Act, and Fair Housing Act, the tent poles of antidiscrimination law in the 1960s. As governor he supported a ballot initiative that would allow housing discrimination, arguing, "If an individual wants to discriminate against Negroes or others in selling or renting his house, it is his right to do so." His arguments, though, were not limited to libertarianism; he called the Voting Rights Act "humiliating for the South," suggesting not just that it was wrong for the government to intervene but that recognizing the history of anti-Black discrimination in the region was an unnecessarily wounding blow to white southerners.[14]

The racial politics of law and order and discrimination, along with an emphasis on crime, riots, and student protest, showed how Reagan developed a social conservatism distinct from the single-issue activism that would emerge in the 1970s. That decade saw the rise of right-wing movements opposing issues like abortion, feminism, gay rights, and school desegregation. Yet, as governor, Reagan loosened abortion regulations, tightened gun restrictions, and supported the Equal Rights Amendment, a constitutional amendment that would bar discrimination on the basis of sex. That disconnect did not mean Reagan had abandoned conservatism. Rather, it showed that those issues had not yet become part of conservative orthodoxy.

Even as issues like abortion became political litmus tests—a shift Reagan helped accelerate in 1980 when he insisted his running mate, George H. W. Bush, drop his pro-abortion politics—the fissure between Reagan and this new set of right-wing movements, loosely organized as the New Right, continued, setting the stage for a rift in the conservative movement that would continue throughout Reagan's presidency.

A small group of political strategists who mobilized social conservatives in the 1970s and 1980s, the New Right had never been enamored of Reagan. Its founders, who included political operatives like Heritage Foundation cofounder Paul Weyrich, direct-mail innovator Richard Viguerie, and Conservative Caucus head Howard Phillips, had grown disillusioned with the Republican Party in the 1970s (Phillips, in fact, left the party in 1974). Like many conservatives, they saw Richard Nixon as too moderate and were aghast when his successor, Gerald Ford, chose Nelson Rockefeller, former governor of New York and avatar of the liberal northeastern Republican establishment, as his vice president in 1974.

These men believed that the future of the party lay in the social issues firing up activists across the nation. These emerging social issues, fueled by racial and religious conservatism, were electric. Part of a backlash to the civil rights movement and the New Left, they tapped a wellspring of fear, resentment, and anger that drove hundreds of thousands of white people, men and women, to rallies and protests across the country. "We organize discontent," as Phillips put it. And in particular, they organized the discontent of newly mobilized religious activists by framing disparate social issues as part of a cohesive set of morality politics. Weyrich, the thin-faced, sharp-featured religious conservative in the New Right's leadership, coined the term "moral majority" to describe this upswell of activism, drawing like-minded preachers like Jerry Falwell and Pat Robertson into the coalition.[15]

If morality was the New Right's theme, resentment was its emotion. Richard Viguerie, who had made his fortune targeting Goldwater voters with direct-mail advertising, understood that almost instinctively. Providing direct-mail services to George Wallace's campaign in the early 1970s, Viguerie grew increasingly excited about the ardent segregationist. "I'm realizing as each day goes by that George Wallace and I have more in common than I thought," he told *New York* magazine in 1975. "I'd like to see less government in people's lives than Wallace does, but when it comes to social issues, we're together." But it wasn't just Wallace's stances on things like busing, policing, schools, and pornography that attracted Viguerie. It was his style: his anger, his invective, his clear sense of who the enemy was. And for Viguerie, that was good for business. "In an ideological cause like this, people give money not to win friends, but to defeat enemies," he said, laying out a philosophy that would leach from the world of direct mail into right-wing politics more broadly in the 1990s.[16]

While Reagan would become the unintended beneficiary of much of the New Right's activism—the activists it helped organize would become enthusiastic supporters of his presidential run in 1980—the leaders of the New Right showed only passing interest in the California governor. When the 1976 presidential election rolled around, many in the New Right were more interested in

Wallace, even though Reagan provided a conservative alternative to Ford within the Republican Party. Ford was no liberal, but he looked quite moderate compared to Reagan, who pledged to slash the federal budget and rethink Social Security, while attacking a group he called "welfare queens." Yet Reagan also understood he would need moderate Republicans to win the nomination. So, in an effort to unseat Ford at the convention, he pledged to choose a moderate Republican as his running mate. The New Right recoiled in disgust: it wanted technicolor conservatives, not pale-pastel imitations.[17]

New Right frustrations with Reagan grew in the years that followed, particularly after Reagan came out against Proposition 6 in California. The initiative would have made it legal not only to fire teachers for being gay but also to fire any teacher who spoke in support of gay rights. The vicious campaign, which echoed singer turned antigay activist Anita Bryant's successful efforts to repeal Miami's employment protections for gay workers, compared same-sex attraction to bestiality and child rape. It had the full support of people like Falwell and much of the New Right but met with stiff opposition from Reagan, who swatted it down from every angle. The initiative was unnecessary and costly, Reagan the pragmatist argued, while Reagan the libertarian insisted it was an infringement on privacy and constitutional rights. He made clear he was not offering broad support to gay Californians—"I don't approve of teaching a so-called gay life-style in our schools," he said in his statement opposing the initiative—but he worried about the initiative's "potential for real mischief."[18]

Though a newly organized part of the conservative coalition, the New Right rapidly established institutions and media outlets that would help it wield political power in the 1970s and 1980s. Those included the Heritage Foundation, a think tank established by Paul Weyrich in 1973; the Conservative Caucus, an advocacy group created by Howard Phillips in 1974; the National Conservative Political Action Committee, an innovative money group founded in 1975 that figured out how to funnel millions in independent expenditures to conservative candidates without violating campaign laws; and the Moral Majority, Jerry Falwell's religious right organization created in 1979.

These organizations provided space for the New Right to build its political identity—one distinct from Reagan's—and its independence within the movement. So when the 1980 Republican primaries rolled around, the New Right was on the hunt for a candidate to the right of Reagan. It landed first on Phil Crane, the forty-nine-year-old Illinois representative who had Reagan's leading-man looks, though not his Hollywood history. Since the early 1970s, Crane had worked closely with New Right leaders like Weyrich, then a congressional aide, to establish the Republican Study Committee, the conservative caucus in the House, which Crane chaired throughout the 1970s and 1980s. When Crane dropped out early in the 1980 primary, the New Right shifted its support to John Connally, the former Texas governor and treasury secretary who had become a Republican just a few years earlier. Only once Connally lost to Reagan in South Carolina did New Right leaders begrudgingly fall in line—and then, only until Reagan won the presidency.[19]

The support for alternatives put the New Right at odds with much of the Republican Party. Reagan had led polls of possible candidates for the 1980 nomination throughout 1979, with only former president Ford and former CIA director George H. W. Bush providing any real competition. Bush squeaked out a victory in the Iowa caucuses, but Reagan quickly bounced back and secured the nomination. The Republican Party leadership, which had fought so hard to avoid conservative capture of the party in the 1964 election, saw far less danger in Reagan's nomination.

That was due in part to Reagan and in part to changes that had fundamentally transformed the GOP and US politics. Reagan's folksy rhetoric, Hollywood charisma, and bright-side attitude were worlds apart from Goldwater's dour apocalypticism. And the party's base had shifted firmly to the right in the intervening sixteen years, as the Great Society foundered and the post–World War II economic boom finally petered out. When it became clear that Reagan would win the nomination, John Anderson, a Republican representative from Illinois, launched an independent bid for president. His campaign attracted a chunk of moderate Republicans who could not stomach voting for a staunch conservative like Reagan. He captured 6.6 percent of the popular vote, a respectable showing for an independent candidate. But Reagan still walked away with more than 50 percent of the popular vote, burying President Jimmy Carter in a landslide and demonstrating just how popular Reagan, and Reaganism, could be.

A FEW HOURS before Reagan ambled onto that makeshift stage in Los Angeles on Election Night 1980, President Jimmy Carter made his way to a podium at the Sheraton Hotel in Washington, DC, to concede the race. "I promised you four years ago that I would never lie to you," he reminded his supporters, his face stretched into a pained grimace. "So, I can't stand here tonight and say it doesn't hurt." He understood that his overwhelming loss reflected not simply a preference for Reagan but a rejection of him. Even though he'd had the better part of a day to come to terms with the defeat—his pollster Pat Caddell had told him overnight that they were expecting at least an eight-point loss—the sheer size of Reagan's victory seemed to overwhelm him.[20]

But then, the presidency itself had seemed to overwhelm Carter. He had inherited a crush of intractable problems. By the time he came into the White House, inflation and the oil crisis had eaten away at Americans' earnings, while Watergate and the war in Vietnam had eaten away at their faith in American institutions. The surge in violent crime that began in the 1960s continued unabated. Severe fiscal crises fueled by white flight and deindustrialization left several US cities on the brink of bankruptcy. The international scene was no better: if the Cold War had once presented an existential threat to the United States, it had also provided a sense of purpose and moral clarity. Thanks to the policy of détente, the threat had eased, but the loss in Vietnam and agitation over the apartheid regimes in America's Cold War allies of South Africa and Rhodesia had muddied the moral waters around US involvement abroad. Throughout his four-year presidency, Carter often seemed outmatched by these broad historical forces.

While Carter struggled to address these challenges, Reagan swooped in with simple explanations and clear, if fantastical, solutions, from deep tax cuts that would magically refill government coffers to reheating the Cold War in order to win a final victory over communism. It was a vision that showed how the events of the previous decade had influenced his presidential aspirations. If his governorship had been shaped by the sense that the 1960s had gone too far—an excess of civil rights, protests, and government aid—his presidency would be shaped by the sense that the 1970s had delivered too little: too little patriotism, too little strength, too little vision, too little hope. Reagan was convinced that his landslide victory had given him a mandate to infuse the United States with all those things, as well as to enact the conservative philosophy that he had developed over the past three decades.

In the campaign and during his two terms as president, Reagan clarified the qualities that made Reaganism distinct from Cold War conservatism. Part of it was attitudinal. Reagan has long been considered an optimist, a trait held up as a defining feature of his presidency. And he was. This attitude set him apart from the anger, fear, and resentment that had fueled the conservative movement of the 1960s and 1970s, including the New Right. It also separated him from the sense of national decline that dragged on the country in the 1970s. "They say that the United States has had its day in the sun, that our nation has passed its zenith," he said in his 1980 acceptance speech. "They expect you to tell your children that the American people no longer have the will to cope with their problems; that the future will be one of sacrifice and few opportunities. My fellow citizens, I utterly reject that view." Beaming out at the audience, Reagan brought the convention to its feet with that line, promising a brighter future if only Americans would consent to a change in leadership.[21]

As that line suggests, optimism was as much a political tool as a personal quality. And it was a core component of Reaganism. During his presidency, his optimism colored both his vision for a bright future and his longing for a nostalgic past, making Reaganism a place where wishful thinking met wistful thinking. Such optimism often tipped over into a stubborn unwillingness to reckon honestly with the past or deal frankly with the limits or downsides of his policies. That could be seen in his support for supply-side economics, which held that large tax cuts for wealthy Americans and corporations would rapidly expand the economy and return dividends to lower- and middle-class Americans. Reagan had learned that economic philosophy from its main proponents, journalist Jude Wanniski, economist Arthur Laffer, and Republican representative Jack Kemp. Their tutelage filled him with a blithe certitude that slashing taxes for the wealthy would expand the tax base so dramatically that government revenue would actually grow (it did not; the Reagan years saw exploding deficits).[22]

That sunny-side approach to politics also infused Reaganism with a kind of blindness to the lingering consequences of past wrongdoing. This was especially clear in his opposition to affirmative action, a key part of the colorblind racism that defined Reaganism. Reagan seized on affirmative action, as many on the right did, as evidence that the civil rights movement had moved on from the noble quest for equality of opportunity to the pernicious pursuit of what the right labeled "reverse racism." That interpretation, which required Reagan to ignore that he had opposed the "noble" civil rights legislation of the 1960s, presented racism and Black oppression as a problem that had already been solved. It also allowed Reagan to argue that white Americans were the victims of new civil rights legislation.

No one pursued the administration's opposition to affirmative action more forcefully than William Bradford Reynolds, whom Reagan appointed to head the Civil Rights Division at the Department of Justice. Reynolds, who served all eight years, carried out a public relations campaign against affirmative action, which he referred to as "reverse discrimination."[23] Calling affirmative action "morally wrong," Reynolds not only denounced efforts like targeted hiring and minority recruitment programs but served as the bulwark within the administration against any sort of compromise, challenging everyone from Clarence Thomas, then head of the Equal Employment Opportunity Commission (EEOC), to Reagan himself whenever he felt they were softening on the policy. Yet, while the administration argued that its opposition to affirmative action was an extension of its commitment to the Civil Rights and Voting Rights Acts of the mid-1960s, it actually targeted those as well. During Reagan's time in office, steep cuts to the EEOC budgets led it to eliminate 12 percent of its staff, limiting enforcement efforts for civil rights violations. At the same time, the administration fought to water down the 1982 reauthorization of the Voting Rights Act, arguing that violations should require proving *intent* to discriminate rather than simply showing discriminatory outcomes. (The administration lost that battle.)[24]

Another feature of Reaganism was an ideological flexibility that allowed Reagan to stay popular. Though he embraced a constellation of conservative ideas and policies that shaped his agenda, when he faced too much pushback and risked losing public support, he would abandon right-wing policies in favor of the status quo.

That ideological flexibility showed in his approach to racial politics. In effecting his own southern strategy, Reagan understood that he had to find a way to appeal to those who had flocked to segregationist George Wallace in 1968 without alienating the more moderate suburbanites who bristled at overt racist appeals, which a growing number of white suburban voters considered somewhere between impolite and offensive. So Reagan adopted a dog-whistle strategy, signaling to Wallace voters that he would look out for them, while maintaining plausible deniability of his motives. During the campaign, that strategy landed him in Neshoba County, Mississippi, not far from where three civil rights workers had been murdered in 1964, to give a speech in defense of "states' rights." Similar high-pitched invocations of racism ran through Reagan's rhetoric about "welfare queens" and "young bucks" using food stamps to buy expensive steaks, an appeal to white grievance that also helped blend anti-Black politics into antigovernment politics.[25]

That effort to thread the needle between hard-line conservatism and popular appeal had defined his tenure as governor and would follow him into the White House. Ideological flexibility reshaped his most defining policies: tax cuts and Soviet engagement. On the campaign trail and even in his early days as president, Reagan held firm to radical ideas about both the economy and the Cold War. He wanted to slash taxes to the bone as part of his supply-side theory of economics, and he wanted to abolish communism through an aggressive approach to the Soviet Union.

Soon after taking office, he put his economic plans into action. On a foggy August morning at Rancho del Cielo, his private retreat in California that also served as a tax shelter, he signed into law one of the largest tax cuts in US history. After those massive tax cuts, combined with enormous growth in the military budget, ballooned the deficit, Reagan went back to the bargaining table. A year later, he was back at Rancho del Cielo signing a bill to raise taxes by $98.3 billion over the next three years (unlike a year earlier, journalists were barred from witnessing the second signing ceremony). Reagan would raise taxes again in 1984 in an effort to get deficits under control. Ultimately the two bills would raise more revenue than any other peacetime tax hikes in history.[26]

The same shift happened in foreign policy. Once it became clear that his apocalyptic rhetoric toward the Soviet Union was pushing the two nations closer to conflict, Reagan pivoted toward diplomacy. In January 1984, he outlined his softened approach, calling for "a policy of credible deterrence, peaceful competition and constructive cooperation" and even then downplaying deterrence in favor of cooperation and peace. He regularly engaged with Soviet leaders, though he grew frustrated that they kept dying on him (three died in the span of four years). The arrival of Mikhail Gorbachev—at fifty-four, a much younger, more forward-looking leader than the Soviet Union had had in some time—led to a policy of engagement that resulted in new treaties and, ultimately, Reagan's declaration at the Kremlin in 1988 that his attacks on "the evil empire" were the product of "another time, another era."[27]

The Cold War dominated far more than just US-Soviet relations. It was the atmosphere of the Reagan presidency, shaping
nearly every aspect of his foreign and domestic policies. Its influence
was most clear in the ways he wielded ideas of freedom and democracy, not just as ideas but as the motivation and justification for
his policymaking, often with perverse results. Anticommunism, for
instance, excused antidemocratic activities throughout the administration's foreign policy: the decision to evade congressional restrictions on aid to the Contras in Nicaragua, a scandal so breathtaking
in its scope that it surpassed Watergate in terms of its deceit and
corruption; the decision to prop up the racist apartheid regime in
South Africa in the face of calls for self-government; and support
for Ferdinand Marcos's dictatorship in Philippines, even as Marcos
tried to steal an election.

But as empty as the rhetoric of freedom and democracy appeared on the world stage, it had a genuine impact on how Reagan viewed other policy areas like immigration and trade. Reagan
believed in the ideas of free trade and free movement and saw an
openness to immigration as a bedrock value of the treasured "city
on the hill" philosophy he promoted frequently as president. In his
1979 campaign announcement, he proposed a "North American
Accord," a common market created by the removal of high tariffs
between the United States, Canada, and Mexico. Though leaders in
both Canada and Mexico expressed skepticism about the idea, wor-
rying that it would simply expand the economic dominance of the
United States, Reagan eventually negotiated a free trade agreement
with Canada, which would ultimately be replaced with the North
American Free Trade Agreement in the 1990s.[28]

Reagan also saw the free movement of people as part of the democratic ideal. He bristled at the idea of a border wall, arguing in 1980,
"You don't build a nine-foot fence along the border between two

friendly nations." An early draft of the speech, which emphasized even more clearly the connection with the Cold War, read, "We cannot erect a Berlin Wall across the southern border." He spoke about immigration, including undocumented migrants, in emotional, aspirational terms. "We are talking here not just about statistics but human beings, families, and hopes and dreams for a better life." While the 1986 immigration bill he signed into law did include more sanctions on employers who hired those in the country without authorization, it also granted amnesty and a path to citizenship to millions of people living and working in the United States.[29]

The Cold War framework did not always translate into an embrace of immigrants and refugees. Reagan brought an anticommunist, not human rights, view to foreign policy. Because he was unwilling to acknowledge atrocities committed by right-wing anticommunist governments in El Salvador and Guatemala, for instance, the administration refused to recognize refugees from those countries. But Reagan maintained the rhetoric of freedom even as he at times ignored its implications.[30]

At a naturalization ceremony in 1984, Reagan spoke at length about freedom, which he saw as the pull factor that drew immigrants to the United States, a notion of a piece with his determined belief in American exceptionalism. But he also shared his belief that immigration benefited the United States as well, not only economically but with the infusion of new cultures, ideas, and experiences. "So, you know, every now and then academics talk about assimilation and how our various ethnic groups have, with time, dropped their ethnicity and become more 'American,'" he said. "Well, I don't know about that. It seems to me that America is constantly reinventing what 'America' means. We adopt this country's phrases and that country's art, and I think it's really closer to the truth to say that America has assimilated as much as her immigrants have. It's made for a delightful diversity, and it's made us a stronger and a more vital nation."[31]

While Reagan espoused a shallow view of diversity, found in a new word or cultural artifact, he had come to embrace the idea that diversity represented a positive good for the United States. He saw the political value in it as well: he relished appointing the first woman to the Supreme Court and readily pointed to the (admittedly few) high-ranking nonwhite officials in his administration—even if he could not recognize his Black cabinet member on sight, mistaking his secretary of housing and urban development, Samuel Pierce, for a Black mayor he was supposed to be meeting.[32]

Reagan's pro-diversity, pro-freedom, pro-democracy language, developed as part of his Cold War perspective, underscored another defining quality of Reaganism: its conflation of popularity and democracy. Reagan trumpeted majoritarian democracy as a cornerstone of US governance—and why not? His back-to-back landslide wins told him that he, and possibly his approach to government, had the broad support of the American people. When he left office in 1989, he had the highest approval rating of any outgoing president since World War II. Popular democracy seemed to have worked pretty well for him.

Majoritarian democracy may not sound like something so unusual for an American president to embrace, but the conservative movement had treated it with suspicion for decades. Rooted in the suppression of Black majorities in some parts of the South, support for minority rule appeared in the pages of National Review and in the rallies for Barry Goldwater. The claim that the United States is "a republic, not a democracy" gained popularity in the 1960s in response to the democratic rumblings of the Black freedom struggle. But with the rise of Richard Nixon's "silent majority" and his and Reagan's massive electoral victories, conservative majoritarianism was having a moment.

Reagan's popularity had limits, though, and even during his presidency the seams of conservative majoritarianism were starting to show. He was deeply unpopular with Black Americans, winning just 14 percent of their vote—which, while the highest a Republican presidential candidate had earned in two decades, was still meager. Only around one in four Latinos voted for Reagan, according to a 1981 analysis by the Southwest Voter Registration Education Project. The 1980 race was also the first in which a sustained partisan gender gap appeared, with women favoring the Democratic Party and men the Republican Party. While Reagan spoke about an inclusive conservatism, not many nonwhite Americans felt included in his vision. But while he was in office, the overwhelming support he received from white Americans ensured that his overall support remained high.[33]

Popularity also guided Reagan's policy choices. He did not want to be associated with unpopular policies, so he often either hid them in the bureaucracy or dropped them altogether when backlash began to build. After the administration cut funding for school lunches by 40 percent in 1981, public outcry and ridicule followed. Noting that children were now allotted four ounces of milk instead of six and that a squeeze of ketchup counted as a serving of vegetables, Richard Cohen at the *Washington Post* wrote, "The spirit of Marie Antoinette infuses the administration of Ronald Reagan." Reagan, embarrassed, suggested that someone deep in the bureaucracy must be trying to sabotage him and that he'd canceled the cuts. None of this was true: the cuts were part of the president's agenda and were not canceled, simply scaled back. But he could not abide the backlash.[34]

The same was true of the massive deficits that accompanied Reagan's tax cuts. In theory, he would have coupled the lowered taxes with significant spending cuts to major programs, perhaps making

Social Security voluntary, as he recommended before running for president, or dismantling Medicare and Medicaid, programs he had railed against as "socialized medicine." But the programs were popular, and the one time Reagan tried to touch Social Security—floating the idea in 1981 that the government should significantly reduce payments for those who retired between ages sixty-two and sixty-five—even his advisors recognized the idea's toxicity. They forced the head of Health and Human Services to announce it rather than Reagan and abandoned the bureaucrat when the backlash began. The Senate later voted 96–0 against any cuts for early retirement, and Reagan once again pretended to oppose his own idea.[35]

Unwilling to cut any popular spending programs, Reagan instead went after programs for the poor, including food stamps and Medicaid. While those programs helped support millions of impoverished Americans, they made up such a small portion of government spending that the cuts, though devastating to those who relied on the programs, did little to reduce the rate of government spending. So during the Reagan era, deficits grew. This infuriated David Stockman, his head of the Office of Management and Budget, a doctrinaire deficit hawk who joined the administration believing Reagan really did want to cut the budget. After Stockman resigned in disgust, he publicly excoriated Reagan, writing a book in 1986 titled *The Triumph of Politics: How the Reagan Revolution Failed.* "There is a startling disconnection between Reagan the campaigner, the scourge of big government, and Reagan the chief executive officer of the American government," he said in an interview with *Omni* magazine. "There's no consistent, credible or serious intellectual content to Reaganism, only a very popular kind of rhetoric—and by content I mean ideas, a sense of reality and facts."[36]

Stockman was right that Reaganism was "a very popular kind of rhetoric," but it was a rhetoric that shaped policies and defined the Reagan presidency. It was the unique fingerprint of a presidency at the tail end of the Cold War, molded by more than three decades' worth of anticommunist ideas, antiliberal politics, and new conservative policy experiments. It was rooted in the broader conservative movement but also distinct from it, defined far more by its optimism, popularity, and ideological flexibility. One of the clearest indications that Reaganism was not synonymous with conservatism came from conservatives themselves, who were divided on the Reagan presidency. The New Right in particular railed against the administration, howling over the betrayals meted out by the White House. Though Reagan would later become a conservative saint, during his years in office, for many on the right, he was the god that failed.

But if Reagan divided conservatives, his successor in the Oval Office would bring them back together—united in their belief that George H. W. Bush was the man who betrayed the Reagan revolution.

CHAPTER TWO

THE APOSTATE

TWO EVENTS IN 1989 SWIFTLY UNSETTLED THE
right's tenuous consensus on Reaganism: in January,
Ronald Reagan left the presidency, and in November, the
Cold War came to a sudden end. The two forces that held together
the Reagan coalition shuffled offstage, one after another. And the
man overseeing the transition was the one least suited, by temperament and politics, to hold the fragile, fracturing coalition together:
George H. W. Bush.

The New England blue blood turned Texas oilman who served
as Reagan's vice president embodied the broader transformation
happening in the Republican Party. Over the course of the 1960s
and 1970s, the base of party leadership shifted from wealthy East
Coast elites who tended to be political moderates to wealthy Sunbelt elites who were far more conservative. Bush reluctantly made
that same transition. In 1980, when he joined the ticket, he dropped

his support for abortion rights and vowed to back Reagan's agenda. Yet, while he fully embraced Reagan's program as his running mate and then vice president, he never won the right's trust—and never cared much for them, either.

In conservative lore, Bush was the wimpy, whimpering end of the Reagan revolution. He was everything Reagan was not: taciturn, moderate, uncharismatic, indecisive, weak. But if the men diverged in their styles, their politics as president were actually quite similar. Bush, whose decisive election margins in 1988 were only slightly smaller than Reagan's in 1980, spoke about freedom and democracy in the aftermath of the Cold War as forcefully as Reagan did in the midst of it. He touted free markets, securing support for the North American Free Trade Agreement (NAFTA), and flexed US military might, assembling a multinational coalition to repel the Iraqi invasion of Kuwait in the first major military action of the post–Cold War era.

And the things the right loathed about Bush were the very things that they had criticized about Reagan. Negotiating with the Soviets, appointing moderate Supreme Court justices, raising taxes—both Reagan and Bush stood guilty of these conservative heresies. Even the charge of weak leadership applied to both men, though the right saw it as an innate flaw in Bush—"the wimp factor," as *Newsweek* called it—and an external problem for his predecessor, one that could be cured if aides "let Reagan be Reagan."[1]

Yet most conservatives portrayed Bush's presidency as a betrayal of Reaganism, not a continuation of it. For New Right leaders and others who had been critical of Reagan during his presidency, that approach allowed them to do two things: to build a broader co-alition for their complaints about Reaganite governance without criticizing Reagan himself and to rescue Reagan from his record, helping to construct the Reagan mythology that would become a key component of post–Cold War conservatism, even as Reagan-ism itself faded away.

————

BEFORE THE NEW Right sharpened its teeth on Bush, it cut them on Reagan.

For eight long years, leaders of the New Right hammered away at Reagan. They were always ready with a snarling soundbite whenever journalists rang them up. Three weeks into the first term, direct-mail guru Richard Viguerie griped to a group of clergy, "I knew conservatives would get the short end of the stick. I just didn't know it would be this short." When Reagan nominated Sandra Day O'Connor to the Supreme Court, they wailed. When he appointed Jim Baker as his chief of staff, they gnashed their teeth. When he agreed to a tax hike after his historic tax cut emptied government coffers . . . well, almost all conservatives opposed that. But for the New Right, it was a sign that whatever conservatism Reagan had professed, he had not brought it with him to the White House. Viguerie's magazine, *Conservative Digest*, ran a story in July 1982 whose headline asked, "Has Reagan Deserted the Conservatives?" (The answer was yes.) And he told whomever he could in 1984 that the New Right was keen to find someone to challenge Reagan in 1984, a project that ultimately went nowhere.[2]

On social issues in particular, the New Right felt the Reagan administration placated its supporters with lots of pretty words but little actual policy. Reagan voiced his support for two amendments, one to restore school prayer and the other to ban abortion, but devoted little political capital to passing either. He instead used the proposed amendments to unite the Christian right, which began the administration fractured on the question of school prayer (the Southern Baptists opposed the initiative, fearing that schools that were allowed to mandate school prayer would infringe on their religious freedom). The administration's lobbying efforts not only brought the Southern Baptist Convention around on the question of school prayer but helped secure the place of white religious conservatives in the Republican Party—even though the school prayer amendment failed by eleven votes in the Senate and the antiabortion amendment never got off the ground. Nor did the administration deliver the death knell to affirmative action as the New Right wanted. They even thought Reagan was too sympathetic to people suffering from HIV and AIDS, and they were appalled when his surgeon general recommended the use of condoms and sex education to help slow the epidemic.[3]

When it came to foreign policy, the New Right threw even harder punches, especially when it came to Reagan's approach to the Soviet Union. Newt Gingrich, a young history professor turned Georgia representative who in the 1980s was steadily working his way up the Republican leadership ladder in the House, came out swinging when Reagan announced his first summit with new Soviet leader Mikhail Gorbachev in 1985. Never one for rhetorical restraint, Gingrich called it "the most dangerous summit for the West since Adolf Hitler met with Chamberlain in 1938 at Munich."[4]

When Reagan went a step further and agreed to limited disarmament as part of the Intermediate-Range Nuclear Forces (INF) Treaty, conservative critics were apoplectic. New Right leader Howard Phillips denounced Reagan as "a useful idiot for Soviet propaganda," while fellow activist Paul Weyrich called him "a weakened president, weakened in spirit as well as clout." They argued that he had been co-opted by the Washington establishment, abandoning the people and the principles that had put him in office in two consecutive landslide elections. (They did not note that the INF Treaty was immensely popular, with 80 percent of Americans supporting

his approach to the Soviet Union in the last year of his presidency.)
Reagan sat for interviews with New Right outlets like the *Conservative Digest* and spent time in private conversations with its leaders,
but it did little good. They were already turning their eyes to the
1988 race.[5]

That search for a new candidate was shaped by a sense that the
problem wasn't just, or even primarily, Reagan but Reaganism. All
the features of Reaganism that had fueled two landslide victories
had become liabilities in the New Right's eyes: the optimism, the
popularity, the pragmatism. The Heritage Foundation, founded by
Weyrich in 1973, charged that Reagan was "a prisoner of his optimism": rather than do the hard work of cutting government spending, he pinned his hopes on the magical higher revenues that tax
cuts were supposed to generate. The revenues never appeared, and
deficits swelled under Reagan. That sunny-side conservatism was
perhaps the first component of Reaganism to be cast aside, quickly
crowded out by the politics of resentment. "Reagan's boundless optimism has had its day," Sid Blumenthal wrote as the 1988 Republican primary got underway. "In the line of history, that day may be
seen as a short one."[6]

His popularity and pragmatism also got marked down as liabilities. Pat Buchanan, who had served as the representative of the
party's right wing in the Nixon, Ford, and Reagan administrations,
argued in 1988 that the president had cared too much about how
policies polled. "Had Ronald Reagan consulted his convictions
more and his pollsters less, he would not be going home with politicians clucking about 'the Reagan deficits,' or with the press calling
him the biggest spender in history." The *Wall Street Journal* also saw
Reagan's popularity as a sign of weakness, not strength. He left office as the most popular president in a half century, meaning "he
settled for less change than either he or his supporters wanted or

could have gotten." His penchant for pragmatism likewise weighed his presidency down, according to conservative critics, leading to what Buchanan called "the transformation of Ronald Reagan from a pivotal and revolutionary figure in American politics into a traditional, middle-of-the-road pragmatic Republican president."[7]

The New Right was convinced the Reagan revolution had failed, and they had a clear diagnosis for that failure. Buchanan, writing for *National Review* in the months before the 1988 election, put it plainly: "The Republican moment slipped by, I believe, when the GOP refused to take up the challenge from the Left on its chosen battleground: the politics of class, culture, religion, and race." On economics, in his view, the White House had clearly delineated the stakes: low taxes and smaller government or more taxes and bigger government. "That same clarity and conviction," he wrote, "were rarely present when the subject was patriotism, nationalism, religion, or race." Those battles were left unfought.[8]

And so, while Reagan left the presidency in a haze of popular approval and would soon take his place among the pantheon of conservative saints, during his presidency a core group of conservatives saw him as an apostate, someone who had abandoned the conservative creed for the priesthood of the Republican establishment.

Next time, they vowed, they would back a true believer.

———

WHEN IT CAME to true believers, none was truer than Pat Robertson. Over the 1960s and 1970s, he had become the country's foremost televangelist, overseeing a media empire that elevated him as one of the most recognizable leaders of the religious right. In September 1986, he announced—via a sprawling closed-circuit satellite television network that connected 216 sites around the country—that he would run for president if three million people signed a petition supporting him. It was not quite a formal declaration, because campaign finance regulations meant he would have to give up his television show when he announced officially. And television was a big part of his identity. Facing questions the next day on *CBS Morning News* about whether the country would elect a right-wing religious leader as president, he deftly reframed the question. "Well, you know, really what I am is a morning talk-show host. And so I guess the question would be, 'Is America ready for a morning talk-show host to be president?'"[9]

That unusual mix of roles—television personality, preacher, politician—would be on display when he finally launched his presidential bid in the fall of 1987. He announced his run from an unexpected locale: the heart of the Bedford-Stuyvesant neighborhood in Brooklyn. The makeshift stage where he declared his candidacy sat in front of the old brownstone where he, his wife, and their three children had lived for a few months in 1959. Though Robertson now celebrated it as the starting point of a mission that had become an international media sensation, it had been an awful time for the young family, crammed into the squalid apartment while Robertson, bouncing from scheme to scheme, contemplated buying the brothel next door in a fit of missionary zeal.[10]

The brothel idea had, at the time, seemed like the final stage of Robertson's collapse. Son of a powerful political family—his father represented Virginia as one of its two arch-segregationist senators—he had graduated from Yale Law School a few years earlier but failed the bar. He then spent nine months in a management position at a chemical company, which he quit to run an electronics components business with some friends. He divested from that company to enter the ministry, ending up in the cramped and crumbling home in Bed-Stuy. But that's when fate—or, rather, his patrician parents—intervened. They connected him with a man trying to sell a rundown television station in Virginia. Seeing the dilapidated space, Robertson decided to "claim it for the Lord," turning it into a religious broadcasting station and, eventually, a televangelism empire.[11]

Over the next three decades, Robertson built the Christian Broadcasting Network (CBN) into a hub of conservative evangelical programming. By the 1970s, it was one of three Christian networks drawing tens of millions of viewers. Those networks emerged along with a sprawling religious right radio empire that included sixty-six nationally syndicated shows that reached millions of Americans. And while the religious right may have had a reputation as fusty traditionalists, their media institutions thrived on new technologies. An early adopter of cable, Robertson continued to expand his reach, and as he did, he pulled in bigger and bigger stars for his tent-pole program, *The 700 Club*. In the 1970s, guests included people like Israeli prime minister Yitzhak Rabin and President-Elect Jimmy Carter.[12]

As his media empire grew, so too did his political involvement. Still a Democrat, he supported Carter in 1976, believing that because they were both southern evangelicals, their interests overlapped. But over the course of the Carter administration, Robertson tapped into the network of New Right leaders and conservative evangelical pastors who had begun to organize their followers into a political force. That included people like fellow televangelist Jerry Falwell, who founded the Moral Majority in 1979 and whose *The Old-Time Gospel Hour* aired on 373 stations across the country. Copying the patriotic political rallies that Falwell convened in the nation's capital, in 1980 Robertson held a "Washington for Jesus" rally, bringing two hundred thousand Christians to the Capitol for a gathering that blended preaching and policy, as speakers denounced abortion, gay rights, and the bans on mandatory prayer in schools.[13]

As the face of the Moral Majority, Falwell starred in most contemporary accounts of the relationship between Reagan and the religious right. Robertson was a TV host; Falwell stood at the head of
an organization that promised to organize millions of activists for
the Republican Party. But Robertson was a key player in Reagan-era
politics as well, embedding himself in the courtship between the
movement and the administration. In 1984, in a sign of approval for
the administration during Reagan's reelection campaign, Robertson announced his conversion from Democrat to Republican. But
while he enjoyed his access to the president and the sense of power
that came with it, he shared the religious right's frustrations with
Reagan's policies. On everything from school prayer to abortion, the
president had said all the right things but achieved no real change.[14]

So in 1987, Robertson resigned his ordination with the Southern Baptist Convention and stepped away from CBN to run for
president. Savvy enough to understand his reputation as a religious
leader was as much a liability as an asset in his campaign, particularly after a spate of scandals had rocked the televangelist world, he
led with economic and foreign policy: he was first a deficit hawk
critical of Reagan's profligate spending; next a Cold War hawk critical of Reagan's turn to détente; and only then a religion hawk, ready
to push hard to outlaw abortion and return mandatory prayer to
public schools. Though to the right of Reagan, he tended to stress
how *normal* he was. He knew how easy it would be to portray him
as a wild-eyed extremist, so he angled to be reassuring in every public appearance.

Including his campaign launch. He had prepared a speech
shorn of any mentions of religion and promising a "government
for all people," signaling his intent to wage an expansive, inclusive
campaign. Even the location had been carefully chosen to show he
was not just the candidate of white charismatic Christians from

middle America but someone whose presidency would be a ministry to Black Americans as well. He selected Rosie Grier to introduce
him to the crowd. The former defensive lineman for the Los Angeles Rams had a post-football career full of unexpected turns: as
a bodyguard he had disarmed Robert Kennedy's assassin in 1968;
he'd then had a lengthy television and singing career, started an
inner-city ministry, promoted needlepoint and macrame as hobbies
for men, and, in 1984, endorsed Ronald Reagan. And now he was
the warm-up act for Pat Robertson's presidential campaign.

But carefully planned as it was, the announcement went wrong
right from the start. First, Grier flubbed Robertson's name, introducing him as "Pat Robinson." When Robertson and his wife, Dede,
emerged from the brownstone onto the stage, they were greeted with
a mix of cheers and raucous boos. While his supporters clapped
from their folding chairs in the middle of Monroe Street, two other
groups looked on with a mix of bewilderment and revulsion. Black
Brooklynites crowded on the nearby stoops, some laughing, some
jeering, some looking politely confused by Robertson's presence in
their neighborhood. And out on the street just yards away from the
stage, a group of about fifty protesters from the gay rights group
ACT UP shouted "Bigot!" and "Go home, Pat!" as Robertson started
his speech. The chants were so loud that he almost immediately
went off script, struggling throughout the ten-minute speech to be
heard over the protest. As he finished, in one last, small indignity, he
stumbled backward off the small dais.[15]

The campaign fared a bit better, but only because the launch
went so badly. Robertson finished second in the Iowa caucus, behind Bob Dole, the Republican leader in the Senate, and ahead of
Vice President Bush. But he flatlined nearly everywhere else. By
trying to convince voters he was a level-headed, something-for-
everyone candidate, he couldn't exploit the vein of resentment that

Pat Buchanan would so ably tap four years later. Nor could he truly shake what television host John McLaughlin called the "wacko factor." Networks played clips of Robertson engaged in faith healing and speaking in tongues. Reporters pointed to his past statements that there should be no wall between church and state and that only Christians and Jews should be able to hold office in the United States. And while Robertson could claim to run as a unity candidate representing everyone, he had quite recently compared non-Christians to termites and defended discrimination against people with AIDS, which he falsely claimed was airborne.[16]

Robertson's campaign showed the limits of the power of the religious right. Ascendant during the Reagan years, it would steadily increase its share of the Republican coalition. But that greater representation did not directly translate to policy. While white evangelicals would remain an influential constituency in the conservative coalition, they would find it difficult to exercise more power in the post-Reagan era than they had during his presidency. In fact, they would increasingly find themselves foot soldiers for the Republican Party rather than its leaders, devoted more to securing political power than promoting devout leaders.

Robertson's campaign collapsed in early 1988, and soon, so did many of the institutions of the New Right. The Moral Majority closed up shop in 1989. Viguerie was forced to sell off the *Conservative Digest* that same year, and the National Conservative Political Action Committee, which had been considered one of the most important New Right organizations for its innovations in independent expenditures, dissolved soon after. The New Right had spent its energy on Reagan and had little left for the fight to come. But in keeping alive the strain of conservatism that people like Pat Buchanan and Pat Robertson embodied, it had set the stage for the end of Reaganism.

Ultimately the nomination went to George H. W. Bush—an outcome that, while the New Right mourned it at the time, turned out to be a boon for their longer-term objectives. Because while they couldn't quite find their footing running against the Reagan legacy, they found in Bush a repository for all their discontent. Part of a monied family from Connecticut, he was the eastern establishment personified. And given his late conversion to social conservatism—a conversion that coincided with his selection as Reagan's vice president—his ideological bona fides were always in doubt. Bush made it much easier to illustrate the stark contrasts between their conservatism and that of the Reagan-Bush administrations. And while the New Right wouldn't be leading the charge, they had paved the way for the rise of a new nationalist, populist, resentful right that would move the party away not only from Bush but from Reagan.

———

PICK THROUGH THE threads of George H. W. Bush's presidency, and you can make a case that he should have been as much a darling of the conservative movement as Reagan was. For all the talk of wimpiness, on the campaign trail in 1988, he rarely pulled his punches. Moderate Republicans, in fact, were distraught that the man they had known as unfailingly gracious and kind had turned snarling and sarcastic as he fought for the presidency.[17]

That snarl came courtesy of two men devoted to the art of political warfare whom Bush had brought onto his campaign: Roger Ailes, a media consultant, and Lee Atwater, a political strategist. The two worked to mold Bush into the kind of populist fighter that conservatives craved, a tall order given his Brahmin background. But he was a quick study. Just before the Iowa caucus, he appeared on the CBS Evening News to do a live-via-satellite interview with Dan Rather. Ailes and Atwater spent hours drilling into Bush the idea that he had to treat Rather as the enemy. After an opening package raised questions about the Iran-Contra scandal, in which Bush was deeply implicated, Bush came out swinging. He charged that Rather had violated the terms of the interview, dredging up long-settled questions rather than focusing on policy and Bush's vision for the nation.

But tellingly, Bush never pivoted to policy or vision. Instead, he spent the ten-minute interview insisting that Rather and CBS were treating him unfairly. To ensure he didn't come across as whiny, he also made sure to hit back at Rather with a brutally effective line, saying his whole career shouldn't be judged by Iran-Contra, any more than Rather's should be judged by the infamous moment months earlier when he had walked off the set in a snit, leaving CBS to air a black screen for nearly seven minutes. After the interview, a hot mic picked up Bush gloating, "The bastard didn't lay a glove on me."[18]

The fight with Rather readied Bush for the upcoming general election against Michael Dukakis. He excoriated Dukakis—whom he referred to only as "the liberal governor of Massachusetts"—as soft on crime, weak on military commitments, and unpatriotic. "What is it about the Pledge of Allegiance that upsets him so much?" Bush asked, hammering Dukakis on his veto of a bill that would have made it mandatory for teachers to lead students in the Pledge of Allegiance each day. Bush also denounced him as a "card-carrying member of the American Civil Liberties Union," a bit of Red-baiting that echoed McCarthyite attacks on "card-carrying Communists." He went after Dukakis on the death penalty, abortion, gun control—emotionally charged social issues that became the central focus of the 1988 campaign.[19]

The campaign was ugly. Bush highlighted the case of William Horton, a Black man he called "Willie" at his rallies, to argue that the prison furlough system in Massachusetts was evidence that Dukakis was too weak on criminals. Horton, who had committed rape and murder while on furlough, became a symbol not just of crime but of Black criminality, which the Bush campaign and its allies emphasized again and again in a series of racist ads. Campaign consultant Roger Ailes also pushed a story that Dukakis had sought mental health treatment after the death of his brother fifteen years earlier, a charge that, at the time, still carried considerable stigma.[20]

Those efforts to keep the skeptical right on board during the campaign led to perhaps the most regrettable line of Bush's career, his "no new taxes" pledge. When Reagan had promised to cut taxes, the right readily believed him. And he delivered . . . until he reversed course and started raising taxes a few years later. Tax-cut absolutism—embodied in activist Grover Norquist's no-new-tax pledge, which debuted in 1986—seized the party in response. Bush would bear the brunt of it. Already deeply skeptical of his conservatism, the New Right pressed Bush again and again to commit to not raising taxes. The Bush team scrambled to find a way to convince them: in 1987, Bush signed the Norquist pledge, and at the convention in 1988, he uttered his famous promise: "Read my lips: no new taxes."[21]

Yet, despite these efforts to win over the hardline conservatives of the New Right who had been so critical of Reagan, they remained even more skeptical of Bush. After Bush clinched the nomination, Viguerie mused that it might not be the worst thing for Republicans to lose in November. Representative Vin Weber, who was working with Representative Newt Gingrich to start pulling the House caucus in the direction of the New Right, explained the right's resignation: "We're beginning to recognize that the sort of aggressive conservatism we've been pushing doesn't have any leadership or any visibility anymore." Not even Bush's choice of running mate, charismatic conservative senator Dan Quayle, convinced the right that he would govern as one of them.[22]

Even though he pledged to pursue a "kinder, gentler" politics once in office, Bush labored to keep the Republican right on board as president, serving up a steady stream of policies and pronouncements to please his conservative critics. While he worked to establish his administration as distinct from Reagan's—no Reagan appointee was allowed to retain their same position in the Bush administration—he nonetheless governed much like his predecessor. He kept slugging away at domestic issues that kept the conservative base engaged and enraged: abortion, affirmative action, crime. Out of forty-four vetoes during his time in office, ten were of bills related to abortion. He also deployed his veto powers to strike down the Civil Rights Act of 1990, which sought to strengthen workers' ability to sue for discrimination. Bush argued that, if implemented, the bill would "introduce the destructive force of quotas" into the workplace.[23]

Given that Democrats controlled both houses of Congress, vetoes were the primary way Bush could intervene in legislation. But the bully pulpit offered him an opportunity to introduce and shape ideas. While nowhere near as compelling an orator as Reagan—he knew better than to try to compete with a trained actor—he could spark debate simply by mentioning a topic, especially a topic that reframed conservatives, who had spent a decade in power, as victims of liberal elites. No matter how weak and ineffectual Bush seemed, he still found success with conservatives by tapping into the grievance politics of the American right.

In Bush's case, the topic was political correctness. The phrase, which the New Left had used jokingly for years to poke fun at a style of doctrinaire activism, transformed in the late 1980s into a new framework for conservative complaints about liberalism in higher education. Those complaints were not new: William F. Buckley Jr. had made his reputation in the early 1950s attacking what he saw as the secularism and liberal economic orthodoxies at Yale. But political correctness, often abbreviated "p.c.," hinted at a novel threat, one that the right would turn into a moral panic in the early 1990s.

The term "political correctness" only entered the mainstream political lexicon in late 1990, helped along by high-profile incidents in which students using racist and homophobic slurs at their colleges faced significant consequences. In October, the *New York Times* ran a piece on "the rising hegemony of the politically correct," a sympathetic examination of the p.c. debate on college campuses. Journalist Richard Bernstein described the evolution of the phrase "politically correct" into "a sarcastic jibe used by those, conservatives and classical liberals alike, to describe what they see as a growing intolerance, a closing of debate, a pressure to conform to a radical program or risk being accused of a commonly reiterated trio of thought crimes: sexism, racism and homophobia." But Bernstein suggested that political correctness had consequences far beyond higher education, with adherents demanding support for everything from affirmative action to environmental regulations to Palestinian self-determination. Cover stories in national magazines like *Newsweek* and *The Atlantic* quickly followed.[24]

Around six months later, in May 1991, Bush gave a commencement address at the University of Michigan in which he attacked political correctness as an assault on free speech. Noting that it was the two hundredth anniversary of the Bill of Rights, he warned that an "Orwellian" campaign against wrongthink was sweeping across the United States. "What began as a crusade for civility has soured into a cause of conflict and even censorship. Disputants treat sheer force—getting their foes punished or expelled, for instance—as a substitute for the power of ideas." He argued that politically correct culture was a corrosive blend of bullying, censorship, and reverse racism, stressing that, like Lyndon Johnson's Great Society, it was noble in motives but catastrophic in outcomes.

He did not often talk about the topic after that, but the address signaled the return of Bush the Campaigner, who replaced the promise of a "kinder, gentler politics" with hard-nosed rhetoric and hard-line politics. To prepare for the 1992 race, he brought aboard Tony Snow, a writer for the conservative *Washington Times*, to begin infusing his speeches with the grievance politics that he had deployed in his 1988 race. Judging from the Michigan speech, it was a smart move: suddenly Bush was drawing favorable comparisons to Reagan.[25]

And yet, for all these Reaganesque moments, Bush faced constant accusations that he had abandoned—no, *betrayed*—the conservative movement and deserved a serious challenge from the right when he ran again.

<hr />

THE PROBLEMS FOR Bush's reelection campaign had started early, arguably before he'd ever become president. At the Republican National Convention in New Orleans in 1988, he had stood before the roaring crowd of delegates and served up his legendary promise: "Read my lips: no new taxes."

That six-word campaign pledge defined so much of Bush's relationship to the right, encapsulating the blend of insincerity, compromise, and betrayal that they found so off-putting about the president. To a certain extent, they were right: his team had always considered the promise to have a time limit. They wouldn't push for increased taxes in the first year but would readily consider them later to begin chipping away at the mammoth deficits he inherited from Reagan. For many on the right, though, Bush's pledge was ironclad. They

doubted his conservatism, and he could not prove it to them by simply reciting the words of the conservative creed; he had to live up to
them every day of his presidency. The slightest deviation would be
confirmation that he never truly was one of them.[26]

Given this history, the Bush administration knew its 1990 budget deal, which included a tax hike, would elicit howls of outrage
from the grassroots right. They were less prepared for the opposition in Congress.

Bush's congressional problems could be traced to a change in
the House of Representatives shortly after Bush took office. When
he plucked Dick Cheney out of Congress to serve as his secretary
of defense, Bush created an opening in the House Republican leadership. Though Bob Michel, the House minority leader, had hand-
picked Cheney's replacement, the caucus had a different choice in
mind. Having spent more than three decades in the minority, many
members were growing restless. Landslide victories for Republican
presidential candidates had failed to translate into a majority in the
House. So they selected as the new whip someone who had an aggressive plan to change that: Newt Gingrich.

Gingrich, whose mop of white hair belied his youth, had been
in the House for a decade, steadily building up a base of support.
His plan? To force greater confrontation between Democrats and
Republicans, confrontation that, he hoped, would shake Americans
out of their habitual preference for Democrats and force a real party
realignment.

That plan was not without its problems. For one, Gingrich had
no experience whipping votes, leaving Minority Leader Bob Michel
to *very* grudgingly pick up the slack for his lieutenant. ("I'd like to
be relieved of handling two chores, but maybe my role will have to
be somewhat adjusted to that," Michel grumbled to the *Washington
Post*, acknowledging that he heard the message that the caucus was

sending by voting for Gingrich: they wanted leadership "to be more activated and more visible and more aggressive.") But it also put Gingrich on a collision course with the White House. That's because Bush, facing a Democrat-controlled Congress and eager to see his agenda enacted, planned to embrace bipartisanship. Gingrich had more of a scorched-earth approach in mind. Even before ascending to whip, he had used ethics charges to engineer the downfall of Democratic Speaker Jim Wright. And Gingrich saw that as just the start: he wanted to turn future elections into referenda on the party of corruption versus the party of reform, and he planned to take down a few more Democrats to ensure that the charge stuck.[27]

The difference in strategies ensured that, at some point, Bush and Gingrich were going to come into conflict. When it happened, it happened spectacularly—and in public. The issue was the 1990 budget deal, which was the backbone of the Bush administration's efforts to rein in the massive deficits of the Reagan years. It included a raft of new revenue provisions, closing tax loopholes, increasing IRS enforcement, and, of course, hiking tax rates. Gingrich had been signaling support for the bill for months, assuring the White House that the caucus would back moderate tax increases. The promise of easy passage for the legislation was a moment of relief for the struggling administration: by 1990 the boom economy of the Reagan years had given way to a sudden recession, and Americans were feeling it, first with the oil shock caused by Iraq's invasion of Kuwait in 1990, then in the job losses as the manufacturing sector contracted. The administration needed a win. With congressional leadership on board, Bush planned to announce the deal in the Rose Garden flanked by the leadership of both parties. But at the last minute, Gingrich veered off, instead leading a revolt against the bill that would result in a brief government shutdown and—because Bush had to rely on more Democratic votes once

Republicans fled—higher tax increases than Bush had initially negotiated.[28]

In agreeing to the budget deal, Bush was following in Reagan's footsteps, agreeing to a tax increase despite being an avowed anti-taxer. But conservative suspicions, coupled with the Gingrich revolt, ensured that Bush's support of the budget bill would get him tarred as a heretic. A few days after the walkout, Gingrich—never short on gall—angled to have his and his second wife's picture taken with the president at a fund-raising event; Gingrich, abandoning any sense of agency, told Bush, "I'm really sorry that this is happening." Bush grimaced in response, "You're killing us, you are just killing us."[29]

The revolt had other consequences as well: Reagan's heretical tax increases had caused grumbling on the right but not a full-on revolt. With the number two Republican in the House standing firm against the revenue increases in the budget bill, however, Bush appeared as though he had not just broken a promise but breached an inviolable conservative principle. In fact, the decision to sign the budget bill in the face of Republican opposition helped cement the idea not only that Bush had betrayed the right but that any increase in taxes, no matter the size or the source, was anathema to the conservative cause.

The budget deal alone was likely reason enough for the right to sour on Bush. But the heresies quickly stacked up. Bush had scored points with conservatives for vetoing the 1990 Civil Rights Act, which would have made it easier for employees to sue for discrimination by, in part, requiring not that they prove hiring processes were crafted with the intent to discriminate, just that they had that effect. But his veto had only bought him a little time. He soon was back in negotiations with House Democrats, who reintroduced the bill as their first act in 1991. Bush repeatedly threatened to veto the new bill too, but he ended up signing compromise legislation in November 1991. Though he insisted the bill protected employers from quotas based on race and gender, the right was unimpressed.[30]

They were even less impressed with a last-minute snag in the legislation, when reporters and members of Congress caught wind of a draft signing statement related to the bill. The signing statement, a tool used by presidents to instruct agencies on how to interpret and implement legislation, would have abruptly ended many of the federal government's affirmative action programs. The news led several Democrats and civil rights leaders to boycott the signing ceremony. To win them back, Bush withheld the directive and reiterated his support for affirmative action—a move that riled his detractors on the right.[31]

If that wasn't enough, Bush also crossed swords with the right on cultural issues. During the Bush years, right-wing activists began campaigning against what they saw as obscene and profane art supported by the federal government grants. They demanded greater oversight—if not the outright dismantling—of the National Endowment for the Arts (NEA). Bush agreed that artists like Robert Mapplethorpe, whose black-and-white photos depicted explicit images of sadomasochism and gay sex, produced revolting "filth." Yet he argued that the federal government had no business telling artists what sort of art they should produce. Congress took a stronger stand, introducing a decency standard into funding for the NEA in 1990, leaving NEA chair John Frohnmayer to reluctantly institute a decency test for artists who were receiving endowment funds. Bush eventually fired Frohnmayer, but not before he had been thoroughly bashed on the subject during the 1992 campaign.[32]

Even foreign policy, where Bush felt far more at home, proved tricky ground to navigate, despite the fact that so many of the administration's signature foreign policy achievements should have thrilled the right. But when the Cold War came crashing to an end in Berlin one night in November 1989, everything changed—and not just for foreign policy. The Cold War had conditioned the entirety of US politics for decades. For conservatives, it meant their central organizing principle had disappeared. The modern right had been knitted together by anticommunism and, more explicitly, opposition to the Soviet Union, only to find that structural reality undone practically overnight.

Which is why the joy that greeted the end of the Cold War was shot through with apprehension. First, unwinding Soviet control of Eastern Europe and the Soviet Socialist Republics was a delicate, at times dangerous process that unfolded over the course of the Bush administration. It was, on the whole, a success, with credit due to leaders across Europe and Asia. Among conservatives, Reagan got most of the credit, but Bush earned some grudging respect as well.

Second, the end of the Cold War unwound the underlying logic of the conservative coalition. Bush, who was already struggling to keep conservatives happy during his presidency, found keeping the conservative coalition united was especially difficult without the glue of the Cold War to bind them together. With the Cold War no longer providing the motivation for a kind of conservative internationalism, or at least a conservative interventionism, suddenly there was room for the reappearance of the Old Right of the 1930s and 1940s, back when the nationalist strain in conservatism promoted protectionism and treated foreign intervention with skepticism if not alarm. The new Old Right, which would eventually be rebranded as paleoconservatism, did not fully emerge in the Bush years but was quickly coalescing as the Cold War ended. That meant there was very little opposition on the right to US intervention in Iraq, which followed Iraq's invasion of Kuwait. Convinced by British prime minister Margaret Thatcher that this was a Munich moment—when appeasement would only empower a brutish, expansion-minded dictator—Bush began building the international coalition that would push Iraqi troops out of Kuwait. The invasion inspired a temporary truce between Bush and the right: "Obviously the Iraq war has changed the atmosphere from what otherwise would have been a revolt against Bush on domestic policy," conceded one long-time conservative activist in early 1991.[33]

Yet the seeds of the truce's demise were sown in the buildup to war. As Bush began making the case for intervention against Iraq in late 1990, he described one objective of war as the creation of a "new world order" marked by freedom, justice, and peace. Those three words, meant to evoke the historic possibility of a moment when the United States had emerged as the world's sole superpower, fed into right-wing conspiracies and fear of a single global government that would fill the vacuum the Soviet Union left behind. A year later, Pat Robertson published *The New World Order*, a best-selling book crammed with every flavor of internationalist conspiracy: the Illuminati, the Freemasons, the Trilateral Commission, the Rothschilds. At one point he suggested Bush was "unknowingly and unwittingly carrying out the mission and mouthing the phrases of a tightly knit cabal whose goal is nothing less than a new order for the human race under the domination of Lucifer and his followers." Elsewhere he mused that the Bush administration may have pushed for the Iraq War in order to advance the cause of global governance. And while not everyone on the right went quite as far as Robertson, he was tapping into a vein of antiestablishment and anti-internationalist politics that would become central to right-wing politics in the 1990s.[34]

Programs like the North American Free Trade Agreement, which fulfilled Reagan's vision of a North American accord, triggered expected resistance from the labor sector of the Democratic

Party. But NAFTA also drew surprising opposition from parts of the conservative movement as well. Pat Buchanan saw the treaty as an attack on US sovereignty. Roger Milliken, a major conservative donor whom Buchanan later credited with persuading him to abandon free trade, favored a more protectionist economy. And New Right leaders like Paul Weyrich and Phyllis Schlafly believed that opposition to NAFTA was a way to expand the movement's populist base and keep Reagan Democrats, particularly the white working class, tied to the Republican Party. The promise of "free trade" did not override growing concerns about economic competition and, increasingly, immigration, especially in the middle of a recession.[35]

By late 1991, things were looking grim for Bush. The economic recession had deepened, his approval numbers had cratered, and the conservative coalition he was so desperate to court was unraveling around him. In January 1991, the Heritage Foundation denounced Bush as a heretic, saying, "We know Ronald Reagan, and George Bush has shown he is no Ronald Reagan." And in December of that year, National Review broke with him as well. The editors told readers that "unless President Bush makes a major, explicit, and convincing turn to the right"—something they did not count on—they would be unable to support his reelection.[36]

They hoped, instead, to see him challenged from his right. And they were in luck: he was about to face a challenger who was not only far more conservative than Bush but had rapidly adapted to the conditions of post-Reagan, post–Cold War politics and would pioneer the model for the new right-wing politics of the 1990s.

CHAPTER THREE

THE POPULISTS

D ID I NOT TELL YOU THAT WE WOULD MAKE HISTORY?"
The crowd, packed into the Courtyard restaurant in the
south end of Manchester, New Hampshire, let out a boisterous, and maybe a bit inebriated, cheer. Pat Buchanan soaked it in
before launching into his next line, hastily written just hours before,
when exit polls showed him neck and neck with President George
H. W. Bush in the state's primary. "Today from dawn to dusk, the
Buchanan brigades met King George's army all along the Concord-
Manchester-Nashua line, and I'm here to report they are retreating
back into Massachusetts!" Now a broad smile broke across his face as
the crowd roared again. The populist revolt had begun.[1]

This was not how Buchanan had expected his evening to go.
Bush, the sitting president, was supposed to be a shoo-in for the
party's nomination in 1992. Public polling showed Buchanan well
behind the president in the New Hampshire contest, and over the

course of the day he had tinkered with a speech announcing his withdrawal from the race. Then an aide burst into his hotel room with a poll showing him just four points behind the president. Buchanan, perched on the edge of the hotel bed, sat stunned for a moment, then asked, "Well, what the fuck do we do now?"[2]

One of the first things they did was figure out when the networks planned to start their campaign coverage. After learning that NBC and CNN would cut to New Hampshire at 10 p.m., Buchanan planned his speech for 10:01. Then he got to writing. That's how Buchanan snagged live prime-time coverage on the major networks, while Bill Clinton, who spoke at a little past 9 p.m. after finishing second in the Democratic primaries, was stuck with C-SPAN. All those years in front of the camera as a television pundit were paying off for Buchanan in more ways than one.[3]

Buchanan didn't win in New Hampshire—he ended up sixteen points behind Bush—but in claiming 37 percent of the vote, he upended not only the Republican primary but the entire presidential race. Because down in Texas, Ross Perot, once described by the *Wall Street Journal* as a "populist billionaire," sensed an opportunity. If a talk show host could rally anti-Bush forces in the primary, maybe he could do the same in the general.[4]

Two days later, Perot showed up on CNN's *Larry King Live* with a challenge: if his supporters could get him on the ballot in all fifty states, he would run for president.

As Buchanan stalled in the polls over the next few months, attention turned to Perot, whose third-party bid would be one of the most successful in US presidential history. The two men were riding the same wave of discontented populism: both opposed the Iraq War, both pushed for more economic protectionism, and both railed against a political establishment that failed to serve "the forgotten man." They also shared unusual qualities in a presidential candidate:

neither had ever held elected office, and both had built their political reputations and their political bases primarily through media.

There were differences too. Buchanan modeled an exclusionary right-wing populism built on white racial anxieties, disdain for feminism, and disgust for gay rights. Buchanan's politics were recognizably conservative, even though they broke sharply from Ronald Reagan's. Perot, on the other hand, defied categorization. Unlike Buchanan, he was anathema to the New Right: he supported abortion, sex education, and higher taxes.

Yet, despite their differences, their campaigns revealed the transformation underway in US politics. The tectonic plates of American politics were shifting in ways that would break apart the Reagan agenda and remake the contours of conservatism. Political fault lines were being redrawn in a way they had not been since the 1960s, when advances in Black civil rights had first splintered the Democratic coalition, then realigned the two parties.

Buchanan's pitchfork populism and Perot's erratic campaign reflected the distinct political climate of the early 1990s, a moment of transition before the intense polarization and partisanship that followed. A significant portion of the voting public hungered for a protest vote, railing against establishment politics and eager for disruption. That discontent, though, was inchoate. It flowed toward Buchanan, toward Bill Clinton, toward Ross Perot, crossing ideological and partisan identities as politicians scrambled to capture an up-for-grabs electorate. Though Buchanan and Perot both lost their races, their campaigns laid the groundwork for the politics of the post-Reagan era.

———

LONG BEFORE PAT Buchanan launched his presidential campaign, he joined Richard Nixon's. It was a heady time for Buchanan, who was still in his twenties when he met Nixon in late 1964 (technically their second meeting, since Buchanan had once caddied for Nixon during his vice presidency). He had been writing for the *St. Louis Globe-Democrat*, and his fiery right-wing editorials and political instincts seemed like a perfect fit for Nixon, who was eyeing the 1968 presidential race. Barry Goldwater's nomination showed Nixon he needed to be attuned to the conservative base. So he brought Buchanan on board, first to help campaign for Republicans in the 1966 midterms, and then to help win over conservatives for his own presidential run.[5]

Over the next few years, Buchanan grew close to Nixon, whom he called the Old Man, and became a lifelong Nixon loyalist. In 1968, he labored hard to bring the right into the Nixon camp—a difficult thing to do, as many conservative leaders distrusted Nixon as an establishment Republican and wanted the new governor of California, Ronald Reagan, to be the nominee. But a few marquee conservatives, including *National Review* editor Bill Buckley, came out for Nixon, and when he won the presidency, Nixon brought Buchanan into the White House as a speechwriter, political consultant, and ambassador to a wary and restive right-wing.[6]

While his position in the administration required persuading conservatives to go along with policies they may not have liked (like the decision to open relations with China in 1972), Buchanan's personal conservatism was hard-line and pugilistic. He absorbed his political impulses from his father, an Irish-Catholic accountant with three personal heroes: General Douglas MacArthur, Spanish dictator Francisco Franco, and anticommunist senator Joe McCarthy. That lineage may explain why he was concerned less with the size of government than with its ideological bent; right-wing authoritarianism did not bother Buchanan much. He celebrated his Confederate ancestry and remained opposed to integration long after the passage of the Civil Rights Act. His conservatism was attitudinal as well. He virulently opposed any trace of institutional liberalism, whether in journalism, universities, the Catholic Church, or the Republican Party. And he never passed on a fight—he was expelled from Georgetown University for a year after brawling with police officers who had pulled him over for speeding.[7]

That fighting spirit and instinctive antiliberalism played well in the Nixon administration, whose president and vice president were always spoiling for a fight. Buchanan penned some of Vice President Spiro Agnew's most barbed attacks on media bias, delighting in his role as the go-to writer for the administration's hard-hitting speeches. Though the Nixon administration lost many conservatives when Nixon opened relations with China, Buchanan's sense of loyalty to the president kept him on board. He would stay through the bleak days of Watergate and continued on, briefly, as an adviser in the Ford administration.

But with Nixon no longer in office, Buchanan's interest in public service quickly waned. He lobbied to be made ambassador to South Africa (he strongly believed the apartheid regime was a key Cold War ally and a model government), but the idea was too controversial for the new president. Buchanan quit the month after Gerald Ford took office, returning to where he had started: the media.[8]

Buchanan landed his first television show in 1980, when he turned the call-in radio show he cohosted with liberal commentator Tom Braden into a local late-night television show called *After Hours*. When *After Hours* was dropped in 1982 for low ratings, CNN, a new twenty-four-hour news channel hungry for content, rushed in to pick it up. Rebranded as *Crossfire*, the show gave CNN some entertaining political sparring and gave Buchanan a national audience. Though CNN founder Ted Turner reportedly was skeptical of the show, it became a programming staple for the network. And if you weren't one of the 23.7 million American households with cable TV, you could still find Buchanan on your dial. Over on PBS, he was a regular on *The McLaughlin Group*, part of its weekly pundit roundtable since its launch in 1982.[9]

Though Buchanan had been a columnist since his days as an editorial writer for the *St. Louis Globe-Democrat* in the early 1960s, no print outlet could match the fame power of television. With a spin of the dial (or, if their TVs were high-tech enough, a click of the remote), Americans could see and hear Buchanan as he went on the attack, brawling with his liberal sparring partners. While the verbal fisticuffs turned some people off—the high-volume crosstalk, not yet a mainstay of cable news, could be jarring and unpleasant— others saw the show as a new, captivating kind of political entertainment. Conservatives especially delighted in seeing their views so aggressively defended on national television.

Buchanan's arrival on television came just as a major transformation was happening in television journalism. Responding to accusations of liberal bias, which had reached a fever pitch during the Nixon administration (thanks to speeches by Vice President Agnew that Buchanan helped write), network news began experimenting with new forms of punditry, pitting liberal and conservative commentators against one another in the name of balance. ABC had done this as a one-off during the 1968 convention with memorable results: liberal writer Gore Vidal had called conservative columnist William F. Buckley Jr. a crypto-Nazi; Buckley had called Vidal a queer and threatened to sock him in his "goddamn face." But the format wasn't formalized until 1971, when *60 Minutes* launched its "Point/Counterpoint" segment with conservative James J. Kilpatrick and liberal Nicholas von Hoffman. Suddenly there was space for political commentary that was openly, proudly biased, giving conservatives a platform for punditry that spoke not just to other conservatives but to the entire country.[10]

The rise of conservative punditry in the 1970s modeled a new vision for what "fair" coverage looked like. But it had the added effect of introducing an element of entertainment into political coverage. After a few decades of radio and television journalism that drew its credibility from the neutral tone and professed objectivity of the white male host, the sparring style of left-right debate was a jolt to the system. While white men still predominated, the shows were a startling shift from network news: loud, opinionated, full of shouting and laughter. Audiences were hooked, so much so that spoofs of "Point/Counterpoint" became a regular feature on the new skit comedy show *Saturday Night Live*. For Buchanan, that new model meant an opportunity to hop from the printed page to broadcast: the shows *Crossfire* and *The McLaughlin Group* were modeled after— and made possible by—the popularity of "Point/Counterpoint."

For all his success in punditry, Buchanan was not done with political work. In 1985 he left both *Crossfire* and *The McLaughlin Group* for a stint as Reagan's communication director. He spent that time not just working with Reagan but plotting to succeed him. "The greatest vacuum in American politics is to the right of Ronald Reagan," he noted in early 1987 as he tested the market for a Buchanan campaign. As soon as he floated the idea of a presidential bid, he won the backing of New Right leaders, who were hungry for a scrappy political fight.[11]

Buchanan quickly realized, however, that even his supporters saw him more as a source of disruption than as a viable presidential nominee. Polling bore that out. His name recognition was sky-high, but more people held negative views of Buchanan than positive ones, even in polls limited to Republicans and independents. His television career meant people knew who he was; it also meant they didn't like him very much. Within a few weeks of releasing his presidential trial balloon, Buchanan withdrew from the race.[12]

Soon after, he left the Reagan administration to return to television. While that might have seemed to some a sign that he was abandoning his presidential ambitions, Buchanan understood television was a far better platform for building a political following than a job toiling in the bowels of the White House. As the Reagan years gave way to the Bush years, Buchanan nurtured on air a brand-new, post–Cold War conservatism, one that squarely marked Reagan as a president from another, now obsolete era. He still adored Reagan, of course. He could recall that day in the Oval Office when he introduced his extended family to the president. The two men stood side by side for pictures, then headed over to the Roosevelt Room for Buchanan's farewell party, where the president presented him with a pair of bronzed running shoes (Buchanan was an avid jogger). He'd stood next to Reagan and declared, "We're all Reaganites now."[13]

But Reagan retired, Bush took over, the Cold War ended, and the economy sagged, and suddenly all those old arguments no longer cohered. Go save Kuwait from Iraq? Why? What business was it of the United States' how the Middle East arranged its affairs? Whom did free trade benefit? Certainly not the factory workers in Manchester, New Hampshire, or Detroit, Michigan, whose jobs had made their way to Japan and, if the Bush administration had its way, would soon relocate to Mexico. And speaking of Mexico, why should American workers compete with migrants for work? Especially if those migrants didn't come from western Europe: "We are a European country," Buchanan insisted, before suggesting that the United States would benefit far more from English immigration than African.[14]

During the Bush administration, Buchanan abandoned the Reaganite positions on free trade, interventionism, and immigration. But the Cold War consensus Buchanan questioned most was the idea that democracy was an unqualified good. He made the point baldly in a column in early 1991. "The American press is infatuated to the point of intoxication with 'democracy,'" he wrote, not only in fanning the dreams of democracy abroad in the former Soviet Union but in encouraging it at home as well. Democracy, he suggested, led to poor governance. Comparing institutions like IBM and the Marine Corps to the government in Washington, DC, he noted, "Only the last is run on democratic, not autocratic principles. Yet, who would choose the last as the superior institution?" To drive the point home, he concluded, "If the people are corrupt, the more democracy, the worse the government."[15]

These complaints about democracy, though odd coming from someone eying a presidential bid, had precedence within the conservative movement he sought to represent. Conservatives, after all, had hoisted signs proclaiming, "A Republic, Not a Democracy," during Barry Goldwater's campaign in 1964. They also challenged the Supreme Court's standard of one-man, one-vote and rejected the Voting Rights Act (which Buchanan never warmed up to). But in the Reagan years, paeans to democracy had shaped both foreign policy and celebrations of the broad majorities that swept Reagan into office.

Buchanan led the way in returning the right to those antidemocratic roots. The political philosophy he honed during the Bush years would become known as paleoconservatism for the ways it harkened back to the Old Right of the 1930s and 1940s. The end of the Cold War and invasion of Iraq shaped his determinedly noninterventionist politics: no need to fund Contras or prop up teetering regimes abroad, positions he had supported during the Reagan years. Buchanan believed the United States did not need to go abroad to find foreign enemies to fight, for they were already on America's shores, in the form of cheap goods from China and Japan and foreign workers from Latin America, Asia, and Africa. And Bush's support for expanding the North Atlantic Treaty Organization and entering the North American Free Trade Agreement (NAFTA) convinced Buchanan that the president was a proponent of a "new world order" that threatened US sovereignty as well as its white cultural heritage.

So Buchanan vowed to throw it all out: no more free trade, no more democracy promotion, no more celebrations of diversity. And he was ready to make the case that he couldn't make with Reagan in office: that the United States was in decline and needed a revolution to stop its slide. "The people of this country need to recapture our capital city from an occupying army of lobbyists and registered agents of foreign powers hired to look out for everybody and everything except the national interest of the United States," he told a rambunctious crowd in late 1991, as he laid out his America First agenda during his announcement speech in New Hampshire. Nor was this just a revolution against the New Deal and Great Society, the issues that had fueled Reagan's run. No, this was a war against the Republican establishment, including Bush and Reagan.[16]

> We Republicans can no longer say it is all the liberals' fault. It was not some liberal Democrat who declared, "Read my lips! No new taxes!," then broke his word to cut a back room budget deal with the big spenders. It was not Edward Kennedy who railed against a quota bill, then embraced its twin. It was not Congress alone who set off on the greatest social spending spree in 60 years, running up the largest deficits in modern history.

> No, that was done by men in whom we placed our con-
> fidence and our trust, and who turned their backs, and
> walked away from us.

Republican leaders had betrayed conservatives, and his campaign would be the instrument of the right's revenge.[17]

The speech drew from Buchanan's considerable talents as a pundit. But to win the nomination, he would have to show political skill as well. It was one thing to build a television career; it was quite another to leverage that platform into a campaign for president. That's what was so remarkable about Pat Buchanan's rise in 1992. He'd never held elected office, and his time in government had not been spent in high-profile cabinet positions or major policymaking roles. He was a TV personality, not a politician. And yet conservatives flocked to him, at least in part because he *was* a media personality.

Buchanan's media base might make him appear to be a natural heir to Reagan, who, after all, had been a movie star in his pre-presidential days. But Reagan had laundered his movie star reputation through the California governor's office. By the time he made his 1980 run, his third attempt at the Republican nomination, Reagan had become part of the Republican establishment, even as he ran a sideline in media through his radio commentaries. And even though Reagan was a creature of media, he was part of the old media: the films for the Hollywood studio system in the 1930s and 1940s, the starchy hosting gig on prime-time network television in the 1950s, the scripted three-minute radio commentaries in the 1970s.

No, Buchanan was much more like Pat Robertson than Ronald Reagan. Robertson's run showed that a combative media figure who had never held office could leave a mark on the race—in his brief 1988 campaign, Robertson managed to win a few states and force Bush to appeal to white evangelicals.

Yet, despite these similarities, Buchanan and Robertson came from very different media backgrounds, resulting in quite different campaigns. Robertson spent much of his campaign taming his brimstone prophesies and charismatic oddities. A man with a record of faith healing and speaking in tongues had a long way to go to convince nonevangelicals that he could be a mainstream politician. Buchanan, having come up through the world of political entertainment, had far more transferable skills. Debate and provocation were his tools on television and on the campaign trail. And while his commentary was often incendiary, he saved his most controversial statements for the printed page. A newspaper column, it turned out, was a bit more difficult to turn into an attack ad than a soundbite like "Read my lips: no new taxes."

Just as important as the stylistic advantages his media training gave him were the political advantages. Though Buchanan had served in three Republican administrations, he was hardly a party apparatchik. Nor was he an activist lashed to a particular constituency. When he entered the presidential race, he did so with an audience, not a faction. And while it wasn't clear that an audience could be molded into a voting base, his background gave him considerably more room to navigate in the primary campaign. He could adapt to the realities of a post–Cold War politics and forge a new style of post-Reagan conservatism because he wasn't bound to the party's platform or to an organization's agenda.

Instead, Buchanan built his appeal on his populist style. Claiming to speak for the forgotten man, he raged against "King George" and promised to take on the establishment. While the pitchfork wouldn't become the emblem of his candidacy for another four years, that energy coursed through his 1992 campaign. His position—the outsider—would come to matter more than his platform. Unburdened by a voting record or party loyalties, Buchanan had more room to deviate from the Reaganite line.

Still, it was apparent early on that, while there was a real appetite for Buchanan's message and an intensity among his supporters not found among Bush's backers, Buchanan could not topple a sitting president. He had revealed a hefty lode of discontent embedded within the party, but he struggled—as Reagan had in 1976 when he challenged Ford for the nomination—to convince Republicans that he was better positioned to defeat the Democratic nominee in the general election.

Buchanan was not running to win, though. He believed that, with the Cold War over, his conservatism represented the future of the Republican Party and that his was a message Americans needed to hear. So while Bush won every primary after New Hampshire with more than 60 percent of the vote, Buchanan stayed in the race, determined to keep his issues in the mix.

And by the end of spring, while Bush was running away with the nomination, Buchanan was ready to make his last stand at the US-Mexico border.

———

DUST CLUNG TO Buchanan's suit as he clambered out of the four-wheel-drive vehicle, fresh from a Border Patrol tour of the terrain near the San Diego–Tijuana border. He could do little to neaten up before he spoke to reporters: dust seemed to cling to everything—his shoes, the truck, the air itself. There was little relief from it or the bright blaze of the sun on the ridge overlooking Smuggler's Gulch, the dip in the land where migrants passed between Mexico and the United States.[18]

It was May 1992—spring, but already heating up. A jumble of people had gathered to see him, though the crowd was much smaller than in those days back in February when he had, for a moment, seemed poised to upend Bush's reelection bid. The reporters, microphones and notebooks in hand as they waited for the press conference to begin, were easy to spot, as were his supporters, clad in suits and ties, buying sodas from a pop-up refreshment stand on the other side of the border. A clutch of migrants looked on with mild interest.

The group on the edge of the crowd, though . . . they were a problem. Already his aides were eying them warily. They wanted some of the same things Buchanan did—more patrols at the border, fewer migrants crossing into the United States—and they too warned of an "invasion" transforming America. But the presence of their leader, a man named Tom Metzger, threatened to spoil the presser before it began.

Metzger, formerly a member of the Ku Klux Klan and the White Aryan Resistance, had just done a stretch in prison for cross burning in Los Angeles. He had founded a Klan Border Watch in California back in 1979, one of several efforts by white-power groups to police the southern border. He would happily offload that work to the National Guard—something Buchanan had called for as well—but he wanted guardsmen to "shoot to kill" when they saw a migrant. While Buchanan quickly informed reporters he wanted nothing to do with Metzger, the Klansman's presence was a reminder of the challenges Buchanan faced in transforming the Republican Party.[19]

Buchanan had come to the border to talk about building a wall. He had a ten-point plan, one that included erecting a two-hundred-mile wall ("the Buchanan fence"), doubling the Border Patrol, and denying citizenship to children born on US soil to undocumented immigrants. Those were novel ideas for a Republican presidential candidate in May 1992. They were even new to Buchanan, who in 1984 had been lauding "undocumented aliens" as tax-paying, bootstrapping workers who, unlike their native-born counterparts, avoided "the Venus fly trap of the welfare state."[20]

But ever alert to shifts in the white electorate, Buchanan sensed an opportunity at the border. The group he called the "Wallace vote" (named for segregationist George Wallace, a popular third-party candidate in 1968 and 1972, when Buchanan had been working for Richard Nixon) had been content enough within the Reagan coalition. Without that charismatic conservative in the White House, though, their grumblings were growing louder. Affirmative action, the Los Angeles riots, decades of rising crime rates—all seemed to Buchanan to be issues ripe for exploitation. Buchanan had seen Reagan welcome the Wallace voter into the party, but only as a junior partner in a broader coalition. What if, he thought, these racial conservatives were not just a part of the party but its base? The party should be putting their needs first, not merely offering a wink and a nod now and again to soothe their tempers.

So when Buchanan walked up to the bank of microphones set up near the chain-link fence that crossed the gulch, he sounded very different than he had in 1984. "I am calling attention to a national disgrace," he said: "The failure of the national government of the United States to protect the borders of the United States from an illegal invasion that involves at least a million aliens a year." Throughout the speech, Buchanan blamed immigrants for the nation's economic and social woes. He also deftly tied them to another issue near and dear to the Wallace voter's heart: the Los Angeles riots.

Just as Reagan had seized on the political benefits of social unrest, Buchanan saw opportunity in the uprising, which had been triggered just a few weeks earlier by the acquittal of four white officers who had brutally beaten Rodney King, a Black man, while a witness recorded nearby. He headed straight to Southern California to meet with police officers, guardsmen, and the Korean storeowners lionized as the first line of defense against Black rioters. There, he praised the jury that had acquitted the officers and came out against any new social programs for inner-city communities. "This orgy of violence and lynching"—yes, he said lynching—"cannot be used to shake down the American taxpayer for another Great Society."[21]

While the unrest in Los Angeles might seem a world away from the border crossings at Smuggler's Gulch, Buchanan forged a connection. At the border, he cited Attorney General William Barr's claim that fully a third of the six thousand people arrested during the early days of the riots were undocumented immigrants and that the unrest in Los Angeles could be directly connected to the lawlessness at the border. "Foreigners are coming into this country illegally and helping to burn down one of the greatest cities in America," Buchanan alleged, abandoning his vision of undocumented immigrants as peaceful workers for one of illegal foreigners as criminal agents.[22]

It was pure Wallace: a tale of Black criminality and invasion and the pressing need for tough, even brutal force to reinstate order. That story was the foundation upon which Buchanan had built his America First campaign, a campaign that warned of moral degradation and the collapse of "Western civilization." His America was a nation under siege, one that had to pull up the drawbridge and reinforce the ramparts.

It was a good message, Buchanan believed. If it weren't for those damn Klansmen.

Tom Metzger and his crew, buzzing around the edges of the press conference, were a reminder of the Klansman who had been darting on the edges of the Republican primary. A week before Buchanan launched his presidential bid, David Duke launched his.

Duke spent much of the 1970s in either a Nazi uniform or a Klan robe, part of the white-power movement in Louisiana. Early on, he figured out how to leverage national media to his advantage, presenting himself as a Klansman in a suit on programs like NBC's *Tomorrow* with Tom Snyder. Snyder marveled over Duke during his 1974 interview, calling him "intelligent, articulate, young, and charming."[23]

In the years that followed, Duke, his face smoothed and sharpened by plastic surgery, decided to set aside his old political affiliations—but not his political goals—in order to gain more power. He spent several years as a Democrat, briefly detoured to the white-supremacist Populist Party, and then in 1989 became a Republican. He won a special election for a seat in the Louisiana House of Representatives and, after failed bids for Senate and governor, joined the Republican presidential primary in December 1991.[24]

Buchanan had had his eye on Duke since 1989, when Duke won the Republican primary for that special seat in the state legislature. Duke had only just become a Republican, and GOP leaders—including President Bush and former president Reagan—quickly denounced him. Consider that: a president and former president weighed in on a special election for a state legislature seat because they understood how dangerous it was for a party that had learned to dog-whistle racist appeals to suddenly have a Klansman and neo-Nazi in its ranks.[25]

Buchanan, however, had a different take. Writing just after Duke's win in 1989, he taunted the Republican Party for using overwhelming force against the former Klansman. "It saw in Duke's candidacy a glorious opportunity to burnish its civil rights credentials," he wrote, a ploy to win the Black vote. But, he argued, the Black vote was not what the GOP needed. Instead, the party should do what it did with George Wallace: "Take a hard look at Duke's portfolio of winning issues; and expropriate those not in conflict with GOP principles." Those principles? Lower taxes, crime committed by "the urban underclass," and affirmative action ("i.e., reverse discrimination against white folks").[26]

In fact, Buchanan believed the Republican Party's effort to woo Black voters had caused the situation in Louisiana in the first place. "David Duke walked into the political vacuum left when conservative Republicans in the Reagan years were intimidated into shucking off winning social issues so we might pass moral muster with Ben Hooks and Coretta King," he wrote, naming two Black civil rights leaders. Note how Buchanan talked about "winning social issues." He wasn't talking about abortion or school prayer or gay rights. He was talking about "the injustice and immorality of quotas" and "forced integration of neighborhoods and schools."[27]

Three years later, when Buchanan decided to run for president, these concerns about the white vote were still at the front of his mind. When he got into the race, journalists floated a number of different catalysts for his campaign: the Iraq War, which he vocally opposed; Bush's tax hike; the sharp economic recession. But Buchanan himself pointed to a different motivation. Shortly after he launched his campaign in Concord, New Hampshire, he returned to his home in Virginia to talk with Lally Weymouth at the *Washington Post* about his decision to run. It wasn't the war, he said, that pushed him over the edge, or even Bush's deal making with Democrats. It was the 1991 Civil Rights Act.[28]

The bill, which Bush had reluctantly signed, expanded the rights of employees to sue for discrimination, rights that had been sharply curtailed by a series of recent Supreme Court rulings. Buchanan was livid. He believed that appointing Clarence Thomas, a Black judge, to the Supreme Court had bought Bush room to spike the bill. But the president caved. "Every minority malcontent is going to be suing," he groused to Weymouth. And as for Bush? "I just said goodbye: the final infidelity."

Buchanan wasn't just saying good-bye to Bush; he was saying good-bye to Reaganism. The end of the Cold War had dissolved the logic that bound conservatism together. Free of that, Buchanan was willing to rethink its component parts. Free trade? Out. Military intervention? Gone. Even some of those bedrock ideas about American exceptionalism and democracy and equality—they were all up for review.

He believed he had landed on a winning message. And he had, in fact, managed to quickly outshine Duke, boxing him out as the candidate of white grievance.

Duke's presence in the race remained a problem, though. Reporters couldn't help but take note of the similarities between the two men's campaigns, right down to their shared "America First" slogan. Buchanan had known the slogan was a provocative choice. He consciously drew the name from the original America First Committee, formed to oppose US intervention in World War II. While the original group had encompassed a wide swath of political orientations—conservatives, liberals, socialists, fascists—its reputation was defined by its most outspoken right-wing promoters, including Charles Lindbergh, the famed aviator who gave antisemitic and pro-Nazi speeches under the America First banner.[29]

Buchanan faced accusations of racism, antisemitism, and even Nazi sympathies throughout his campaign, and not just because of his proximity to Duke or the "America First" slogan. A few months before heading to Smuggler's Gulch, when the crowds were still large and boisterous, he made a swing through the South. There he railed against the 1965 Voting Rights Act, calling it an act of "regional discrimination" against the South, and made a pilgrimage to Stone Mountain, Georgia, where the Klan had been reborn in 1915.

While there he visited the Confederate Mount Rushmore, a rock-face with engravings of Confederate leaders Jefferson Davis, Robert E. Lee, and Stonewall Jackson. As he fielded reporters' questions in front of Stone Mountain, he praised former Georgia governor Eugene Talmadge, a rabid white supremacist. The visit was reminiscent of Reagan's visit to Philadelphia, Mississippi, with an important difference: the Reagan campaign created plausible deniability around its invocation of states' rights at the Neshoba County fair. Pat Buchanan was venerating the Confederacy outright. The dog whistle had been replaced with a bullhorn.[30]

Buchanan faced suspicions of pro-Nazi and antisemitic sympathies as well. He dabbled in Holocaust denial, questioning whether people really had been gassed to death at the Treblinka concentration camp in Poland. He defended former Nazis being rounded up in the 1980s and argued the US government should not be involved in hunting them down. And though he supported US-Israel relations during the 1970s and 1980s, he suddenly reversed course after leaving the Reagan administration. He publicly sided with Palestinians against Israel as early as 1989, called Congress "Israeli-occupied territory," and blamed Israel for the US decision to go to war in Iraq.[31]

In response to those statements, William F. Buckley Jr. devoted a full issue of *National Review* to exploring antisemitism, including the charges against Buchanan, and concluded that he had indeed been antisemitic (though Buckley wrote it in his astonishingly convoluted way: "I find it impossible to defend Pat Buchanan against the charge that what he did and said during the period under examination amounted to anti-Semitism, whatever it was that drove him to say and do it: most probably, an iconoclastic temperament").[32]

Buchanan dismissed the charges of antisemitism as part of a "preplanned, orchestrated smear campaign," but he was never able to fully shake them, especially with Duke in the headlines and men like Metzger latching onto his rallies. He worried that these associations would not only throw up roadblocks to his campaign but slow the acceptance of his ideas as well. And by the time he reached the border that May, his ideas were all he was fighting for. He had effectively lost to Bush but, as he told a small gathering in San Diego the next day, would take the fight all the way to the convention to ensure his ideas not only had a hearing but left a mark on the Republican Party. And it worked. Later that August, at the Republican National Convention, the party's platform was amended to call for "structures" on the southern border—the first time the GOP backed a border wall. Buchanan may not have won the nomination, but his politics were already taking root in the institutional structure of the Republican Party.[33]

REPUBLICAN VOTERS WEREN'T the only ones looking to shake things up in the 1992 election. In the Democratic Party, primary voters opted for Bill Clinton, the forty-six-year-old Arkansas governor whose southern roots, baby-boom demographics, and centrist politics made him a sharp departure from the previous nominee, Michael Dukakis, a Massachusetts governor who was easily caricatured as a soft-on-crime, tax-and-spend liberal. But restive voters would have another unconventional option as well: Ross Perot.

The eccentric billionaire was not entirely unknown to Americans. He had leveraged his fortune to stage some pretty wild stunts over the years. In 1969 he became a household name after organizing a food-and-gift drop for prisoners of war in Vietnam (even though the planes never made it to their destination). The same year that American hostages languished in Tehran, he mounted a commando raid to rescue two of his company's employees also being held in the country. That ballsy episode, which he later conceded was "more lucky than smart," was memorialized a few years later in the TV miniseries *On Wings of Eagles* (Richard Crenna played Perot). And in 1987, much to the frustration of the Reagan administration, he entered into private talks with the Vietnamese government to recover missing and captured US soldiers.[34]

Perot knew how to create a media moment, and he knew how to leverage those moments into access. After his airdrop stunt in Vietnam, he was in constant—weekly—contact with the Nixon White House. But he wasn't a pundit or media innovator. Unlike Buchanan, who was a media personality, Perot was a *mediated* personality, someone whose image was carefully crafted in press coverage and popular culture.

If, by conventional measures, Buchanan was an unlikely presidential candidate, Perot was an unthinkable one. Barely five and half feet tall, with Alfred E. Neuman ears and a squeak-toy voice, he appeared more cartoonish than commanding. Yet those features also made him strangely compelling. When he appeared on *Larry King Live* for the first time in 1990 to argue against a US-led attack on Iraq, not only did a cabinet secretary call in to challenge him, but the show's producers fielded a record number of calls. Ross Perot was television gold.[35]

The team at *Larry King Live* took one look at the record-breaking numbers and immediately started working to book him on the show several more times. The game changer was that February appearance in 1992, when Perot announced he would run for president if supporters got him on the ballot in all fifty states. Not only did the show set another record for calls, but over the next three weeks, Perot's team received more than a million calls to the toll-free number he'd shared on the show. Perot continued to stoke interest with well-timed media appearances. A turn on *Donahue* netted a quarter million more calls. Talk radio picked up the Perot banner in the weeks that followed.[36]

These were all interactive media, shows where audience members could call in and be heard—a new phenomenon for national media, made possible by innovations in cable, satellite, and long-distance telephone technology. Perot promised people "electronic town halls," and when he showed up on the talk show circuit, he delivered. Larry King himself marveled at the way technology was shaking up the presidential race. "Today, if you do the full swing of radio and TV, you are going to reach 80% of the public in a week," he told a *Los Angeles Times* reporter. "You could run a whole campaign on TV and move right to the public." Which is exactly what Perot did.[37]

Buchanan watched in dismay as Perot, now an object of fascination for political journalists covering the campaign, sapped the revolutionary fervor he had been riding since New Hampshire. His share of the vote versus Bush began to sag, and he started to reposition himself as the bellwether of the Perot revolution. It was a defensible position. The two men shared a platform that set them apart from the two major parties: opposition to the Iraq War and NAFTA, support for a balanced budget and campaign reforms. There were differences, too, of course, particularly on social issues like school prayer (Perot was against) and abortion (Perot was for), but also on taxes. Cutting taxes became a bright line for the right after Bush reneged on his no-new-taxes pledge, but for Perot the revenue produced by raising taxes was a key component of his plan to balance the budget.[38]

Buchanan understood, though, that issues were only part of the story. Policies and ideology—those mattered less than the act of protest, the expression of anger and disgust that a vote for either man represented. The proof was in the polling. Buchanan, a hard-right candidate, pulled votes equally from conservative, liberal, and moderate Republicans. Exit polls for the California Democratic and Republican primaries showed that, were he on the ballot, Perot would have won *both* races by double-digit margins.[39]

This wasn't an ideological fight—many Perot voters had a fuzzy-at-best grasp of what specific policies their candidate stood for—but a bellow of frustration. Writing in *New York* magazine in mid-May, Joe Klein called Perot "a spokesman for the radical middle." The turn of phrase captured the sense that American politics was shuddering through a moment of transformation. But Buchanan preferred another label for these discontented voters: Middle American Radicals.[40]

The phrase, coined by a political scientist in the mid-1970s, became a favorite of Sam Francis, a friend of Buchanan's who would be fired as a columnist by the *Washington Times* in the mid-1990s for his embrace of the white nationalist movement. "Middle American Radicals" was his way of describing a group that, while sometimes conservative in terms of policy preferences, was actually deeply radical in its rejection—loathing even—of the establishment. Middle American Radicals disdained elites in media, education, politics, and business. That disdain sharpened their populist conviction that they were the "real" Americans, facing off against elites who had bought off the poor using money they'd taken from the middle. These voters were temperamentally radical too, seeking not to conserve but to tear down.[41]

These were the partisans who would become the base of the Republican Party: angry, radical, reactionary, and convinced that they were the victims of a liberal system that included both Democratic and Republican leaders. They were overwhelmingly white and felt that white people had become an oppressed class, losing economic and political power in American society as a result of civil rights, immigration, and economic decline. And in 1992, they had more opportunities than ever before to make clear how dissatisfied they were with their political options.

As his own star dimmed, Buchanan cheered Perot as heir to his own political success in New Hampshire, saying in late May that his campaign had given Perot's "shape and voice and direction." He pointed out that members of the Buchanan brigade were now swarming Perot rallies, decked out in both Buchanan and Perot gear. There was even some personnel overlap, as pollster Frank Luntz hopped from Buchanan's payroll to Perot's.[42]

But Perot's campaign lacked much of the baggage of Buchanan's, and soon Perot was poised to upend the entire 1992 race. Third-party spoilers were rarities in twentieth-century presidential politics. There was George Wallace, who gobbled up 13 percent of the vote in 1968, splitting the Democratic Party vote and helping to elect Richard Nixon. And in 1912, former president Theodore Roosevelt split from the Republican Party to run for a third term, now under the banner of the Progressive Party; his second-place finish threw the race to Democrat Woodrow Wilson.

Perot, though, was different. His hodgepodge of politics didn't seem to represent a clean split in either party or an emerging ideological divide. He embraced some issues that cut against bipartisan consensus, most notably his opposition to NAFTA, but mostly focused on issues like the national debt and political reform. In fact, his campaign focused less on issues than on populist posturing. He was a billionaire with no political experience who embraced those qualities as virtues, arguing that the political system was inherently corrupt and corrosive. He refused to take donations over $5 and preferred to self-finance his campaign, turning his wealth into a virtuous opposition to special interests. He initially opposed hiring any professional campaign staff, under the theory that they were all implicated in the existing political system (he ultimately brought aboard a purposefully bipartisan duo comprised of Jimmy Carter's campaign manager, Hamilton Jordan, and Reagan's campaign manager, Ed Rollins).[43]

Though polls occasionally showed Perot out in front against Bush and Clinton, he led an erratic, unfocused campaign that reflected his own paranoid, authoritarian style (at one point, he required loyalty oaths from those serving on his campaign). He suddenly announced his withdrawal in July, only to reenter the race in October. Though he never quite regained his momentum—the closing month of the campaign included a bumbling appearance by his running mate, Admiral James Stockdale, in the vice presidential debates, as well as Perot's claims that he had initially dropped out because Republican operatives had threatened his daughter's wedding—Perot still received nearly 19 percent of the popular vote on Election Day, more than any third-party candidate since Roosevelt.

Those votes were a howl of protest and of warning: something profound was happening to remake politics in the United States. And while in 1992 that discontent latched onto candidates like Buchanan and Perot, it would ultimately feed a decade of tumult and rancor that would result not in a newfound independent streak in the electorate but in a profoundly partisan politics on the right. And as both Buchanan and Perot showed, it was a matter not just of changing politics but of changing media as well.

CHAPTER FOUR

REAGAN'S HEIR

THE DECISION TO BACK PAT BUCHANAN MAY HAVE been the most consequential of Rush Limbaugh's career. That became clear on the first night of the Republican National Convention in Houston, when Buchanan electrified the delegates with his talk of "a war for the soul of America." The ability of a politician to arouse that much enthusiasm from a crowd was a rare gift, something Limbaugh learned on the second night of the convention, when he settled into his seat next to the vice president's wife. Newt Gingrich, the baby-faced, white-haired minority whip, was halfway through a five-point list of the differences between Democrats and Republicans. The speech was an awkward blend of firebrand language and professorial lecturing. Classic Gingrich: great for the C-SPAN cameras; not quite ready for prime time.[1]

Good as Buchanan's speech had been, it was Limbaugh's name that seemed to be on everyone's lips at the convention. When he'd walked into the vice president's box a half hour earlier, the delegates erupted in chants of "Rush! Rush! Rush!" Buchanan and Pat Robertson, the populist insurgent candidates who sat nearby, had gone unacknowledged. Even now, as Gingrich droned on, people were shouting up at Limbaugh, eager for a wave or a smile from the radio host. Other big names at the convention might have supporters, but only Rush had fans.[2]

No one could question his star power after the day he'd had. He had spent the morning at the KSEV booth in the Houston Astrodome doing his live radio show, a nationally syndicated broadcast that reached 12.5 million Americans three hours a day, five days a week. While on air he read aloud a thank-you note from George H. W. Bush, in which the president observed, "I've been hearing some nice comments about me on the show." (The note did not mention what a novel experience that was, given Limbaugh's support for Buchanan throughout the spring.)[3]

Then he had headed to the Wortham Center in downtown Houston for a party thrown by the Republican National Coalition for Life. Attendees shelled out $75 a person to be there, and they weren't spending that money to see Jerry Falwell or Pat Robertson or even Vice President Dan Quayle, who kicked off the ceremonies. They were there for the headliner: Rush Limbaugh. Phyllis Schlafly acknowledged as much when she introduced him as "the man people really came here to see." Once he'd taken the mic, he doled out all the greatest hits from his show. It was catnip for a room full of fans who knew their cues, shouting "feminazi" when he mentioned Hillary Clinton and booing heartily as he attacked the media. He soaked in their applause, then made his way to the Astrodome to sit in the vice president's box.[4]

And it wasn't even his biggest night. Tomorrow, he would be sitting with the president.[5]

The scene in 1992 was strikingly different from his first convention eight years ago. In 1984 the station manager of KMBZ in Kansas City sent him to the conventions, mostly on a lark. He was just a local host at the time, one who had been fired three times (and was about to be fired again), so he moved through the convention crowds largely unnoticed. For him, the highlight of the Republican convention in Dallas, other than seeing Ronald Reagan speak, had been meeting George Will, a Pulitzer Prize–winning columnist at the *Washington Post*. He had staked out the ABC News truck just so he could introduce himself to the conservative columnist, who would become a friend and casual adviser in the years to come. At the 1992 convention, he would spend a morning having breakfast in the hotel dining room with Will, arguing about Bush's reelection chances.[6]

Though undoubtedly the star of the convention, it would be the last he would ever attend. Truth was, he didn't need the conventions. After 1992, any conservative leader or Republican politician he wanted to see would eagerly come to him—presidents included. His support for Buchanan had ensured as much, prompting a rattled White House to invite Limbaugh for an overnight visit, turning him from a radio host into a kingmaker, the man whose ring Republican politicians would kiss on their road to the White House.

But in 1992, he was in an experimental stage, putting his newfound celebrity to the test. In addition to his convention appearance, he tested out his cross-platform appeal. He made the rounds on all the talk shows, from *Meet the Press* to *Donahue* to William F. Buckley Jr.'s *Firing Line*. He was in talks with the producer of *Designing Women* to guest-star on the show's season opener (the writers envisioned him scrapping with the formidable Julia Sugarbaker). His publishing debut, a book called *The Way Things Ought to Be*, hit bookstores just a few weeks after the convention, and a few weeks after that, his new nightly television show went live. He even had a road show, where he donned a tux and trotted out his best bits from radio. By the fall of 1992, Rush Limbaugh had become an inescapable presence in American life.[7]

No one had ever seen anything quite like it. Limbaugh was pioneering a new kind of political entertainment, one that drew equally from the shock jocks and the political revolution of the 1980s. He would spawn countless imitators, amass unimaginable wealth, and, most surprisingly, become part of the apparatus of the Republican Party. His style didn't just influence political broadcasting; it influenced an entire political party, so much so that, a quarter century later, more politicians would sound like Rush Limbaugh than like Ronald Reagan—and more lived in fear of crossing the radio host than of deviating from the former president's political legacy.

THE 1992 RACE marked the first time Limbaugh got involved in a presidential election. He did so not just because Buchanan offered a compelling alternative to President Bush, whose first term had brought one disappointment after another, but because Limbaugh had admired Buchanan for decades. Growing up in Cape Girardeau, Missouri, he read the *St. Louis Globe-Democrat*, where Buchanan was a young editorial writer crafting fiery conservative columns. After working for Richard Nixon for the better part of a decade, even to the bitter end of his presidency, Buchanan returned with a syndicated column that earned him a national audience. Limbaugh kept up with the column, later praising Buchanan as an "original thinker" and citing him as an inspiration for his own work. Add to that Buchanan's emergence as the most prominent conservative television personality in America, and it's no surprise Limbaugh was singing his praises.[8]

The decision to endorse Buchanan ahead of New Hampshire had really been an experiment. The 1992 presidential primary was the first since Limbaugh's show had gone national. His syndicated show launched in August 1988, and he hadn't even bothered going to the Republican convention a few weeks later. But two things had changed in the intervening years: his listeners were fed up with Bush, and he had achieved godlike status within the movement.

That status had hardly been a given even a few years earlier. When Limbaugh started out on radio as a twenty-year-old college dropout in 1971, he had little to say about politics, spending his airtime spinning records and reporting on sports. He was intrigued by the shock-jock style that gained traction with figures like Don Imus and Bob Grant, whose afternoon drive-time call-in show on New York City's WABC proved that incendiary political commentary could also garner a huge listenership, even if—or because—it was deeply racist and misogynistic. Grant compared "welfare mothers" to "maggots" and suggested they be sterilized. He advocated for "white rights." He used antigay slurs. And despite several firings, he always landed another high-profile gig, because all that controversy kept driving his ratings higher and higher. It turned out that people thrilled at the host's high-wire act, never knowing what he would say next or whether it would go too far.[9]

Limbaugh saw real possibility in Grant's style of political commentary, if he could just tame it a bit. In 1983, he took a job at KMBZ in Kansas City that allowed him, for the first time, to switch from sports and music to political commentary. The politics he took from his father, a staunch conservative, but he remixed those views with the entertaining style he had developed as a sports reporter, plus a few stabs at insult comedy that he'd picked up from shock jocks. His show was popular and enraging—two qualities that he learned went hand in hand—but it also put him on a collision course with the Mormon owners of the station, who liked the ratings but not the style. Ultimately, his sharp criticisms of the management of the Kansas City Chiefs, coming just as the station was trying to win broadcast rights for the team's games, led to his fourth firing.[10]

Limbaugh lost his job just as station owners in Sacramento were looking for a host who could serve up filtered outrage. Having just fired the popular Morton Downey Jr., a shouty right-wing host, for his use of racist slurs, the station owners hired Limbaugh on the condition that he be both authentic and polite, at least when talking to callers. That restriction gave Limbaugh a chance to create something new, a radio personality that borrowed from the shock-jock style but without the reckless disregard for the very real boundaries past which advertisers might lose their nerve.[11]

So rather than try to be maximally offensive, he instead leaned into his sense of self-importance and the conservative politics he had imbibed from his father. Over the next four years in Sacramento, he fine-tuned the Limbaugh persona: bombastic, brilliant, infallible, "with talent on loan from God." He tripled Downey's ratings, and in 1988, he struck a deal to go to New York and begin syndication. *The Rush Limbaugh Show* was going national.[12]

The call-in show gained instant popularity for a variety of reasons. One was Limbaugh himself. He kept things light, aiming to be funny, topical, and controversial, usually succeeding at all three. He matched the sunniness of his idol, Ronald Reagan—styled "Ronaldus Magnus" in Limbaugh-speak—and he often mixed outrage with humor, leaning on satire, parody, and endless nicknames when talking about the people and ideas he abhorred. He quickly developed a patois only intelligible to regular listeners. If he started talking about "The Swimmer" and "Sheets" teaming up with the "feminazis," regulars (and likely no one else) would immediately know he was talking about Senators Ted Kennedy and Robert

Byrd working with women's groups. His listeners developed their own language too, dubbing themselves "dittoheads" in recognition of their constant agreement with each other and the host.

His preference for satire and ferreting out hypocrisy was partly a matter of necessity. Limbaugh had never immersed himself in conservative ideas. He hadn't puzzled over policy or read classic conservative tracts like Friedrich Hayek's *The Road to Serfdom* or Russell Kirk's *The Conservative Mind*. His conservatism was osmotic, absorbed from his father with little reflection and, until his mid-thirties, little interest. That set him apart from someone like Reagan, an autodidact who consumed mountains of conservative literature in his thirties and forties. Rather than getting into the weeds of policy, Limbaugh instead focused on liberal hypocrisy and Democratic excesses. He railed against political correctness, which he called "the new fascism." As a result, his show was less about articulating a fully developed conservative vision than ridiculing the left.[13]

Concerned about the show's longevity while living on the boundary of offensiveness, Limbaugh honed his routine over time. In his early years he delighted in performing "caller abortions," where he played the sound of a vacuum followed by a scream whenever he dropped argumentative callers. Though many listeners enjoyed the gag—one woman at the 1992 convention mentioned it was a favorite—he ultimately dropped it as he sought more mainstream cred. The same went for his mocking attacks on people with HIV and AIDS, one of the few routines he apologized for.[14]

Limbaugh also relied heavily on plausible deniability. His attacks on feminists, gay people, and Black people followed the same pattern: he avoided overt slurs, having learned from Downey's firing, and always claimed he was criticizing "leaders" and "militants," not the broader group. Thus, he argued, "feminazis" were not *all* feminists, just a dozen or so women leading the movement. He wasn't attacking gay people, just "militant homosexuals." He loved Black people—it was their leaders, and the Democrats taking advantage of them, whom he couldn't stand.[15]

By making his statements in ways that allowed him to walk them back if necessary—saying he had been joking, or taken out of context, or misunderstood—allowed Limbaugh to detonate the bomb without ever taking any shrapnel.

But it wasn't just his on-air talent that had gotten him to the top (something journalists always overlooked, to his great annoyance). He'd built a show that took advantage of all the changes happening in radio. Music had migrated to the FM dial, leaving the lower-fidelity AM stations starved for content. Satellite and new long-distance telephone technology allowed him to do an interactive national call-in show and build a devoted base, something that wouldn't have been possible when he was starting out. And while the end of the Fairness Doctrine, a radio regulation that called for balanced political commentary, likely helped, the reason for its end—the Reagan administration—was by far the more meaningful context. Those landslide victories showed conservatism was no fringe phenomenon or regional curiosity.[16]

Not all Reagan voters were conservatives, but his victories alerted broadcasters that there might be a bigger right-wing audience to serve than they had thought. Limbaugh proved that those conservatives were avid and loyal listeners. Though they might represent only 20 to 30 percent of a given market, their propensity for tuning in day after day made them a wildly desirable segment. Across the country, coffee shops and restaurants set up "Rush rooms," where fans could mingle and listen to the show in the dead zone between breakfast and lunch service. Commuters in their cars, workers on the factory floor, retirees whiling away the morning: millions of Americans were not only tuning in but staying tuned in, hour after hour, day after day. Limbaugh didn't just rescue the AM dial. He redeemed it.[17]

And he'd cornered the market. That was the part that really mattered to Limbaugh. As an early innovator, he'd developed a program style that all those who came after would try to copy—and an advertising model that made him incredibly wealthy. He made $3 million the year he went to Houston for the 1992 Republican convention and an estimated $15 million to $20 million the year after that. There was nothing quite like him on radio, and millions tuned in day after day to consume his incendiary commentary—and all the ads that ran during his three hours on air. That more than anything explained why he experimented so much with the style of the show, trying to find the sweet spot between outrage and disgust. He wasn't looking for more people to convert to conservatism; he was looking for new listeners to expand his revenue streams.[18]

In the process, he stumbled across real political influence. In 1991, Limbaugh decided to take his new stature out for a spin by endorsing the conservative challenger. Like Buchanan, he hadn't expected the campaign to go anywhere—it was just a chance for conservatives to protest.

And protest they did, with encouragement from their favorite host. While New Hampshire voters were already unhappy with the Bush administration, Buchanan had seen the Limbaugh effect for himself. "Rush was a big help to us during the primary campaign," Buchanan told journalist James Fallows a few years later. "We used to travel around New Hampshire in the car, and Rush would come on the radio telling everybody that it would be a good thing to vote for Buchanan and shake Bush up."[19]

And the Bush campaign had seen it too. They'd never had to deal with a force like Limbaugh—this was the first presidential campaign during which he'd been a player. He might not have any power; the Buchanan protest vote could well have been an organic expression of discontent that Limbaugh reflected rather than fueled. But with Bush bloodied by the primary fight and another unknown in the form of Ross Perot scrambling the general campaign, the Bush team wasn't taking any chances. After consulting with Roger Ailes, a trusted advisor who had crafted Bush's media strategy in 1988, Bush decided he needed Limbaugh on his side. So he invited the radio host over for dinner and an overnight stay at the White House.[20]

Limbaugh would never forget that visit. In the middle of the night, after the festivities with the president and First Lady had finished, he sat at the desk in the Lincoln Bedroom, staring at a copy of the Gettysburg Address and revisiting the whirlwind day. He and Ailes had hopped on a plane as soon as that day's show had wrapped. After they landed, Ailes had taken him to the Old Ebbitt Grill, a restaurant across from the White House, to eat, explaining about the Bushes, "They eat like birds. If you're hungry and you want to eat something, we better eat before we get in there 'cause dinner is gonna be nothing but a water bowl." So they pregamed dinner, then joined the Bushes at the Kennedy Center before a tiny dinner—Ailes was right—followed by some chat about the election. Limbaugh worried the president wasn't taking the challenge from Ross Perot seriously enough. "While you may know him personally and think he's a little off the wall and a kook," he recalled telling Bush, "he's got a sizable and growing legion of supporters out there."[21]

He'd already called up his mom and brother from the phone in the Lincoln Bedroom to share all this. But one detail in particular lodged firmly in his memory: when Bush saw them into the residence, he'd swooped down on them and picked up Limbaugh's bag, carrying it to his room.

The president of the United States. Carrying his bag.

To Limbaugh, this gesture reflected more than Bush's generations of blue-blooded upbringing. It revealed his own newfound political power: the president *needed* him.

And Bush didn't just need Limbaugh's endorsement. He needed his style. That, at least, was the conclusion some Republicans came to as the Republican primary was coming to an end. Bush's greatest-generation, stiff-upper-lip approach might have played well in the Eisenhower era, but in the early 1990s, politics had been transformed by populism, in both its mood and its media. Patricians had given way to partisans. One Republican leader, the *Washington Post* reported, had been urging the president to mimic Rush Limbaugh, going so far as to urge press secretary Marlin Fitzwater to "compile a tape of Limbaughisms" for Bush to study.[22]

But learning to mimic Limbaugh's rhetoric was only part of the challenge. For Bush to compete against Ross Perot and Bill Clinton, he was going to have to tackle not just radio but television—precisely the medium Limbaugh was branching into as the campaign entered its final months.

———

PRESIDENT BUSH WAS not made for the television culture of the 1990s. But neither was Rush Limbaugh. Always a bit self-conscious about his weight (in the early 1990s, he hovered around 320 pounds), he was never entirely comfortable on camera. But a few years after his radio show went national, he met the man who convinced him television could be a tent pole of a Limbaugh media empire: Roger Ailes.

They met at the 21 Club in 1990, and a year later they finished crafting a proposal for a television version of Limbaugh's radio show, a half-hour syndicated program featuring just Rush—no guests—with occasional audience phone calls sprinkled throughout. Ailes and Limbaugh would have total control of the program, a must-have for Limbaugh, who still felt burned after filling in one night for Pat Sajak, best known as the host of the game show *Wheel of Fortune*, on his short-lived late-night talk show on CBS, *The Pat Sajak Show*. Producers had packed the audience with Rush haters and AIDS activists, leading to jeers and protests and a final segment where the audience had been removed, leaving Limbaugh to speak to an empty room. Limbaugh thought he handled it well, but his mood soured after his father, his idol, called to say he'd been played: "They set you up."[23]

The new syndicated show launched in mid-September, just about a month after the Republican convention. The set was styled like a fancy lawyer's office, with a tufted leather chair for Limbaugh and green-shaded lamps lining the wall (a Freudian might point out that Limbaugh's father and brother were lawyers, and his father had expressed a great deal of disappointment that Limbaugh didn't follow in his footsteps). He used bits of videotape and had a live studio audience, and for an early-1990s talk show, the graphic design was pretty good. It didn't have the pulse-raising slickness of Ailes's later venture, Fox News, but looking back, Ailes was clearly figuring out how to translate conservative talk into conservative television.

Ailes and Limbaugh were not alone in their efforts to translate popular talk-radio programs into television. Cable networks, especially those dedicated to news, experimented with political talk shows throughout the 1980s and 1990s. Larry King scored the first hit with political talk television. He got his start in radio, but in 1985 CNN decided to see if the hit radio show could become a television phenomenon. It could and did: it became CNN's top-rated show in the late 1980s.[24]

Elsewhere on television, daytime tabloid shows with roots in talk radio were all the rage. Shows like *Donahue* and *Sally Jessy Raphael* not only had live audiences but also experimented with taking callers live on air. Though these shows tended to frame discussions as matters of personal experience and culture, they regularly brushed up against political topics. Phil Donahue in particular worked to get hot-button political topics on air, including bringing Limbaugh on in 1992. Though these were not political talk shows, they were evidence of the way entertainment and politics were becoming more deeply entwined.

And while Perot seemed to understand this, leveraging cable shows to get out his message, Bill Clinton was the candidate best suited to the emerging political culture. He was a guest on daytime shows like *Donahue*, on late-night shows like *The Arsenio Hall Show*, and even on MTV, the cable channel best known for its music videos. He didn't just appear on those programs—he spoke their language, playing saxophone on *Arsenio* and taking questions about his underwear preference on MTV. The ease with which he navigated those venues showed the advantage that Clinton, who would become the first baby-boomer president, had over his much older rivals. Like Limbaugh, he came of age in the 1960s, when the space between music, television, politics, and protest collapsed and antiestablishment politics became not only cool but, for many Americans, morally necessary. By the time Limbaugh's and Clinton's careers were taking off in the late 1970s and early 1980s, the moral core of those protest politics had been tempered, but their style— the oppositional stance, the embrace of emotion, the merger with culture—remained.[25]

In that sense, Clinton and Limbaugh swam in the same cultural waters with ease, even as their politics sharply diverged. Theirs was a politics of connection, contingent on creating intimate emotional ties with listeners or voters. When Limbaugh spoke with callers, he helped them tell their sometimes messy and confusing stories, then used those stories to make his point. Clinton did the same: in a telling moment in one townhall-style presidential debate—a format that favored his preference for one-on-one politics—he took an audience member's garbled question about the deficit and reframed it as one about fear and uncertainty caused by the economic recession, allowing him to empathize and talk about his own experiences in Arkansas.

The recession loomed large over the campaign, as did the sense of generational difference. Clinton played in to that by presenting himself as a New Democrat, offering a mix of traditional liberal policies like expanded healthcare access with fiscally and socially conservative stances on welfare, crime, and marriage equality. He also openly courted white voters with anti-Black dog whistles, criticizing civil rights leader Jesse Jackson at a conference for his Rainbow Coalition and traveling to a correctional facility near Stone Mountain, Georgia, to deliver his tough-on-crime message in front of a phalanx of incarcerated men, nearly all of whom were Black. Those messages not only won Clinton the nomination but would deliver him the presidency.[26]

Though Bush hit on those same conservative themes, he could not convey Clinton's cool. With Perot showing up on *Larry King Live* and Clinton making the rounds on *Donahue*, MTV, and *Arsenio*, Bush's aides begged him to join the fight. To Bush, it felt improper, unpresidential. But little by little he edged his way into the new populist media. He agreed to do *Larry King*, though as a prerecorded interview, no phone calls (taking phone calls, he worried, was beneath the dignity of the office). The next day, though, Clinton and Al Gore did a full hour live, so Bush finally capitulated and did the same, phone calls and all. But before he did *Larry King*, he did *Limbaugh*.[27]

Limbaugh rarely had guests, but in the heat of the 1992 campaign, he too switched things up. Dan Quayle stopped by the studio in July, an appearance simulcast on C-SPAN, and at the start of September, the president himself came calling. He joined Limbaugh in studio, where he defended the economy, blaming the media for its focus on negative stories while promising the economy was "poised for a dramatic recovery." And he delivered a sharp new attack on Bill Clinton, saying that Clinton believed the "military was immoral."[28]

Propriety aside, the decision to go on *Limbaugh* should have been a no-brainer. Twelve million people tuned in to Limbaugh's daily broadcast, most of them the type of engaged conservative Bush needed to win. And suddenly Bush wasn't the only one reaching out to Rush for help. Newt Gingrich, who had squeezed past his Democratic challenger by fewer than a thousand votes in 1990, had barely survived a primary challenge in July 1992, requiring a recount before he could advance to the general election. He turned to Limbaugh to help get him over the line that fall, holding an Atlanta fund-raiser featuring Limbaugh just before the November election.[29]

Gingrich survived in November; Bush did not. And while Limbaugh was zero for two in his presidential picks, he had emerged from the Republican loss with the most valuable property imaginable: a letter, signed "Ron," declaring him the number one voice of conservatism in America.

———

THE LETTER LIMBAUGH held in his nicotine-stained fingers probably belonged in a museum—or at least an archive of some sort. He'd read it a hundred times, and one small detail still stuck with him. It was signed "Ron." Not a dashed-off "R.R." or formal "Ronald Reagan." Just "Ron," the way you'd sign a note to a friend.

The two men's paths never crossed, perhaps because they so often ran parallel: entertainers, Republicans, radio men. Reagan had a radio show in the 1970s, in the off years between his governorship and his presidency. It was very different from Limbaugh's: daily three-minute spots, reaching an audience of around twenty million listeners. The content differed too. As a former governor with an eye on the presidency, he focused much more on policy than rabble-rousing. But he and Limbaugh shared an affection for radio, something Reagan had developed in his early days as a sports announcer, as well as a deep understanding of its power. After leaving the governor's office, Reagan had been offered a TV gig, a commentary spot on the CBS Evening News with Walter Cronkite, but opted for the microphone instead. As he explained to his media adviser, Michael K. Deaver, he thought radio had a kind of credibility that television news had lost. And he had seen something in Limbaugh that convinced him they were kindred spirits.[30]

And so the former president had given the radio host an invaluable gift. The letter, which Limbaugh read on his television show, contained a line that he would repeat again and again. He even interrupted his own reading of the letter to make sure his audience was paying attention: "Listen to this," he told them, then read the letter's most important line: "Now that I've retired from active politics, I don't mind that you've become the number one voice for conservatism in our country." Limbaugh paused, marveling over the sentence. "I mean, you know, that's—that's not just a, 'Hey, Rush, nice to know you. Hope you enjoyed my letter' kind of sentence. There's something very serious in that."[31]

With the election just a few weeks behind them and President Bush still in the White House for another month or so, Ronald

Reagan had crowned Limbaugh the number one voice of conservatism in America. He had chosen his successor, and it was someone
who would never hold elected office. Perhaps without meaning to,
Reagan had legitimated a new source of power in the conservative
movement, one the Republican Party would have to compete with,
or try to co-opt, in the coming years.

Reagan was not the only one who saw Limbaugh, a media personality with no political experience and no electoral ambitions, as
the future of the Republican Party. A year later, in the fall of 1993,
National Review put Limbaugh on its cover under the headline
"Leader of the Opposition." The Reagan seal of approval, plus the
now twenty million listeners Limbaugh attracted, made it impossible for James Bowman, author of the cover story, to find any Republican willing to criticize the radio host—especially none of those
eyeing a 1996 bid. Bob Dole lauded him as "smart" and "tough." Phil
Gramm praised his intelligence, saying he "has had a profound impact on conservative thinking in America." Dan Quayle, Jack Kemp,
Bill Bennett—if you were keeping the door open for 1996, you were
gushing over Rush Limbaugh in 1993.[32]

Bowman granted that Limbaugh was a great entertainer, but was
he an *homme sérieux* (a serious man, rendered with the eye-rolling
pretension that was *National Review*'s house style)? Ultimately, he
decided, the answer was yes. Limbaugh was no intellectual, but
Reagan hadn't been either, and Limbaugh was talking to all the right
people: Bill Bennett on morality, Larry Kudlow and Thomas W.
Hazlitt on economics, George Will on all things conservative.

For Limbaugh, the glowing profile and lovingly rendered cover
art marked another career highlight. He had long admired William
F. Buckley Jr., the magazine's founder, an erudite, lock-jawed word-
smith with an eye for the ridiculous. Limbaugh longed for Buckley's
approval, something that would mark him as an *homme sérieux* far

more than a *National Review* cover story. And he received it: Buckley took him under his wing when Limbaugh moved to New York in 1988, inviting him to the sort of society cocktail parties that were, for Limbaugh, an entrée into an elite world that he knew existed but had never really seen. He even appeared on *Firing Line*, Buckley's interview show on PBS, though he came across as nervous and slightly overshadowed by the gimlet-eyed host.[33]

The new title, "leader of the opposition," elevated Limbaugh in the movement, in the party, and on radio. Other hosts could claim massive audiences (though none as large as Limbaugh's) or genre-defining shows, but not even Larry King, with his exclusive Perot interviews and regular sit-downs with the new president, could claim to be heading up a political party in exile. King wanted to interview Clinton; Limbaugh wanted to unseat him.

Limbaugh's success also drew imitators. G. Gordon Liddy, a former FBI agent who spent the 1980s on the reputation-rehabilitation circuit after serving prison time for his role in the Watergate scandal, launched his syndicated radio show in 1993. Oliver North, a conservative hero after Iran-Contra, started his show a few years later. But the most interesting new entrant in the field was the man Limbaugh had endorsed the year before. Pat Buchanan had done a local call-in show back in the 1970s before moving to television. Now he was back, with his new syndicated, three-hour-a-day, Limbaugh-like program, *Buchanan and Company*. And it just happened to air on Mutual Broadcasting in the same morning slot as Limbaugh.[34]

Limbaugh wasn't too worried. Sure, the campaign and the years on *Crossfire* made Buchanan a household name. But Buchanan came to radio to sell a set of political ideas, not to entertain. And in radio, Limbaugh believed, entertainment always came before politics.

Besides, Buchanan was bound to be back on the campaign trail in just a few years. Radio was for him, like it had been for Reagan, something to do to pass time and make waves in the years between elections. And then there was the format: just like with *Crossfire* and *The McLaughlin Group* and all the shows Buchanan had done before, *Buchanan and Company* was a right-left sparring show, with Buchanan going up against liberal cohosts like Bob Beckel and Chris Matthews. There was an appetite for that, to be sure, but Limbaugh knew his most loyal listeners, the dittoheads who tuned in day after day, didn't want him handing half his airtime over to liberals. In fact, they didn't even respond that well to guests or lots of phone calls.

No, he wasn't too worried about Buchanan competing either for listeners or leadership. There was really only one person who could conceivably challenge him for the "leadership of the opposition" title—someone notably missing from the *National Review* story. Someone who saw himself as the real leader of the opposition, even if technically he was just the minority whip and the other party held eighty-two more seats in the House.

Still, Newt Gingrich had a plan. And if he had his way, Rush Limbaugh wasn't going to be considered leader of the opposition for long.

CHAPTER FIVE

THE OTHER LEADER OF THE OPPOSITION

A s Newt Gingrich settled into his palatial new digs on Capitol Hill, he welcomed an unusual neighbor. He had handed over the personal suite of his Speaker's office to conservative radio hosts to use as a temporary broadcast studio as the 104th Congress got underway. And the Speaker's office wasn't the only space he had turned over to media outlets. He had thrown open the doors of the Capitol (well, the doors to the grungy basement of the Capitol) to radio hosts and television networks, inviting the entire array of broadcast media to cover the opening days of the GOP's return to power. It had been forty years since a Republican had called the Speaker's office home, and Gingrich wanted to make sure every moment of the ensuing revolution was recorded for posterity.[1]

One voice was missing as the new Congress convened. Rush Limbaugh had chosen that week to go on vacation, likely a deliberate decision that meant Gingrich would have the spotlight to himself, at least for a moment. His carefully orchestrated rollout of the Republican takeover would unfurl without competition from the man dubbed the "leader of the opposition" a year earlier. The title should have gone to then House minority leader Gingrich, but no matter. No one could question that as Speaker, he, not Limbaugh, now led the opposition.

Beyond vying for the same title, Gingrich and Limbaugh had a lot in common. The new Speaker had long argued that communications was as important as policy. He'd spent most of the past decade training conservative candidates in the rhetorical tricks and media strategies that would boost their electoral odds, and his techniques were not so different from Limbaugh's: be brash, stir controversy, steal headlines, and take the fight right to the liberals. They might have had different roles in the revolution (and possibly disagreed over who was actually leading it), but they were fighting the same battle.

That revolution owed as much to Rush Limbaugh and Ross Perot as it did to Ronald Reagan. Gingrich himself was hardly a Reagan loyalist. In a 1984 symposium in the New Right journal *Policy Review*, published by the Heritage Foundation, Gingrich lit into the administration for paying too little attention to revolutionary rhetoric. "Reagan should have focused more on changing the nation than on governing," he argued. He believed the most powerful tool a president had was not the massive bureaucracy he controlled or the executive powers he wielded but the bully pulpit. And from that pulpit, his sermons should have delivered less conciliation and more fire and brimstone. "Reagan should have prepared for re-election by forcing a polarization of the country. He should have been running against liberals and radicals."[2]

Gingrich later argued the Republican revolution of 1994 was an extension of the Reagan revolution, one that confirmed what the Reagan landslides had shown: that conservatism was a broadly popular political faith. But the actual politics he pioneered were far different. He threw out Reagan's eleventh commandment—"Thou shalt not speak ill of any other Republican"—and kept Republicans in a state of perpetual warfare, not just against Democrats but against each other. He wanted to constantly be in the midst of a battle, no matter how unpopular that battle was, because he believed the fight won headlines and secured loyalties. He sought popular language to sell his policies, but not popular policies. If you had a good sales team, he believed, people would buy your product— especially if you could convince them your competitors were even worse. He drew up the blueprint congressional Republicans would follow for decades, even though his constant revolution finally consumed him as well.

THE 1992 ELECTION had left Newt Gingrich poorly placed in his scheme to amass political power. Not only had Bill Clinton won the presidency, but Democrats retained control of both houses of Congress. It was an era of united Democratic governance, one that seemed to leave little room for effective Republican opposition.

Nor was Gingrich well placed to lead that opposition. He was in the House Republican leadership, but he was still playing second fiddle to Minority Leader Bob Michel, whom he believed to be more attached to compromise than confrontation. And Bob Dole, who had made no secret of his presidential ambitions, led Republicans in the Senate. Though the party was in a distinct minority in the upper house, it was in a better position to thwart a new Democratic president than it had been in decades—Clinton came into office with only fifty-eight Democrats in the Senate, the first Democratic president since World War II to enter office with fewer than sixty, leaving Dole room to make mischief with the filibuster. Gingrich had neither the tools nor the title to claim to be the Republican in charge.

But Gingrich was not one to see such challenges as insurmountable. He was a man of enormous ambition and little self-doubt: in his first year as an assistant professor at West Georgia College, he'd applied to be the college's president. And in his time in office, he had stumbled upon two tried-and-true tactics for grabbing headlines and bringing down politicians: allegations of corruption and overheated rhetoric. He was able to leverage both before Clinton was even sworn in.[3]

He was able to attack Clinton so quickly at least in part because, to many on the right, there was something not quite legitimate about his victory. The presidential election had not been particularly close: Clinton won by more than five million votes and with a comfortable margin in the Electoral College. Nor were there insinuations that the election had been stolen. Rather, the right believed a combination of luck and slickness had landed Clinton in the Oval Office, an outcome he had not earned and did not deserve.

For starters, he had only won 43 percent of the vote. As *National Review* reminded its readers, "Governor Clinton won with a percentage of the popular vote that would assure a landslide defeat in normal circumstances." But conservatives also insisted that voters had been sold a false bill of goods: Clinton had misleadingly presented himself as a centrist. During the campaign, he emphasized themes of personal responsibility, work, and family, which, while sometimes connected to liberal policies like national health care and education, were just as often attached to conservative priorities like cuts to welfare and tougher sentencing laws. He also publicly denounced hip-hop artist Sister Souljah during a speech at Jesse Jackson's Rainbow Coalition, part of an effort to demonstrate he was not beholden to Black civil rights activists. The campaign was determined to show that he was the furthest thing from the 1960s radical Republicans portrayed him as.[4]

Republicans, though, were not convinced. They believed that Clinton's promise to "end welfare as we know it" was a ruse to persuade voters that he was more Ronald Reagan than Lyndon Johnson. Clinton, they argued, was a child of the 1960s, devoted both personally and politically to liberal values. As a young man he smoked pot, dodged the draft, and wore his hair long. Now he supported abortion rights, affirmative action, and the right of gay service members to serve openly in the military. Add to that a wife who worked as a high-powered lawyer and seemed to have embraced all the goals and gains of the feminist movement, and Clinton reflected the entirety of what conservatives saw as the radicalism of the 1960s.

That ability to shape-shift into a more centrist politician, combined with allegations of extramarital affairs and suspicious business deals, earned Clinton the nickname "Slick Willie" during his time on the campaign trail. When he won the election, Republicans set out to prove he truly was a fraudulent, corrupt politician.

For Gingrich, that meant exposing the administration as corrupt right from the start. He zeroed in on the revelation that Zoë Baird, Clinton's nominee for attorney general, had hired two undocumented workers and failed to pay Social Security taxes for their work. At the time, these were unremarkable acts, infractions on a par with going a few miles over the speed limit (in Connecticut, where Baird lived, knowingly hiring an undocumented person for domestic work could result in a fine, but the law had never been enforced). The matter was so noncontroversial that it was included in her nomination file, and congressional leaders from both parties shrugged it off.[5]

Congressional leaders other than Gingrich, that is. Though as
a member of the House he had no role in cabinet confirmations,
he seized on the information as evidence of a kind of elite corruption: wealthy and well-connected politicos who deemed themselves
above the law. "The upper classes obey a different set of laws than
the rest of us," he said, reframing Baird's nomination as the result
of a corrupt system that protected its own. This put him at odds
with most of the rest of his party's leadership—Republicans on the
Senate Judiciary Committee had insisted the issue would not be a
stumbling block for Baird—but it also put him right in line with
right-wing radio hosts like Limbaugh, who began beating the corruption drum nonstop in the days that followed. Listeners turned
their outrage into action, flooding congressional phone lines with an
unprecedented volume of calls. Bewildered and chastened, senators
from both parties returned the day after Clinton's inauguration calling for Baird to withdraw, which she quickly did.[6]

A combination of whipped-up outrage and implacable opposition helped derail the Clinton administration nearly as soon as it
started. The administration barely had time to recover from Baird's
failed nomination before Clinton was back in trouble over his campaign promise to allow gay people to serve openly in the military.
Gingrich raised the issue in his very first meeting with Clinton just
a few days after inauguration, warning him that he was engaged in
"social engineering" and had the support of neither the military nor
his own party. While conservative outlets mocked the idea of gay
service members, mainstream outlets like the *Washington Post* also
amplified Gingrich's message. The *Post* framed the story as one of
a president with no military experience facing off against military
leaders on behalf of a special interest group within the party ("the
gay lobby"). Clinton finally settled on the "Don't Ask, Don't Tell"

compromise, which barred members of the service from disclosing, and military officials from asking about, their sexuality. The policy would be in place for nearly two decades.[7]

That dynamic played out again and again in Clinton's first year: over his stimulus bill, his budget, and ultimately his healthcare bill. Republicans reframed each as an act of radical overreach, unwilling, at least at first, to work with the new president on his agenda. As the Democratic Party under Clinton moved to the right, Republicans did not move to meet them in the middle but instead lurched further to the right themselves, rejecting compromise in favor of perpetual political warfare.

Soon, Republicans would also start pushing for investigations. They had seen Republican presidencies derailed by congressional investigations—first Richard Nixon's by Watergate, then Reagan's by Iran-Contra—and believed they could hamper the Clinton presidency in the same way. And it turned out they had plenty of fodder. Republicans accused the Clintons of making fraudulent real estate investments in the Whitewater Development Corporation in Arkansas. They accused the Clintons of cronyism after mass firings in the White House travel office. And they accused them of even darker wrongdoing after the suicide of their close friend and aide Vince Foster. A year into Clinton's presidency, Attorney General Janet Reno bowed to pressure to appoint a special prosecutor to look into the Arkansas land deal and Foster's suicide.

For Gingrich, there was a certain joy to being in the opposition, loosed from the need to navigate around a Republican president. But he didn't want to languish in the minority—he wanted to lead the majority. And in October 1993, news broke that brought him one step closer. Minority Leader Bob Michel announced that he would not be seeking reelection, giving Gingrich a clear path to the

party's top spot in the House. If he could find some way to launch
the House Republicans into the majority, he had a clear path to the
speakership.

That had been his goal since arriving in Congress in 1979, but at
the time it seemed like a pipe dream. Republicans hadn't won more
than two hundred seats in the House since the 1950s. Not even
Reagan's coattails could get them into the majority.

But maybe Ross Perot could.

Figuring out how to corner the Perot vote had both parties
scrambling to unpack what made his voters tick, then find a way to
woo them into their own coalition. That task was especially difficult
for Gingrich. For one, during the 1992 election he had denounced
Perot as an "extraordinarily dangerous gamble," warning of the Texan's authoritarian tendencies. For another, the Perot platform was
far from conservative. Perot voters supported abortion rights and
gun control, environmental regulations and national health insurance. They wanted the United States less involved abroad and called
for higher tariffs *and* higher taxes. Not exactly Reaganites.[8]

Adding to his troubles in winning over Perot voters, Gingrich
had played a leading role in passing the North American Free Trade
Agreement (NAFTA), a treaty negotiated by President George
H. W. Bush in the closing days of his presidency that would establish
a free trade zone between the United States, Canada, and Mexico. A
sizable chunk of the Democratic Party opposed NAFTA, believing
it would harm US workers, cripple labor unions, and weaken environmental regulations. So Gingrich whipped 132 Republican votes
in the House to help the new Democratic president pass a signature
piece of legislation that his own party didn't want. Perot didn't want
it either, emerging as the face of anti-NAFTA politics. Members of
his United We Stand organization flooded Congress with phone
calls and "Say No to NAFTA" postcards, and Perot himself sent

every member of Congress copies of his book *Save Your Job, Save Our Country: Why NAFTA Must Be Stopped—Now!* To counter Perot's push, Gingrich brought out his own big guns, telling the White House to enlist Rush Limbaugh, who supported NAFTA, to lobby for the bill.[9]

It may have seemed odd that Gingrich was rushing in to save a bill that Clinton, who would become his archenemy, was championing. But trade was an odd issue. NAFTA was not, after all, a piece of Democratic legislation. As Gerald Seib explained in the *Wall Street Journal*, a conservative, pro-trade paper, "Republicans created NAFTA. They have the deepest philosophical bond with it, and they have the most to lose if Ross Perot champions a successful campaign to defeat it."[10]

And so it was that, in early November 1993, Gingrich cheered on Vice President Al Gore as he demolished Perot in a debate on the Texan's favorite cable news show, *Larry King Live*. Viewers— all 16.8 million of them, a record that would stand at CNN until 2015—watched as a relaxed, confident Gore needled Perot, who was testy from the start and had trouble countering Gore's claims about the treaty. When Perot repeated his famous line that passage of NAFTA would be followed by the "giant sucking sound" of US jobs flowing to Mexico, Gore pulled out examples of other dire predictions Perot had made in the past, none of which had come to pass. "The politics of negativism and fear only go so far," Gore said. He also pointed out that a number of side deals had been struck that would enhance environmental standards and protect workers' rights. News outlets and snap polls declared Gore the winner, and Gingrich agreed. "The Perot collapse the other night took a great deal of the energy out of the opponents," he told the *New York Times* afterward. Gore's performance helped Gingrich whip his caucus and, ultimately, pass the legislation.[11]

Gingrich wasn't ready to embrace economic nationalism, much less abortion and gun rights, to win over the Perot voters. But he would do plenty of other things to gain their vote. The first was to make inroads with Perot himself. While most of the Republican leadership in Congress opposed such outreach, still furious that Perot had, they believed, handed the White House to Clinton, Gingrich favored and facilitated it. He encouraged Ohio representative John Kasich's consultations with Perot on issues of deficit reduction. And though Bob Dole, Haley Barbour, and Minority Leader Bob Michel all opposed a May 1993 meeting between Perot and Republican freshmen in the House, Gingrich gave it his full support, a move that not only strengthened his support in the caucus but heightened the differences between himself and Michel, whose job he wanted.[12]

But because the Perot movement was less a cult of personality than an expression of frustration, the real key to winning his voters was not wooing Perot—it was tapping into their anger and discontent. And for that, Gingrich needed Frank Luntz.

Frank Luntz was a new type of political consultant: a pollster who relied heavily on focus groups and quickly made his way into the Republican Party's inner sanctum, from where he would shape the politics of the 1990s. When he first addressed the Republican House caucus in 1993, Luntz stood out in the sea of Republican officeholders. The caucus still looked as it had in the Reagan era: white men in power suits and blue-and-red ties, with pin-straight parts in their hair. Luntz, on the other hand, dressed "like an aging graduate student," as one journalist put it, with an unruly mop of dirty-blond hair and barely pressed pleated pants (when he wasn't wearing jeans). He bucked the party in other ways as well, starting the 1992 campaign with Pat Buchanan's team before joining the Perot insurgency. And while neither of his candidates won, he developed a reputation as a kind of angry-voter whisperer—exactly the kind of person Republicans, uncertain about the populist forces sinking their party, wanted to have on hand.[13]

Luntz also had a particular fascination with language; he was as interested in the words used to sell a product as he was in the product itself. And that made him a man after Gingrich's own heart. Gingrich had spent the last decade convincing Republicans that rhetoric won elections. His work through GOPAC, the political action committee (PAC) he took over in 1986, had an unusual bent: rather than simply giving money to candidates for office, he used the PAC to train and recruit candidates who shared his political sensibilities. Even though Gingrich was a never-ending font of ideas (and never shy about sharing them with whoever would listen), his focus at GOPAC centered on strategy and language. Knowing that campaigns required lots of hours stuck in cars shuttling from place to place, he created audiotapes that outlined the finer points of campaigning. In them, he trained candidates to "speak like Newt," just as George H. W. Bush's staff attempted to teach him to speak like Limbaugh.[14]

Luntz and Gingrich both sought to train Republicans to speak a new language, one that would demonize their opponents and shroud even their most unpopular policies in a gauze of punchy, positive words. In a memo sent to conservative Republican candidates in 1994, Luntz emphasized the need for populist symbols and stories. "Everything 'politicians' do, we must do the opposite," he wrote. "If politicians dress in suits, we must dress casual. If politicians give speeches, we must hold discussions. . . . We win only if we are different." He rejected words like "change," arguing that Republicans needed to use "hard and active terminology" to sell their programs and vilify opponents. His advice tracked precisely with Gingrich's infamous GOPAC memo titled "Language: A Key Mechanism of

Control." Circulated in 1990 to help guide Republican candidates in the midterm, the memo listed sixty-four "optimistic positive govern- ing words" to define their campaigns, words like "pride," "strength," and "vision," and sixty-four "contrasting words" to use for their op- ponents, like "radical," "disgrace," and "traitor." The list, like Luntz's advice, drew from focus groups and their visceral responses to the language they heard. By 1994, GOPAC had hired Luntz as a com- munications consultant.[15]

Even before then, Republicans had been picking Luntz's brain about the Perot vote. In early 1993, they invited him to their three- day retreat in Plainsboro, New Jersey. In his presentation, "The Perot Vote and the GOP's Future," he emphasized that, if Republicans wanted to win Perot voters, they would have to become less partisan in their attacks and spend less time on social issues, focusing instead on economics and political reform. They could attack Clinton, but not for being a liberal or a Democrat. They should make a more procedural, character-driven case, calling him dishonest and cor- rupt, a sign of what was broken in politics. Gingrich may have been the master of partisan attacks, but he quickly saw the possibilities in Luntz's advice. "I'm recommending that every Republican candidate and every Republican official read his presentation," he said after- ward, before stealing away for a private lunch with Luntz.[16]

Over the months that followed, Gingrich and Luntz worked together to map out a strategy for winning the Perot vote in the 1994 election. The purest distillation of that work came in the form of the Contract with America. Gingrich had long hoped to nationalize congressional campaigns, but the Contract was his first full-throated effort to do so. And, notably, even though the election would shift the party hard to the right, the Contract itself was not a Reaganesque agenda or a sop to New Right social issues. It was a Perot document through and through.

Centered on reform, the Contract laid out eight congressional reforms and ten proposed laws that Gingrich pledged to act on in the first one hundred days of Congress if Republicans won the House. The reforms, which ranged from opening committee meetings to the public, to term-limiting committee chairs, to auditing Congress for waste, fraud, and abuse, aimed squarely at Perot's reform-minded campaign. Congress, the Contract argued, was corrupt and sclerotic, and Republicans were prepared to clean it up. And they would clean up the United States too, with legislative priorities like a balanced-budget amendment, tough-on-crime laws, welfare reform, capital gains tax cuts, congressional term limits, and, as always, a larger military budget.[17]

None of these ideas were new to the Republican Party. But the particular way they were arranged and tested revealed quite a lot about how Gingrich hoped to shape the party's message. First, though welfare reform and law-and-order politics reflected the party's social and racial conservatism, the policies near and dear to the religious right had been purposely left out. "There will be no social issues," he insisted, and indeed school prayer and abortion were nowhere to be found. Nor were issues with the potential to split the Republican Party, like health care, immigration, and trade. It was a major shift for the party: the 1992 Republican platform, crafted to woo Buchanan voters, dedicated more than 20 percent of its space to a raft of issues related to families and morality; the Contract, crafted for Perot voters, gave the issues only 6 percent of its space. But Gingrich got the buy-in of the Christian Coalition, convincing them that they needed Perot voters to win a majority, and they could tackle social issues once they controlled the House.[18]

Though deciding which issues to leave out of the Contract was relatively easy, deciding which to include was a more convoluted process. Luntz polled incumbent Republicans and focus groups, and in the end the list was whittled down from sixty-seven issues to ten, based on which would fire up the base while keeping the caucus united. Luntz also insisted that all references to "Republican" and "Clinton" be stripped from the document. Describing the effort later in his book *Words That Work,* he explained that many Perot voters didn't identify with the Republican Party. The Contract would work "if—and only if—the pitch was ideological and philosophical rather than political and partisan."[19]

Then came the sales pitch. The Contract was as much about messaging as it was about policy. Gingrich noted that the very structure of the Contract played well in newspapers, which, every time they covered the Contract, repeated the primary issues, often including them in a breakout box that listed the items in a way that was easy to read and digest. When Luntz talked to journalists, he underscored that all the items in the Contract were what he called "60-percent issues," meaning that they received support from 60 percent of Americans in polls. In making that claim, Luntz was leaning into Reaganesque popularity, associating the Republican Party's platform with ideas pitched as commonsense and popular.

Only . . . it wasn't exactly true. Though media outlets repeated the claims that the Contract items had broad support, research shows that the claim was "misleading at best and specious at worst." A study done by political scientist Michael W. Traugott and communications researcher Elizabeth C. Powers dug into opinion polling around the Contract items and found little evidence that policies like raising the defense budget had significant public support. On that item in particular they found most Americans either wanted the budget to stay as it was or wished to see it significantly lowered.[20]

And Luntz was decidedly unforthcoming when it came to showing the data behind his claims. When pressed by journalists to release the data, Luntz said that only the Republican National Committee (RNC) could authorize its release. The RNC, though, told journalists it had never received the numbers. Luntz still insisted that they were private and proprietary. In 1997, the American Association for Public Opinion Research would formally censure him for refusing to release the results of the surveys he conducted for the Contract with America.[21]

The truth behind the 60 percent claim turned out to revolve around Luntz's obsession with language. Luntz never actually polled the policies—he polled the slogans used to sell the policies. He admitted that he used aggressive push polling to boost measures of public support. As a result, the Contract included calls for things like increased defense spending—a position that no more than 30 percent of Americans had supported since the early 1980s. So, while Republicans had promoted the Contract as evidence of their platform's popularity, that popularity had been manufactured. Their message was a mirage.[22]

But their victory was not. On Election Night 1994, Republicans pulled off a win that a few years earlier had been unthinkable. Even a few days earlier it had seemed improbable. Optimistic Republicans had been suggesting they might pick up thirty, even thirty-five seats. They picked up fifty-four. Not a single Republican incumbent lost their seat. The Republicans controlled the House for the first time in forty years, and for the first time since Reconstruction, they held more seats in the South than Democrats did. Including Newt Gingrich's.

How much the Contract mattered to the 1994 election has been the subject of much debate. According to polling, most Americans hadn't heard of it, and the few who had were split over whether it made them more or less likely to vote for Republican candidates. Other survey data shows that Republicans did significantly better with Perot voters in 1994, suggesting that, Contract or no, they had made serious inroads with the discontented voters who supported Perot. A throw-the-bums-out sentiment still coursed through the electorate, but it only swung against Democratic incumbents, suggesting voters saw four decades of Democratic control as at least partly responsible for their discontent. And even if the Contract had not resonated with most Americans, it had the effect of nationalizing the election, ensuring that it would be a referendum on the embattled Clinton presidency, whose domestic policy wins had been few and far between.[23]

The Republican victory, though, meant the Contract would become even more important after the election. It represented the reformist, nonpartisan framework for the Republican Party, setting the agenda for the party's first one hundred days (they would, in fact, take up all ten Contract items in those first three months, with varying degrees of success). But a contradiction lay at the heart of that approach because the Congress voted in during that 1994 landslide represented the most conservative Congress in modern US political history—and one of the most combative and partisan. The party may have sold itself as the heir to the Perot presidential bid, but in 1994, another figure loomed just as large in congressional politics: Rush Limbaugh.

———

NEWT GINGRICH RESCUED Rush Limbaugh from a bit of a losing streak. In 1992, Limbaugh had backed Buchanan, who, after putting in a good show in New Hampshire, quickly fizzled out. Then he had backed Bush, whose loss with only 37.5 percent of the popular vote was as bad as George McGovern's shellacking in 1972. He'd gotten a reputation as a kingmaker, but he had yet to actually support anyone who'd won the crown. The 1994 midterms changed that.

Limbaugh rode hard for congressional Republicans in 1994. Calling the campaign "Operation Restore Democracy," he sought to elevate Republican candidates, intervene in close races, and tie every Democrat to Bill Clinton (and Bill Clinton to every bad thing in the United States). Behind the scenes, he kept an eye on close races to see which he might be able to boost on air. When a Democratic senator tried to counter Limbaugh's constant campaigning by running ads during the show, Limbaugh singled his ads out for an on-air evisceration. He proved so central to the party's midterm strategy that a week before the election, the national political correspondent at the *New York Times* dubbed him the "national precinct captain for the Republican insurgency of 1994."[24]

The outcome on election night put an end to Limbaugh's losing streak.

Though Gingrich spent the evening celebrating with a local radio host instead of Limbaugh—Sean Hannity emceed the victory party for the soon-to-be Speaker in Marietta, Georgia—the election cemented a mutually beneficial relationship that had developed between the radio superstar and the Republican leader. The roots of that relationship snaked back to 1992, when Limbaugh had joined Gingrich on the campaign trail to pitch in for a fund-raiser in the closing days of the election. A year later, Gingrich gave him an even bigger boost in return, leading the charge against the revived Fairness in Broadcasting Act, a legislative effort to reinstate the Fairness Doctrine.[25]

The Fairness Doctrine had been a key piece of communications regulation in the United States for nearly forty years. Instituted in 1949, it was part of an effort to keep broadcasting from devolving into either propaganda or mindless commercialism. It laid out certain conditions for use of the public airwaves: radio and television stations had an obligation to cover controversial issues of public importance and were required to cover them fairly. It quickly became a bogeyman for right-wing broadcasters, evidence of an overbearing regulatory state intent on silencing conservative voices. Ronald Reagan, himself a radio and television host, set out to repeal the Fairness Doctrine from the start of his presidency, something his Federal Communications Commission (FCC) finally accomplished in 1987.[26]

Unlike Reagan, Gingrich had not always been opposed to the Fairness Doctrine. When Congress first tried to reinstate it, Gingrich signed on as a cosponsor. And he was not alone: in 1987 the Fairness Doctrine had plenty of conservative supporters, from Gingrich and Trent Lott, to Phyllis Schlafly and Pat Buchanan, to the Heritage Foundation and Ralph Reed. These conservatives, though generally fans of Reagan-era deregulation, believed that the Fairness Doctrine could be a useful tool to get conservative voices on air. If it were true, as conservatives contended, that liberal bias permeated US media, then a regulation requiring political balance could be a powerful weapon for conservative activists.[27]

What conservative supporters of the Fairness Doctrine in 1987 did not foresee, however, was the rise of right-wing talk radio. The Limbaugh juggernaut suddenly left the right wary of government regulation that might be used to hem in the popular radio host, who by the early 1990s was on over six hundred stations with an estimated twenty million listeners. Overnight, a bipartisan piece of legislation that had previously passed through Congress handily became anathema to Republicans. Limbaugh and the *Wall Street Journal* dubbed the proposed legislation the "Hush Rush bill," making clear that any vote for the legislation would be considered a vote against Limbaugh. The new bill went nowhere.[28]

Once the Hush Rush crusade had passed, Gingrich and Limbaugh teamed up again to help kill antilobbying legislation. It was an odd crusade for Gingrich, who had built his reputation as a reformer but, in reality, was weaponizing ethics complaints to topple Democratic leaders. His biggest coup was successfully pressuring Democratic Speaker Jim Wright to resign in 1989 after stirring up an ethics scandal. While his intent was obvious—to take out prominent Democrats—he always insisted he was genuinely committed not only to reform but to cutting back on congressional luxuries and privileges. He had been hard at work on the Contract with America's reform agenda, and a few months earlier he'd even given up his chauffeured car after his primary opponent attacked him for the extravagance.[29]

Gingrich understood that opposing the lobbying reform bill cut against his arguments about ethics and reform. But he also knew that lobbyists had become a critical part of the apparatus connecting grassroots conservative organizations (and those that claimed to be grassroots) to Republican politicians in Washington. The reforms wouldn't come soon enough to hamstring the GOP in the 1994 campaign, but they could annihilate the conservative political apparatus if enacted. So Gingrich, in addition to undertaking his own aggressive campaign against the bill, activated the other centers of power within the conservative movement.

The Christian Coalition, the religious right group that grew out of Pat Robertson's failed 1988 presidential bid, eagerly joined the fight. Ralph Reed, the impossibly boyish Ken doll who headed the coalition, used the organization's "state-of-the-art network of computers, telephone trees and fax machines" to alert activists to the (false) dangers of a bill that would force them to register as lobbyists if they so much as tithed in church. Robertson took to the airwaves to warn viewers of the Christian Broadcasting Network that the bill represented "one of the most shocking attempts to limit your freedom of speech and the rights of Christian people" in US history.[30]

Gingrich also called on Limbaugh, faxing the radio host criticisms of the bill, which Limbaugh used on his show. Hours after the bill passed the House 306 to 112, Limbaugh appeared on his television show to argue that it was an attack on grassroots organizers like his viewers. Gingrich also lobbied *Wall Street Journal* editor John Fund (who ghostwrote Limbaugh's first book), resulting in an editorial arguing, "What is being sold as a bill to curb special interests looks to us like a way to discourage people from exercising their Constitutional right to petition their government." The resulting flood of phone calls gave Republican senators needed cover to oppose the bill, which they did. The bill, which initially looked like it would sail through Congress, failed to achieve cloture and died in the Senate.[31]

The effort to kill the lobbying bill showed how keenly Gingrich understood not only the grassroots activists and voters who would lift Republicans to historic victories in November 1994 but also the conservative media apparatus that had become an influential node of power within the movement. Gingrich, who had always considered himself technologically savvy (and, in fact, something of a techno-futurist), felt like he had cracked this new media, finding ways to mobilize it to his own political ends.

That media would become a key part of the new era of partisan politics Gingrich ushered in as Speaker. Though on Election Night 1994 he pledged to reach across the aisle and be "Speaker of the House, not Speaker of the Republican Party," there were already signs of the partisan battles ahead. As emcee at Gingrich's victory party, Hannity opened the night mocking Mario Cuomo and Bill Clinton, and outside the ballroom where the Gingrich crew partied, vendors sold T-shirts reading, "Rush Limbaugh for President" and "Clinocchio." And in a sign that he would continue his attacks on the press, he used the police to bar a reporter and photographer from the *Atlanta Constitution* from the event, still upset over a political cartoon the newspaper had run that depicted the moment he told his wife he wanted a divorce while she was hospitalized.[32]

That partisan turn continued well past election night. Gingrich may have promised to be Speaker for the entire House, but the freshman initiation showed how little he meant it. Normally new representatives gathered for orientation at the Harvard Kennedy School, where they would learn the ropes of the legislative process. But the Republican Party of the 1990s was increasingly less interested in governing and so, in 1994, offered an alternative orientation in Baltimore, hosted by the Heritage Foundation and Jack Kemp's Empower America. The lineup was rabidly partisan: former education secretary William Bennett, Paul Gigot of the *Wall Street Journal*, *The Bell Curve* author Charles Murray, Ralph Reed, and the man of the hour, Rush Limbaugh. With all the new Republican representatives opting for Baltimore and only six new Democrats, Harvard canceled its orientation, leaving the Democrats, who had no appetite for hard-right fare, without an event to attend. Which meant that as Gingrich became Speaker, for the first time there was no bipartisan orientation for incoming representatives.[33]

The Republican orientation was less an introduction to Congress than a victory march on it. Representatives wore pins reading "Majority Maker," a nickname they applied to Rush Limbaugh when they made him an honorary member of their caucus. The six women in the new class presented him with a plaque that read "Rush Was Right," after assuring him, "There's not a femi-Nazi amongst us!" Talk radio received endless kudos, as members cited one of Frank Luntz's postelection polls finding that those who listened to talk radio for at least ten hours a week broke Republican three to one. Mentions of Newt Gingrich triggered immediate cheers, which the *Los Angeles Times* cited it as "ample evidence that a cult of personality—the boon and bane of revolutionaries throughout history—is developing around Gingrich."[34]

In a rollicking evening speech, Limbaugh tossed off a few jokes about White House drug use but mostly stuck to his two main messages: beware of the press, and don't dare to deviate from the conservative line. "Some female reporter will come up to one of you and start batting her eyes and ask you to go to lunch," he warned. "Don't fall for this. This is not the time to get moderate. This is not the time to start trying to be liked." He urged the new representatives to stay "rock-ribbed, devoted, in almost a militant way to your principles." And he had a warning for the soon-to-be Speaker too. He relayed to the crowd that before the speech, reporters asked him, "Do you think Newt will moderate his stance now that he's Speaker of the House?" His response? "Better not."[35]

That warning hinted at one of the major challenges Gingrich would face as Speaker. As the leader of the opposition, he suddenly had a number of new incentives to balance. He could no longer simply throw punches; he would have to herd congressional cats and compromise on legislation. But every time he did, the other leader of the opposition, Rush Limbaugh, would be there to tell his audience of millions how Gingrich had betrayed the revolution.

As a result, Gingrich's tenure would be marked by a mix of careful compromise on legislation mixed with over-the-top rhetoric and extreme procedural obstruction to make it look like he was holding the line. It was a style he had begun to cultivate during the Bush administration's budget-deal negotiations. The deal raised taxes, violating Bush's campaign pledge and the party's general antitax stance. Behind the scenes, Gingrich had joined other party leaders to approve the deal. But when it came time to embrace it publicly, he was nowhere to be seen. Literally: without informing the White House, he skipped the Rose Garden ceremony where Republican congressional leaders joined the president to sign the bill. He then spoke out against the deal he had agreed to, saying, "It is my conclusion that it will kill jobs, weaken the economy, and that the tax increase will be counterproductive. And it is not a package that I can support."[36]

As Speaker, though, he could no longer dodge deals. But those deals would come at a cost. The election had given him a caucus that was well to the right of previous Republican House members. Around thirty to forty members of that caucus, including just-elected representatives Lindsey Graham and Joe Scarborough, dubbed themselves the "True Believers," a boast about their hardline politics. Vin Weber, a conservative activist and former representative speaking to a room full of Republican freshmen, quipped that for the first time in his life, he felt like a moderate. It was in this moment that "RINO," the acronym for "Republican in Name Only," became part of the political lexicon. It had been coined in late 1992 by a writer for New Hampshire's archconservative newspaper, the *Manchester Union-Leader*, to describe moderate Republicans in the state. But it quickly migrated across the party's right wing, used to describe first moderates and then insufficiently conservative conservatives—including, at times, Newt Gingrich.[37]

Though the new contingent of right-wing Republicans supported Gingrich for Speaker, they also harbored serious concerns about him. They had watched him work with Democrats on NAFTA and on the 1994 crime bill, an omnibus bill that included tougher sentences, increased the number of death penalty crimes, and banned assault weapons. Gingrich attacked the bill publicly but behind the scenes worked with moderate Republicans to find a compromise. He had shorn the Contract with America of some of the issues right-wing representatives cared about most, like abortion and school prayer. While those representatives may have understood the decision to downplay those issues during the campaign, they were considerably less understanding when Gingrich downplayed his commitment to social issues after the election, telling a group of Republican governors, "We can't be here suggesting the social engineering of the right will be more clever than the social engineering of the left."[38]

In early 1995, just a few weeks after Gingrich took up the speakership, a congressional aide told the *National Journal* about a faction of thirty to forty conservative representatives who already distrusted Gingrich. "They believe that he has sold them out time and time again, on issues like school prayer and business regulation," the aide explained. Throughout his tenure as Speaker, these conservatives would repeatedly challenge him, including a time in 1997 when they plotted—though ultimately failed—to oust him from the Speaker's position. They had a friend in Limbaugh, who constantly held the line against any compromise. Backed by Limbaugh, the True Believers pushed hard for a balanced budget amendment that included a provision requiring a three-fifths majority for any tax increases. The amendment failed to pass, but Limbaugh held it up as a moment when "the freshmen got to Mr. Newt," applauding their willingness to "stand and act on principle."[39]

This tension wracked the Republican Party throughout Gingrich's speakership, helping to feed tactics like the government shutdown in 1995 and 1996 (which the True Believers fought to continue even as it destroyed public opinion about the party) and, ultimately, Clinton's impeachment. It was not that such tactics were new to Gingrich—he had been a fan of destructive tactics throughout his time in Congress—but that they metastasized under pressure from his right, shredding any instinct toward compromise. "The winning strategy for the minority party in the post-Reagan era was simple," political scientist Thomas Schaller wrote about the

Gingrich House. "Do not cooperate, do not compromise, do not seek bipartisan solutions—ever, on anything."[40]

That ethos led to a transformation within the party when the right was finally in the driver's seat. And it marked the moment when moderates were no longer welcome. It might take a few more years for the remaining moderates to retire, switch parties, lose elections, or adopt hard-line views, but under Gingrich, the party transformed from one that celebrated the broad tent ethos that welcomed Reagan Democrats to one that hunted heretics, dismissing anyone not on board with the right's agenda as a RINO. Yet, as Gingrich would discover, he was not the furthest to the right in his caucus—not by a long shot—and the revolution he had unleashed would come for him too.

CHAPTER SIX

ANGRY WHITE MEN—AND WOMEN

E ARLY ON THE MORNING OF AUGUST 21, 1992, JUST hours after the balloons fell at the close of the Republican National Convention in Houston, US marshals in Idaho picked their way through a thickly forested hillside in a section of the Kaniksu National Forest called Ruby Ridge. They were scouting the property, skirting a ramshackle cabin, looking for the safest way to approach the inhabitants. By the end of the day, two people would be dead, and the federal government would be locked in an eleven-day standoff with the family inside.

Isolated in the far reaches of the borderlands between the United States and Canada, Ruby Ridge was the spot white separatists Randy and Vicki Weaver chose as their outpost. Randy Weaver had holed up there with his family after skipping a court appearance on gun charges, part of a federal entrapment scheme to turn him into an informer against the Aryan Nations. Within a few hours of the marshals' arrival, gunshots rang out across the ridge. A US marshal and the Weavers' fourteen-year-old son were killed in a shoot-out. The next day, Vicki Weaver was killed. The government responded with overwhelming force, sending agents from the FBI, Bureau of Alcohol, Tobacco, and Firearms (ATF), and US Marshals Service to lay siege to the cabin.[1]

The militarized show of force against the small cabin, followed the next year by the federal siege against a militant religious sect in Waco, Texas, in which eighty-six people died, stoked fears of a militarized federal government hell-bent on disarming Americans. Coupled with conspiracies about the new world order and new gun-control legislation, these fears culminated in the militia movement, a conspiratorial antigovernment movement made up of armed paramilitary groups with roots in white-power organizing. Whereas such groups were largely nonexistent prior to the late 1980s, by the mid-1990s, there were 858 known militias in the United States.[2]

As militia membership grew, the lines between the conservative movement and these far-right groups blurred. They were united by issues and emotion: anger toward the federal government, opposition to gun control, suspicion of federal bureaucracies, and hostility toward the successes of Black, feminist, and gay rights movements. And both the far-right and the conservative movement helped give shape to the dominant political type of the 1990s: the angry white male.

Though 1992 was dubbed the Year of the Woman, thanks to the tiny but unprecedented number of women elected to the Senate, the same year saw the emergence of the "angry white male" as a distinct figure in US politics. Though the phrase would not gain traction until the mid-1990s, the type was already shoving its way to the center of political culture in the form of Rush Limbaugh and the universally male shock jocks who dominated talk radio; in the form of Pat Buchanan and his broadsides against immigrants, feminism, and affirmative action; in the form of those militias and Klansmen who had gathered on the border to watch Buchanan speak.

And no one in Congress lobbied more enthusiastically for the angry white male than Helen Chenoweth.

Chenoweth, a representative from Idaho whose district included Ruby Ridge, snatched the seat from a Democratic incumbent in the Republican wave of 1994. Republicans had promised a revolution, and she took them at their word. Hailing from a western state where many residents had long envisioned themselves as at war with the federal government, she wedded their antigovernment fervor to an over-the-top talk-radio style. She loved nothing more than tweaking liberals, insisting on being called "congressman" and festooning the entryway of her office with smoked "endangered salmon" fillets and a rifle-and-ammo handbook.[3]

She was an instant star in the Class of 1994. Journalists reveled in her apparent contradictions. Branded a "fire-breather," she had a distinctly non-bomb-throwing appearance. A fifty-six-year-old grandmother when she entered Congress, she was a sprightly woman who teased her short, dark hair to masterful heights, adding two or three inches to her already tall, thin frame. Her soft voice and measured tone made her an odd spokesperson—*spokesman*, she would insist—for the angry white male of the 1990s. Yet she would be one of his fiercest defenders, dubbed a "poster child for the militias" for her ties to the growing network of paramilitary organizations in the United States. It was, as one writer put it, "Helen's unique brand of demure extremism."[4]

Chenoweth represented the growing part of the right that had little interest in Newt Gingrich's compromises. As a member of Congress, she served as a bridge between the Republican Party and a grassroots faction that took maximalist positions on issues like guns and abortion, who sought not just to shrink government but to dismantle it. Her time in Congress—just six years, because she stuck to her pledge to serve only three terms—showed not only the limited ability of Gingrich to mollify the right but the way a radical, sometimes violent right merged into the broader conservative coalition, even into the highest reaches of the federal government. And it underscored the break from Reaganism, especially when Reagan himself entered the fray to rally for federal gun-control laws.

———

Helen Chenoweth crowded in next to five other women who had just been elected to Congress in the Republican wave of 1994. In a room packed with scores of new legislators, their aides, and their families, this small clutch of women had the spotlight, preparing to give a plaque to the man of the hour, Rush Limbaugh. Even in that group, Chenoweth stood out, several inches taller than the others, in a white pantsuit that popped against the dark blue backdrop.

She stood out in other ways as well. By the end of her first term, the *New York Times* had tagged her as "perhaps the most radical of the 73 freshmen Republicans sent to Congress in 1994." She always met such accusations with "Who, me?" innocence, insisting that she was simply reflecting the concerns of her district.[5]

That district, Idaho's First, stretched nine hundred miles from Nevada to Canada. It was more than 95 percent white, a quality Chenoweth vocally defended. She opposed efforts by the Forest Service to recruit more minority workers to the area, arguing that if Black and Latino people wanted to work in Idaho, they would already be there. ("The warm-climate community just hasn't found the colder climate that attractive," she said by way of explanation.)[6]

Born to Kansas farmers, Chenoweth spent her early years in Los Angeles, where she briefly worked as a child actor before the family relocated to a dairy farm in a small lumbering town in Oregon. A talented string bass player, she went to college in Spokane, Washington, on a music scholarship. Within a year of starting college, she had met and married her first husband, Nick, a conservative from small-town Idaho who grew up obsessed with politics. She dropped out of college, and they moved back to his hometown of Orofino, Idaho, where they opened a ski shop and immersed themselves in right-wing literature by authors like the libertarian Ayn Rand. He would end up in law school, while she managed medical offices.[7]

When it came to policy, the two issues that galvanized Chenoweth were guns and the environment. She traced her entry into electoral politics to 1964, when she first volunteered for Barry Goldwater, a fellow westerner. It was not the Civil Rights Act that spurred her into action but rather the Wilderness Act of 1964. The act designated millions of acres as wilderness, sharply proscribing human activities in those areas and curtailing logging, drilling, and other extractive industries. Chenoweth contended the act would destroy the Idaho economy. She and her husband had already been engaged in low-key rebellion against federal environmental rules when they interfered with the couple's own economic interests. Their plans to build an airport in Orofino had been stymied by two trees that blocked their planned runway. When their federal permits to remove the trees were denied, her husband and father-in-law hacked them down and floated the evidence down the river.[8]

That entanglement of personal profit and political ideology shaped Chenoweth's precongressional career. After she and her husband divorced in 1975, leaving her a single mother raising two children, she found work with the state's Republican Party. After a brief spell as chief of staff to Idaho senator Steve Symms, she started a natural resources and political consulting company, lobbying for the region's extractive industries.

That work placed her at the heart of the Sagebrush Rebellion of the 1970s and 1980s. An effort by western activists to open up federal lands and roll back environmental protections, the movement caught the attention of both the New Right and Ronald Reagan. "I happen to be one who cheers and supports the Sagebrush Rebellion," Reagan declared at a 1980 campaign rally in Utah. "Count me in as a rebel." He backed up this new alliance by appointing James Watt, who also identified as a Sagebrush rebel, to head up the Department of the Interior.[9]

Watt only lasted a few years—after a controversial tenure, he was ousted for racist comments about affirmative action in his agency—and the Sagebrush Rebellion had mostly petered out by the end of Reagan's first term. But in the early 1990s, western discontent came roaring back in the form of the "War on the West." Though the War on the West picked up where the Sagebrush Rebellion left off, it was far more militant than its earlier incarnation. Chenoweth embodied this new, more aggressive, and better-funded political movement made up of religious conservatives, corporate interests, militias, and ranchers united against the federal government and the environmentalists they saw as a liberal special interest group invading their land. Amplified through talk radio and congressional committees, the War on the West was a nationalized version of the Sagebrush Rebellion, and Chenoweth was one of its fiercest defenders.[10]

Chenoweth was an unexpected face for a movement symbolized by men and masculinity: cowboys, loggers, ranch hands, miners. From the War on the West's martial language to its insistence that environmentalism was an effete concern, the movement maintained that the West was a man's world. But the Idahoans who built Chenoweth's campaign were predominantly women. Some were evangelical and Mormon activists whom she mobilized through the Idaho Family Forum, a religious right group she cofounded in

1990. The group, powered mostly by women activists, circulated more than three hundred thousand voter guides to one thousand churches across the district and leafleted cars in Mormon areas. In addition to the women of the religious right, she tapped into a network of women loggers, gun owners, ranchers, and business owners who shared what one writer called a "feminine cowgirl chutzpah," self-reliance and physical labor blended with traditional family structures and notions of beauty.[11]

She also helped forge a new conservative approach to women's rights, serving as a bridge between the antifeminism of Phyllis Schlafly and the counterfeminism of the 1990s. Though she supported many of the same policies as Schlafly, opposing abortion and the Equal Rights Amendment, she spoke the language of second-wave feminism and played with gender expectations in ways that worked to her advantage. During the campaign, when her opponent aired *Thelma and Louise*–inspired ads portraying her as an extremist (and subtly tying her to the film's feminism and anger), she leaned into the gendered attack, responding that she would "show those boys in Washington a thing or two."[12]

Her biography set her apart from traditional antifeminists like Schlafly, whose political identity was explicitly rooted in marriage and motherhood and, despite her decades-long career in politics, the idea that women should find fulfillment primarily in home and family. Chenoweth, a divorced single mother with open ambitions and a clear sense of the discrimination women faced in society and the workforce, more fully embraced a kind of "choice feminism" that argued women should be able to opt to pursue a career or stay at home—and be celebrated for either choice. That put her more in line with the young conservative women making names for themselves in the 1990s, like lawyers turned pundits Laura Ingraham and Ann Coulter and Chenoweth's pollster, Kellyanne Fitzpatrick.

After taking office, Chenoweth described her career to journalist Elinor Burkett in explicitly feminist terms with a conservative twist. "This is a new season for women in America. Women are returning to traditional lives and women are going into public policy, and I bridge that gap because I've done both," she said. "I'm one of the women who broke the glass ceiling." She then veered into a mild attack on liberal feminists. "Now I'm serving in Congress and I'm breaking the glass ceiling that says that women have to be what the National Organization for Women wants us to be." Even her insistence that she be called "congressman" featured this same blend of patriarchal critique and needling of liberal feminists. In an appearance on Pat Robertson's *The 700 Club*, she explained that she chose the title because only the male version commanded respect.[13]

Tweaking and trolling her opponents turned out to be an effective way to garner press and tap into the simmering anger in American politics without herself sounding angry. She spoke instead in a wry, satirical tone, riding the same wavelength as talk show hosts like Rush Limbaugh. Her favorite targets were environmentalists. She showed up at one event wearing a shirt that read on the front, "Earth First!"—the name of a radical environmental group—and on the back, "We'll log the other planets later." Another favorite shirt bore the slogan "Idaho's Endangered Species" above a picture of a farmer and a cowboy. It fit right in with a right-wing culture where Rush Limbaugh introduced his "environmental updates" to the strains of "Born Free" overlaid with the sounds of gunshots and animals screeching in pain.[14]

Chenoweth also mirrored Limbaugh's style of commonsense nonsense, arguments that sounded plausible but fell apart under the slightest examination. During one of her endangered sockeye salmon bakes, she scoffed when asked if she took the species' endangered status seriously. "How can I," she responded, "when you can buy a can of salmon off the shelf at Albertson's?" At another event she argued that global warming was not actually occurring and that the spike in temperatures was instead related to the decision to measure the official temperature at airports, where acres of concrete raised the ambient temperature. She also mimicked Limbaugh's habit of backing away from outlandish statements whenever they were repeated back to her. When pressed about her airport theory, she told NBC Nightly News that she had been attacking fearmongering, not climate science. "Don't make me look silly!" she admonished the reporter who followed up on her claims.[15]

But life out west wasn't just about logging and ranching. It was also about guns. And there too Chenoweth would take the maximal position, in a way that earned her a reputation as one of the most radical members of a radical Congress.

———

LEE ANN CALLEAR sat near Helen Chenoweth on a stack of bleachers in Orofino, Idaho, one fall day during the 1996 campaign. Callear worked as the campaign's regional coordinator, and while she and Chenoweth watched the annual town auction, she chatted with journalist Elinor Burkett, who was writing a book on conservative women. Like Chenoweth, Callear deviated from the Schlafly-era housewife activism, embracing a hodgepodge of issues, from the North American Free Trade Agreement and sex education (she was for both) to abortion (she was against). That jumble of positions showed how a range of policy preferences could be smuggled under the same ideological label. She broke with religious conservatives on sex ed but agreed with them, mostly, on abortion, an issue that still split libertarian and social conservatives in Idaho. Chenoweth was sensitive to those splits, working to bar federal funding for abortion without calling too much attention to the issue, given its divisiveness among her supporters.

But if abortion split Idaho conservatives, another issue united them: guns. Callear, who denounced abortion as murder, nonetheless admitted that if she had to, she'd trade abortion bans for gun rights. "I'm no compromiser," she assured Burkett. "But if we don't guard the Second Amendment, we can't guard ourselves against tyranny. I don't hunt. I don't carry a gun. In fact, I'm afraid of guns, just like I'm afraid of bears. But Americans better wise up and realize that gun control imperils their liberty."[16]

Sitting a bleacher row above her, Chenoweth smiled—and for good reason. Callear had just voiced an ideological commitment to guns divorced from their own role in her life. That had been the project Chenoweth, her fellow right-wing Republicans, and groups like the National Rifle Association (NRA) had been pushing for almost two decades—and in the 1990s, they were finally breaking through.

Like abortion, guns had not been a litmus-test issue prior to the 1990s. While the religious right had fallen into lockstep on abortion, the party was slower to come around. It was even slower to come around on guns. As governor, Ronald Reagan had signed into law strict gun-control measures following armed Black Panther protests in the state. But by the time he became president, he had come to see gun owners as an important constituency and reluctantly worked to placate the NRA. The first presidential candidate to receive an NRA endorsement, he spoke at the association's 1983 convention in an effort to shore up his support with gun owners before the 1984 campaign.[17]

It wasn't just the Republican Party that was evolving—so too was the NRA. Founded in 1871, the organization supported gun-control regulations until the 1970s, believing they were necessary to prevent violent crime and to protect gun ownership for hunters. After World War II, the NRA quietly lobbied against the strictest gun regulations, but it mostly focused on things like gun safety and recreational shooting. Only in the 1970s did the NRA make the Second Amendment and individual gun ownership central to its activism. In a swift coup in 1977, the group's moderate leadership was overthrown by hard-line gun-rights activists who believed that every individual had a constitutional right to unrestricted gun ownership—and the ability to carry those guns wherever they wished (to keep *and* bear arms).[18]

At the time, that was considered a radical idea. In 1990, Chief Justice Warren Burger, a conservative jurist appointed by Richard Nixon, called such a claim to unrestricted gun rights "one of the greatest pieces of fraud on the American public by special interest groups that I have ever seen in my lifetime." The Second Amendment applied to state-organized militias, not individuals. Reagan agreed, and despite his willingness to woo gun activists, he also found plenty of carve-outs for gun regulation. While he supported the use of guns for sport, his administration restricted loaded guns in national parks and wildlife refuges. Reagan saw a firm right to gun ownership only for private personal protection, assuring gun owners that his administration would "never disarm any American who seeks to protect his or her family from fear and harm."[19]

But something shifted in the early 1990s. The passage of the 1993 Brady Handgun Violence Prevention Act, which required background checks and a waiting period for gun sales, and the 1994 federal assault weapons ban, which prohibited some semiautomatic weapons and large-capacity magazines, not only superheated but polarized the gun debate, turning it into both an absolutist cause and a partisan one. And as it shifted, it put Reagan at odds with his party.

That's because Reagan supported the passage of both bills, even as the majority of Republicans in Congress, including soon-to-be Speaker Gingrich, opposed them. More than that, Reagan, who weighed in on very little in the years between his presidency and his retirement from public life in 1994, publicly lobbied for both pieces of legislation, seeing them as reasonable restrictions in an era of significant gun violence. The Brady Bill had been named for Reagan's press secretary, James Brady, who had been permanently impaired after being shot in the head during the 1981 assassination attempt against Reagan. In 1991, when the bill was first introduced by Representative Chuck Schumer, Reagan wrote an op-ed endorsing the legislation and pointing out that such a law could have prevented the assassination attempt in which he, Brady, and two others were shot. Reagan also joined former presidents Jimmy Carter and Gerald Ford in an open letter calling for its passage. In both cases, Reagan had public opinion on his side: 77 percent of Americans supported the federal gun ban, and 90 percent supported the Brady Bill, including 80 percent of gun owners.[20]

That public pressure nearly enticed even the NRA to support the Brady Bill—as late as the 1970s the organization had supported waiting periods—but it ultimately continued its opposition, with one eye on public sentiment and another on an even further-right gun-rights organization called Gun Owners of America. Founded in 1975, Gun Owners of America was led by Larry Pratt, who also founded English First, part of the neo-nativist movement, as well as an organization that paid the legal bills for Operation Rescue, a militant antiabortion group. Gun Owners of America constantly nipped at the NRA from the right. That pressure hastened the NRA's turn toward gun-rights absolutism. Under the leadership of Wayne LaPierre, the hard-liner chosen to run the NRA in 1991, the organization shifted to a policy of recriminations and ultimatums, pouring money into the campaigns of pro-gun candidates and running ads against members who voted for gun control.[21]

After the assault weapons ban passed—part of the Violent Crime Control and Law Enforcement Act of 1994, which most Republicans voted against—the NRA reconfigured its donations. The organization, which had previously given more than a third of its campaign donations to Democrats, now tilted even more heavily toward Republicans. In 1994, it dropped donations to Democrats by $200,000 and raised donations to Republicans by $625,000. The NRA gave more money to House Republican freshmen like Chenoweth in 1994 than any other political action committee (PAC), funneling more than twice as much money into Republican campaigns as right-to-life groups, the second-largest PAC category, did.[22]

That intensive focus on the Republican Party did not mean that the NRA supported all Republicans. Rather, it used its ratings system and spending to help pro-gun Republicans defeat members of their own party who suddenly found themselves in the moderate camp as the pro-gun movement moved to a position that opposed all gun regulation and pushed for expansive concealed-carry and open-carry laws. For instance, when New Jersey state senator Charles Gormley, a Republican who had voted for a state-level assault weapons ban in 1990, ran for Congress in 1994, the NRA shelled out $18,000 in negative ads against him, helping boost his opponent to victory. The strategy was not as simple as the NRA buying members of Congress; Gormley's opponent didn't accept any NRA donations. Rather, the NRA would target any lawmaker deemed insufficiently pro-gun, even in primaries. As a result, the NRA was transforming guns into not just a partisan issue but a litmus test for Republican candidates.[23]

NRA funds also helped boost Bob Barr, a newcomer running in 1994 in a tight race for a House seat in Georgia against an incumbent Democrat whom the NRA had targeted as one of its "dirty dozen." Barr won the race and would go on to head up the House's new Firearms Legislation Task Force, which was created as part of an effort to repeal the assault weapons ban (a near-impossible task with a Democratic president in the White House). Both the NRA and the attempts to repeal the assault weapons ban were broadly unpopular in the United States in the 1990s. But the organization was more concerned with influencing legislators and empowering a small but vocal pro-gun movement within the party's base.[24]

Chenoweth, who fit in well with the NRA's new position on guns, snagged a seat on the task force as well. Always on the hunt for ways to repeal restrictions on gun ownership, she spearheaded an effort to end the law barring people convicted of domestic violence from owning guns. To counter the negative press around the domestic violence bill, she organized a press conference featuring women gun activists who supported the bill, introducing the language of women's rights into the gun conversation. The press conference included Women Against Gun Control, a Utah-based group whose president argued, "The Second Amendment *is* the Equal Rights Amendment."[25]

For Chenoweth, unrestricted access to guns was not just about a rural way of life, as some advocates argued. It was connected to a broader antigovernment ethos that held armed self-defense was about protection not just from other people but from the government itself: from Bureau of Land Management officers, from ATF agents, from any arm of the federal government that might turn up in her home state of Idaho. And she represented constituents who not only agreed with that philosophy but had been radicalized by Ruby Ridge and the new gun restrictions.

These were Helen Chenoweth's constituents—not her only ones, of course, but a vocal part of her district. Her close ties and steadfast defense of the militia movement led a local newspaper to call her a "posterchild for the militias," a label that stuck throughout her time in Congress. The ties ran deep, in part because she had built her constituency in Idaho's grassroots right, and a significant portion of that grassroots movement backed the militias. The militias themselves even pitched in on her campaign, with members of the US Militia Association serving as volunteers. And Chenoweth, once in office, continued to pay attention to their concerns. In her first weekend back in Idaho, she held a daylong hearing in Boise on the "excessive use of government force," featuring Randy Weaver's attorney. She detailed any number of stories she had heard featuring out-of-control federal agents before assuring the crowd, "People in the West fight back."[26]

Chenoweth won militia support because her hard-right politics and rhetoric aligned with their own. A VHS tape of one of her speeches, in which she warned that environmental regulations were causing a "breakdown in state sovereignty and possibly leading to a one-world government," sold in a Militia of Montana catalog next to bomb-making manuals and conspiracy videos. (Her spokeswoman made clear that she did not give permission for the sales and did not share the group's beliefs.)[27]

But she had, in fact, intervened on behalf of militias in the early days of her first term. Immediately upon taking office, she pursued policies promoted by the "constitutional sheriffs" movement, which held that local sheriffs were the highest-ranking law enforcement officers in the country, to which state and federal officials had to defer. The idea had its origins in the Posse Comitatus movement of the 1970s, a white-supremacist organization that believed the federal government was part of an illegitimate Jewish plot and that power thus devolved to the county level and the sheriff (who could be overthrown if local citizens felt he had not acted in their interest). The idea of sheriff supremacy seeped into the militia movement, and Chenoweth sought to enshrine it in federal law. She first hoped to write legislation that disarmed federal officials unless the local sheriff granted them explicit written consent to carry weapons, then compromised with a draft bill that she called the Civil Rights Act of 1995, which required federal officials to gain permission from local authorities before acting in an area. (Neither bill was introduced to the floor.)[28]

She also played into far-right militia conspiracies. At a hearing for the House Subcommittee on Resource Conservation in February 1995, she quizzed the undersecretary of agriculture for national resources and environment about "black helicopters," the symbol of federal and one-world-government conspiracies in the 1990s, supposedly spotted in Idaho. She warned that she would become his "worst nightmare" unless the helicopters were grounded. The agency pushed back, saying that while its agents occasionally moved around the sprawling region in civilian crafts, they had never made use of the black, military-style helicopters of lore. When pressed for proof, Chenoweth admitted she hadn't seen them but added, "Enough people in my district have become concerned that I can't just ignore it."[29]

Chenoweth also fanned the flames of conspiracies about the United Nations. Long loathed by the right, who saw the intergovernmental organization as a threat to US sovereignty, the UN returned to the center of right-wing conspiracies at the end of the Cold War. In particular, conspiracy theorists claimed that it was secretly planning to institute a "new world order" of one-world government, a conspiracy popular among militia members that seeped into the nonmilitia right. Pat Robertson latched onto the idea in his best-selling book *The New World Order*. In it, he reworked old antisemitic conspiracies, mixing in Freemasons, the Illuminati, and Satan, to stoke fears of a unitary government that would destroy both Christianity and the United States. The idea caught on, and a new US sovereignty movement sprouted up alongside the local sovereignty movement of the militia world.

Chenoweth joined the UN bashing. She voted to remove the United States from the United Nations, a longtime goal of the John Birch Society, with which she had close ties (her first campaign manager belonged to the society, and she gave speeches to its chapters). She also spread conspiracies about the United Nations. "It is true, about 20 national parks have been taken over by the U.N.," she told constituents, turning the designation of eighteen parks as World Heritage Sites, part of a nonbinding UN program that offers guidance on preservation, into part of a deeper conspiracy.[30]

In addition to the antisemitic thread running through these conspiracies, they also tapped into a thread of racism that ran from the explicit white supremacy of many militia and far-right groups to the slightly—but only slightly—more coded appeals that Chenoweth made. She branded herself a fan of the Confederacy, holding it up as an exemplar of the sort of states' rights politics that she preferred. At one of her endangered salmon bakes during the campaign, she declared, "It's the Anglo-Saxon male that's endangered today." It was a swat both at environmental regulations and at affirmative action. When her comments drew criticism, she doubled down. "I think it speaks for itself," she said, adding that civil rights laws protected "everyone but the white Anglo-Saxon male." Not only did she double down, but she attacked the claims that her comment was racist. "To even equate this with any kind of racism is extremely unfortunate."[31]

Still, racist organizations understood her remarks. A former
Klan leader in Georgia celebrated her 1994 win as a victory for "race-
based campaigns," pointing to it as evidence "of a sea change in the
mood of the white voter towards candidates who offer frank solutions to America's growing nonwhite chaos." Though Chenoweth
rejected the endorsement, the recognition that racist groups saw
in her remarks, which whistled a little more loudly than Reagan's,
underscored the increased blurriness between Republicans in office
and the radical racist grass roots.[32]

Chenoweth was not the only member of Congress who blurred
those lines. Washington representative Linda Smith, a fellow freshman elected in 1994, met with militia representatives and allowed
militia members to volunteer on her campaign. She shrugged off
press questions about the meetings, noting that militia members
were constituents just like everyone else in her district. Another
Washington representative, Jack Metcalf, regularly spoke to militia
groups on his pet topic, abolishing the Federal Reserve. That work
led him to serve as cochair for Redeem Our Country, a far-right
organization with an antisemitic newsletter. And Steve Stockman, a
Texas representative, harbored close ties and sympathies with militias. In March 1995, he warned Attorney General Janet Reno not to
carry out a federal raid on armed citizen militias, rumored to be in
the works on militia message boards online. He also wrote an article
for *Guns & Ammo* magazine arguing that the federal government
staged the raid at Waco in order to push through the assault weapons ban.[33]

It was Stockman who received a fax on the morning of April 19,
1995, from a member of the Michigan Militia. Cryptically written,
it suggested that federal agents had been behind the massive explosion that had just taken place in Oklahoma City—an explosion that

would put an intense spotlight on the new members of Congress with close ties to the militia movement.

———

THE OKLAHOMA CITY bombing, a devastating attack carried out by white-power activists Timothy McVeigh and Terry Nichols, had the potential to crush not only the militia movement but the officeholders and political leaders who supported it. In the wake of the terror attack, news outlets closely examined lawmakers' ties to militia groups, while the incendiary rhetoric that had become so popular on the right suddenly struck even supporters as dangerous and unpatriotic. Just six days before the bombing, Wayne LaPierre had sent out a fund-raising letter for the NRA in which he called government officials "jack-booted thugs" empowered to "break in our doors, seize our guns, destroy our property, and even injure or kill us." When the letter became public after the bombing, LaPierre initially held firm, arguing that his words were "a pretty close description of what's happening in the real world." But after former president George H. W. Bush announced he had resigned his lifetime membership after reading the letter, LaPierre relented, offering a public apology. He also publicly distanced the NRA from the militia movement, saying, "We don't train for a revolt in the woods; we train for safety."[34]

LaPierre was not the only one having trouble navigating the aftermath of the attack. A week after the bombing, President Bill Clinton denounced "promoters of paranoia" for fostering a climate of hate and anger that made the violent attack possible. Though he did not mention anyone in particular, and his aides hastened to clarify that he did not mean mainstream right-wing voices, Rush Limbaugh seized the opportunity to take offense. Arguing that

Clinton and liberals were using the deaths of 168 people for politi-cal purposes, Limbaugh complained, "The insinuations being made are irresponsible and are going to have a chilling effect on legiti-mate discussion." For years after, he would contend that Clinton had blamed him for the bombing.[35]

Limbaugh did, however, seek to put some distance between himself and the far right. In the months after the bombing, he started poking fun at certain types of conspiracy theories (not all of them, because he himself spread conspiracies that Clinton aide Vince Foster, who died by suicide in 1993, had been murdered). On one show he did a bit he called "The Kook SATs." Sample question: "If Trilateralist A traveled east at 30 miles an hour and Trilateralist B traveled west at 50 miles an hour, how long would it take them to take over the Federal Reserve?"[36]

Limbaugh also seemed to be cozying up to Republican lead-ers, aligning himself with the mainstream of the party. He often had Newt Gingrich on the show or talked about his conversations with "Mr. Newt." He flashed his insider connections with marquee conservatives like Bill Bennett and Bob Dole, the Senate minority leader who was on his way to becoming the Republican presiden-tial nominee. Freighted with those personal connections, he seemed less in line with the Chenoweths of the party and more in line with the new Republican establishment. After a caller complained about the compromise-laden politics of career politicians like Dole, Lim-baugh spoke up in their defense. "Washington politics is a career," he shrugged. "Somebody who's never done it before is not going to excel or succeed." He went on to defend deal making as the basic currency of politics, sounding far more like an insider than a bomb thrower.[37]

Even this mild moderation by Limbaugh and LaPierre opened a space on their right that neither man was comfortable with. They knew not only that they had competitors willing to exploit that space—in the case of LaPierre, the Gun Owners of America; in the case of Limbaugh, upstart radio shows all across the country—but that at least part of their base still wanted hard-right content, even if it meant they would be attacked as militia-loving malcontents.

That hunger was evident in the way conspiracy theories and militias continued to thrive in the wake of the bombing. One prime example that unfolded in the months after the bombing was the cancellation of the Conference of the States, the brainchild of conservative governors and state representatives who wanted to stage a conference to symbolically reclaim the Tenth Amendment. That amendment, which said that any powers not explicitly given the federal government in the Constitution belonged to the states, was the second-favorite amendment of the militia movement and states' rights advocates, who saw it as a tool for rolling back federal power. Gingrich embraced the effort, seeing it as just the kind of media event that he liked.

Yet right-wing activists became convinced that the conference was a plot to rewrite the constitution and open the door for one-world government. Activist Linda Liotta, an artist and Clinton voter living in Potomac, Maryland, was one of the first to seize on the Conference of the States, convinced that not just Clinton but Republican leaders like Gingrich and Dole were selling out US sovereignty to establish a global government. She and other activists spread the conspiracy theory via fax trees, a favorite mode of communication for right-wing groups in an era when internet connectivity was not broadly available throughout the country. They also forged alliances with a few state-level Republican officials active in groups like the Constitutionalists' Networking Center and the Tenth Amendment Movement. Though militia groups also spread the conspiracy, the main activists were a much different alliance spread across the country. The *Washington Post* described them as a "coalition of small business owners, insurance agents, airline employees, engineers and stay-at-home mothers."[38]

The journalist reporting on these fax-tree activists seemed surprised at their middle-class status, but he shouldn't have been. For decades groups like the John Birch Society had drawn from the same type of white, economically comfortable activists who resented their portrayal as wild-eyed, ill-informed conspiracists, even as they trafficked in wild-eyed, ill-informed conspiracies. He also seemed surprised at the "angry white mothers" in a movement generally associated with "angry white men." But that too was not so abnormal. From the 1920s Klan, to the 1950s Massive Resistance movement, to the 1970s antibusing activism, women had been front and center in right-wing politics. In the militias, too: about a third of the militia activists in Idaho were women.[39]

The activists ultimately reached thousands of people through their fax trees, and by enlisting talk radio, they reached countless more. Angry messages flooded statehouses, so much so that the organizers relented, calling off the conference.

Their success, and the bewilderment of officials who thought they were engaging in the very theatrics that grassroots activists seemed to love, showed the tensions that ran through a movement in which the lines between fringe and mainstream were blurred beyond recognition: you could be a bomb thrower one day and an establishment shill the next. Many of the activists had flirted with the Perot movement and marinated in talk radio. But they kept evolving. "I was never involved in politics until 1992, when I worked for Perot and discovered I had a voice," said one Manhattan-based fax-tree activist. "A great many of us have gone beyond Perot since then." They had gone beyond many parts of the right, past Reagan and Gingrich and Limbaugh.[40]

Yet for right-wing representatives like Chenoweth, these activists were still her base. After Oklahoma, she didn't denounce militias but continued to express her support. She made clear she did
not support the bombing but suggested the federal government
shared culpability. "We still must begin to look at the public policies
that may be pushing people too far," she said. And as a result, she
found herself with a new national platform: she received invitations
to appear on *Face the Nation* and the network news and garnered
mentions in all the major papers. Ties to extremists led not to Chenoweth's being ignored as a fringe figure but rather spotlighted as
someone unusual, intriguing, and insightful. Chenoweth leveraged
that journalistic bias to great effect, becoming, if not a household
name, then an increasingly influential Republican lawmaker.

She also faced no consequences in Congress, where she was elevated to her preferred committee in her second term. After a close
campaign in 1996, she easily won reelection in 1998, leaving Congress in 2000 only because she had pledged to limit herself to three
terms. Embracing extremism hadn't cost her a thing—it had made
her a media darling, cemented her popularity with Idaho voters, and
revealed an emerging dynamic within the conservative movement:
the boundaries between fringe and mainstream were disappearing,
and those who still acted as if they were operating in a world that
rewarded compromise and condemnations of extremism would be
sorely disappointed.

CHAPTER SEVEN

RACE SELLS

MILITIAS REPRESENTED ONE EXPRESSION OF THE angry white male of the 1990s: gritty, conspiratorial, violent. But there was another side as well, one filtered through the intellectual elites of the conservative movement. These writers and think tankers believed the colorblind racism of the Reagan era was ill-suited to both the realities and the mood of the 1990s. They looked at the United States and saw Black people rioting in Los Angeles and Latino migrants slipping across the southern border, automobile factories shuttering in the Rust Belt and aeronautics factories closing on the West Coast, and women and people of color claiming more spaces in universities and corporations. In short, they saw plenty of reasons for the angry white male to be angry—as well as a chance to cement his place in the conservative coalition.

The cause of all these problems, they believed, was the social and political activism of the 1960s: the liberation movements for Black,

Latino, Indigenous, and Asian people; the feminist movement; gay rights activism; and the antipoverty programs of the Great Society. The Civil Rights Act and Voting Rights Act had sought to secure equality for Black Americans and opened the door to more activist programs like busing and affirmative action. The Immigration Act of 1965 had shifted immigration from Europe to the Global South, changing the demographics of immigrants from almost entirely white to an unprecedented mix of Asian, African, and Latino. And antipoverty programs had sustained cultures, lifestyles, and even groups of people they believed the government should discourage.

Embedded in those beliefs was a criticism not only of liberal egalitarianism but also of Ronald Reagan's colorblind racism. An earlier generation of Reaganites and neoconservatives (liberal social scientists, writers, and politicians who moved right in the 1960s and 1970s in reaction to the liberation movements of those years) had criticized Great Society programs because they interfered with a set of natural systems that, if allowed to operate unconstrained, would in time promote greater freedom, purer meritocracy, and a kind of natural equality. But for this new generation that adopted what they thought of as a "race realist" approach, equality was not possible. Nor could race be ignored, because it contained vital information about limitations of culture, IQ, and assimilation.

This pessimistic racism had profound consequences for policy, as well as for more foundational ideas like democracy. Nativism became central to an anti-immigrant backlash that began reshaping US politics in the early 1990s. Familiar appeals to end affirmative action now came with calls to roll back the Civil Rights and Voting Rights Acts. There were even recommendations for eugenicist policies to encourage higher birthrates for white women while limiting them for poor minority women.

When such ideas came paired with a white robe or a swastika, they were easy to dismiss as radical. But the popularizers of this new racism, who wrote books like Richard Herrnstein and Charles Murray's *The Bell Curve*, Dinesh D'Souza's *The End of Racism*, and Peter Brimelow's *Alien Nation*, presented their ideas with all the trappings of intellectual respectability. Their heavily footnoted books brimmed with charts and references to scholarly works. And they touched a nerve: each was treated seriously by established news outlets and at times even caught the eye of Democratic moderates who found the scientific-sounding books to be a modern alternative to rank bigotry in their efforts to appeal to white voters.

"TIME TO RETHINK immigration?"

That was the question *National Review* asked on its cover in June 1992—a moment when, other than Pat Buchanan, not many Americans were thinking about immigration at all. Just a few years earlier, George H. W. Bush had signed bipartisan legislation to increase immigration to the United States with a focus on family reunification and skilled workers. The legislation had also created a commission to study immigration policy, which was quietly at work in Congress. But as a political issue, it did not appear to be top of mind for most Americans, garnering little notice in the 1992 election.

Still, the cover story caused a stir. The author, Peter Brimelow, was an immigrant himself—he grew up in Lancashire, England, before eventually settling in New York City—as was the editor who commissioned it. Brimelow had been through the process of becoming a US citizen, and what he saw as he waited in the offices of the Immigration and Naturalization Service (INS) revolted him. Comparing the INS waiting room to the tenth circle of hell, he declared there was "something distinctly infernal about the spectacle

of so many lost souls waiting around so hopelessly, mutually incom-
prehensible in virtually every language under the sun."

So far, he could be describing the frustrations of any bureau-
cratic experience. But he had some other thoughts on the inhabitants of the room. They struck him as docile in the face of the
INS's opaque and seemingly arbitrary rules, and he mused that
such docility may have been "imbued in them by eons of arbitrary
government in their native lands." One other thing struck him about
that waiting room, something he'd noticed elsewhere in his adopted
home of New York: "Just as when you leave Park Avenue and de-
scend into the subway, on entering the INS waiting rooms you find
yourself in an underworld that is almost entirely colored."[1]

He elaborated on that idea of a colored underworld in his book
Alien Nation, released in 1995. The book revolved around what
he called "a plain historical fact": "the American nation has always
had a specific ethnic core. And that core has always been white."
The immigration patterns of the past quarter century, however, had
threatened to change that, triggering a "demographic mutation" that
was steadily replacing the country's "specific ethnic core" with one
that looked more like the people waiting alongside him in the INS
offices. To defend that white ethnic core, Brimelow concluded, the
United States would have to enact restrictive immigration laws that
heavily favored white Western countries.[2]

Doing so would require repealing the Immigration and Nation-
ality Act of 1965, which did away with a racist quota system that
limited immigration to almost exclusively white European migrants.
Brimelow wanted that system back. Even though he argued that immigration—both authorized and unauthorized—had grown much
too quickly and should be dramatically scaled back, he also railed
against any limits on eastern European immigration, believing that
the United States could easily assimilate those white migrants. He

insisted that this was about not *race* but *culture*: immigrants from the "Third World," if they arrived in large numbers, simply could not fully assimilate into US culture and, being poorer and less educated, would tax every system in the country, from welfare, to jobs, to health care, to the environment.

Brimelow's insistence that his argument was not about race was undercut not only by his repeated emphasis on whiteness but by his distinction between earlier waves of immigration and the post-1965 pattern, which he described as dangerously dominated by "visible minorities." He nonetheless swatted back the charge of racism in his introductory chapter. "Because the term 'racist' is now so debased," he wrote, "I usually shrug such smears off by pointing to its new definition: *anyone who is winning an argument with a liberal.*"[3]

That preemptive claim did not, of course, stop reviewers from pointing out the racism in the book. But it did show how Brimelow approached his critics: by framing his ideas as controversial truths that had been walled off from the realm of acceptable conversation. "The country is being transformed against its will, by accident, in a way that's unprecedented in the history of the world, to no visible economic gain," he told Brian Lamb in an interview about the book on C-SPAN. "And you're not supposed to talk about it, so of course I couldn't resist," he added, his thin lips curling into a smile, as though he'd dipped into a tempting dessert rather than engaged in handwringing about the shrinking white majority.[4]

Brimelow's book grabbed attention for a number of reasons. His journalistic bona fides (he was a senior editor at *Forbes* and an editor at *National Review*), his lilting northern English accent, his branding as a controversialist—all of these allowed him to present his arguments about race and immigration on national platforms throughout the mid-1990s. He had learned something that Pat Buchanan had figured out when he first contemplated a presidential run: "The principal press bias is not a liberal bias. It's a bias for a good fight. The press loves to see a fight start, and hates to see it end." Both men understood how media worked because they had been part of the journalism world for decades, connections that won them a hearing for their arguments about the superiority of white Western civilization and how best to defend it.[5]

But *Alien Nation*, which *Newsweek's* Jerry Adler described as "one of the most widely discussed books of 1995," also grabbed attention because it landed in the midst of a newly politicized debate over immigration. Across the United States in the 1990s, the politics of immigration were rapidly changing. Buchanan's call for a border wall in 1992 looked prescient two years later, when California state politics exploded over Proposition 187. The proposition, if enacted, would strip undocumented immigrants of access to any social service, including public education. It passed with overwhelming majorities and the support of Democrats as well as Republicans. With the new bipartisan embrace of immigration restriction, Buchanan went even further, calling for new limitations on authorized immigration as well. He also veered away from economic arguments against immigration and toward something different: arguments about culture, whiteness, and the American identity that would become a defining feature of the neo-nativism of the 1990s.[6]

The road to that new nativism ran through California. The early 1990s had not been kind to the state. The heart of the country's military-industrial complex, California had seen its population and prosperity mushroom in the Cold War era as federal funds flooded the state's universities, military bases, research centers, and corporations. When the Cold War ended, the recession that wracked the United States hit California particularly hard. Yet few people pointed to immigration, which was rising rapidly in the state, as the cause of California's problems. Pat Buchanan's barnstorming at the border had generated little more than a shrug in the state. While many Californians, when asked, may have said immigration levels were too high, as late as March 1993, only 2 percent of Californians ranked immigration as their top concern. Which meant that immigration restriction was not a natural consequence of the economic recession—it required an intensive campaign to transform it into a hot-button issue.[7]

That campaign started with Republican governor Pete Wilson, who was staring down grim approval ratings halfway through his first term: in October 1992 only 28 percent of Californians approved of the job he was doing, an all-time low among California governors. Desperate to shake things up, he first tried attacking welfare. His numbers barely moved. Then in August 1993, he switched tactics. He published an open letter to the federal government, arguing that California was going broke because the federal government was doing little to control undocumented immigration, leaving the state to pay for their welfare benefits, public education, and medical care. He not only proposed that the federal government no longer burden the state with those payments but that it also abolish birthright citizenship for children born to undocumented immigrants (something that would require a constitutional amendment).[8]

Within a few months, a small group of anti-immigration activists met to discuss developing an initiative—a legislative proposal voters could weigh in on in the 1994 election—that paralleled Wilson's open letter. If enacted, it would create a citizenship database and bar all undocumented immigrants from accessing social services, public education, nonemergency health care, and welfare. They lobbied for it under the name "Save Our State"—a callback to the right-wing grassroots campaigns of the 1970s like the antigay Save Our Children campaign in Miami—though once they acquired enough signatures to get it on the ballot, it would become known simply as Proposition 187.[9]

The drafters found, just as Wilson had, that Californians responded strongly to the idea of immigration as a fiscal problem, an approach that fit in neatly with the Perot movement (in fact, the California branch of United We Stand, Perot's political organization, played a significant role in organizing signature drives for the initiative). Nor was it an idea that appealed solely to Republicans— Wilson was seizing on a narrative of immigration and fiscal responsibility already percolating in the national Democratic Party. His replacement in the Senate, Democrat Dianne Feinstein, wrote an op-ed in the *Los Angeles Times* just a few months before his open letter calling for beefed-up immigration enforcement and stiffer penalties for border smuggling.[10]

Both parties would shift right on immigration in 1993 and 1994. Both tended to frame the debate in fiscal and economic terms that, on their surface, were unemotional hard-numbers appeals. Yet, in both parties the actual debate over immigration took on a darker tone of invasion, criminality, and decline. When talking about immigration, Feinstein emphasized overcrowded schools and housing shortages. And while she never said, "They're stealing your jobs," "They're cheating your children," "They're why you can't afford to buy a house," the implications were clear. They were even clearer in Wilson's infamous border-crossing ad. It featured grainy video of migrants crossing the border while a narrator gravely warned of the ceaseless flow of Mexican migrants, evoking images of an invasion from the south. The ad added a layer of animus to the debate that began to drive down Latino and Asian support for Proposition 187.[11]

Democrats in California and nationally opposed the initiative, noting that the Supreme Court had already ruled that undocumented children had a right to public education. But they found other ways to make clear they were ready to crack down. In the months before the 1994 election, Attorney General Janet Reno announced the launch of Operation Gatekeeper, a plan to beef up border patrols on the stretch of the border from San Diego to the Pacific Ocean.[12]

For Republicans, the fight over Proposition 187 revealed a deep fault line in the party. The California GOP was firmly united in favor of it heading into the 1994 election. But the national party quickly splintered. The Reaganite wing, led by people like Jack Kemp and Bill Bennett, saw the initiative as a serious threat to the long-term interests of the party. In the closing days of the election, they wrote a joint op-ed in the *Wall Street Journal* warning that not only was Proposition 187 "fundamentally flawed" and "constitutionally questionable," but it was "broadening into an ugly antipathy toward all immigrants." Their argument wasn't just about the initiative: it was about the future of the party. If those pushing Proposition 187 had their way, Republicans would be abandoning Reagan's "city on a hill" for "an isolated fortress with the drawbridge up." Thumping on immigration might help in the short-term, as evidenced by Wilson's sprightly poll numbers, but as Kemp and Bennett said in a separate statement, in the long run the party would be worse off if it gave in to a growing segment that was "pessimistic, angry and opposed."[13]

Those pessimistic, angry, and opposed Republicans were not at all impressed with Kemp and Bennett. At his first public appearance following the statement, Kemp had to face down a crowd of angry Californians, with one audience member asking, "Why didn't you just keep quiet?" California representative Dana Rohrabacher expressed the same sentiment, making clear that he thought Kemp had irreparably harmed his political future. "His act of stupidity has knocked him right out of the presidential race," he told reporters at a nearby fund-raiser. "If he disagreed with it, he should have kept his mouth shut." And of course, Pat Buchanan came out swinging. He took particular aim at Kemp and Bennett's claim that the initiative was nativist. "The truth is the exact opposite," he insisted. "It is not bigotry to put your own country and your own family first. That is the essence of true charity and patriotism."[14]

Despite these divisions, and despite Democratic leaders' tough-on-borders stance, immigration restriction was quickly becoming seen as a Republican issue. That's because, on the institutional level, Proposition 187 drew its support almost entirely from the GOP. And when it won big on Election Day, part of the red wave that swept Newt Gingrich into the Speaker's office, it ensured immigration would be a major part of the shifting landscape of post–Cold War politics in the United States.

IF HARD-LINE, RACE-BASED immigration restrictions were a deviation from the Reagan era, an opposition to Great Society civil rights and poverty programs, particularly those aimed at helping Black Americans, seemed very much like a continuation of it. But the new writing on Black Americans, inequality, and government intervention deviated sharply from Reagan's libertarian-minded approach. Reagan asserted these programs failed because they were a matter of government overreach, interrupting the natural state of the market and social relations. He offered an optimistic (even Pollyannaish) view of what would exist without government interference: a colorblind, meritocratic, and equality-based society.

Writers like Charles Murray, Richard Herrnstein, and Dinesh D'Souza painted a much bleaker picture. When they looked at Black inequality—in wealth, in educational attainment, in life expectancy, in political power—they saw the root cause not as racism or ineffective government intervention but as problems that existed within the Black community—in Murray and Herrnstein's case, an intelligence deficit; in D'Souza's, a cultural one. Those arguments would not only lay the groundwork for a more pessimistic, color-conscious racism on the right but also provide a more respectable version of anti-Black politics than that of someone like David Duke (who, for all his efforts to appear respectable, could never truly disassociate himself from the Klan).

Murray and Herrnstein's *The Bell Curve* became an instant sensation when it hit shelves in 1994. In it, they offered a number of arguments about IQ, societal problems, and race. The core contentions were that IQ was, to a significant degree, heritable and unchangeable; that low IQ correlated to both race and negative social behaviors, leading to poverty, crime, and out-of-wedlock children; and that policy should take those correlations into account. Though crammed full of charts and equations, *The Bell Curve* was not a scientific tract—the authors were a political scientist (Murray) and a psychologist (Herrnstein), not scientists or geneticists. It was instead a policy book that used poorly interpreted and dubiously sourced pseudoscientific data to build its arguments.[15]

The Bell Curve was a broadside against the Great Society and a call for new policies that, while not explicitly race based, would have profound consequences for Black people and nonwhite immigrants. The authors called for, among other things, elimination of aid to poor mothers so they would stop having children; an end to the use of affirmative action in college admissions, which they argued raised low-IQ people of color above their ability levels; and a shift in immigration law from family-based immigration to merit-based immigration in order to favor higher-IQ immigrants.

These were not new ideas, of course. Scientific racism had been around for centuries, confidently asserting schema for racial classifications and racial superiority. Herrnstein himself had been on the race-IQ beat for almost a quarter century, part of a renaissance of scientific racism repackaged around contemporary intelligence research. In a 1971 piece for *The Atlantic*, he argued government spending on education and antipoverty programs could not promote equality, because they did not address racial groups' inherited differences in IQ. The article proved as influential as it was controversial. In the White House, Pat Buchanan, then an aide to President Richard Nixon, drafted a memo arguing against federal programs focused on integration and poverty. "The importance of this article is difficult to understate," he wrote to the president, confusing "understate" with "overstate." "If correct, then all our efforts and expenditures not only for 'compensatory education' but to provide an 'equal chance at the starting line' are guaranteeing that we wind up with the intelligent ones coming in first. And every study we have shows blacks 15 IQ points below whites on the average."[16]

Nixon sent the article to presidential counselor Daniel Patrick Moynihan, who a few years earlier had authored the Moynihan Report, which argued Black poverty was a function of failings in Black culture. Moynihan told the president that Herrnstein's arguments rang true. Yet, while both men agreed with Herrnstein, in a private Oval Office conversation about the article, the sense of taboo hovered: "Nobody must think we're thinking about it," Nixon told Moynihan, "and . . . if we do find out it's correct, we must never tell anybody." Nixon, whose racism is well documented, stressed that he hadn't wanted to agree with Herrnstein and other race-IQ researchers like Arthur Jensen, but he ultimately did. "I've reluctantly concluded, based at least on the evidence presently before me, and I don't base it on any scientific evidence, that what Herrnstein says, and what was said earlier by Jensen, and so forth, is probably very close to the truth."[17]

It mattered that Moynihan and Nixon did not declare their agreement with Herrnstein publicly. They may have agreed, but their agreement did not shape the public debate about social and economic programs. The trajectory for *The Bell Curve* was markedly different: controversial as it was, it entered mainstream political discourse and became part of the right's conception of race, IQ, and policy.

Like Herrnstein, Murray had begun influencing policy before the 1990s. His first book, *Losing Ground*, came out in 1984 and hewed closely to the Reagan line. In it, he directly attacked the Great Society's antipoverty programs, arguing they increased poverty and inflicted moral damage on those who used them. Deliberately conflating poor people with Black people, he argued that despite the billions spent on poverty programs, the ranks of the poor had actually grown. The solution: end all affirmative action programs and all welfare for poor people of working age. The project was an instant hit within the conservative movement and the Reagan administration—and Bill Clinton would eventually profess agreement with it as well (his Third Way politics were at times indistinguishable from Reaganism).[18]

Both authors of *The Bell Curve* had trafficked in racist ideas before the book's publication. Herrnstein's were more explicitly racist, while Murray's were subtler. Their shared dedication to finding ways to both explain away racism and undo Great Society programs brought them together for *The Bell Curve*, a book that pushed Murray in particular past a Reaganite critique of antipoverty programs and toward something more sinister.

Dinesh D'Souza, an immigrant from Mumbai who spent his years after college working in the Reagan administration, disagreed with Murray and Herrnstein's conclusions—but not because he still clung to the Reaganite line. In a chapter of his 1995 book *The End of Racism* titled "The Content of Our Chromosomes," he laid out Murray and Herrnstein's argument, carefully picking through the controversy about race, intelligence, and genetics. In the end, he agreed that the fifteen-point gap between white and Black Americans on IQ tests was significant and had serious implications for policy. But he disagreed that it was rooted in genetic difference. Instead, he argued that the issues were cultural: specifically, a failing of Black culture.[19]

In *The End of Racism*, D'Souza insisted that structural racism was largely the invention of "race hustlers," both inside the university and out, and that the ideology of multiculturalism and cultural relativism had poisoned discussions about race in the United States. He argued for the supremacy of Western (white) culture, maintaining that problems of high incarceration rates and poverty stemmed not from racist institutions but from a corruption at the heart of Black society, which he labeled "self-defeating" and "irresponsible."[20]

D'Souza described inner cities as places where "the streets are irrigated with alcohol, urine, and blood." Racism, he argued, is simply "rational discrimination," the ability of observers to detect that Black culture is worse than white culture. It was not racism but antiracism that was to blame for African Americans' plight, he maintained, arguing that Black civil rights activists and white liberal Democrats had a vested interest in keeping "the black underclass" down.[21]

D'Souza's work fit into a developing discourse about race that centered on affirmative action, political correctness, and multiculturalism. Handwringing over multiculturalism became a national pastime in the 1990s, and not only on the right. The end of the Cold War triggered a fear of national disintegration as old empires and nation-states began unravelling. Not only had the former Soviet Union begun the process of breaking up, with a number of formerly occupied states gaining independence, but other non-Soviet states began to break apart as well, most notably Czechoslovakia and Yugoslavia. In the 1991 book *The Disuniting of America*, liberal historian Arthur Schlesinger Jr. worried that the United States would encounter a similar type of shattering with the demise of a common culture, driven not just by migration from across the globe but by ideas of multiculturalism that celebrated the presence of distinct cultures rather than emphasizing assimilation into the dominant one, something he called the "cult of ethnicity."[22]

The most energetic rejections of multiculturalism, though, came from the right. A flood of books, including D'Souza's *Illiberal Education*, which spent fifteen weeks on the best-seller list, railed against the ideas of multiculturalism and diversity. The authors believed such ideas had not only infected US higher education but were seeping into the culture at large. They saw these ideas as a threat to America itself: challenging the notion that Western civilization, with the United States as its greatest practitioner and defender, was the superior culture. To battle back against these ideas, they began to argue that racial differences not only existed but presented a genuine threat to white Western culture.[23]

Like Murray and Brimelow, D'Souza cloaked his arguments in academic garb: extensive citations, lengthy expositions, detailed history. And like their books, *The End of Racism* was about promoting conservative policy, starting with the premise that the problems Black Americans faced were not the result of racism and that no outside intervention—especially not affirmative action—could solve them. He even recommended repealing the Civil Rights Act of 1964, arguing that nondiscrimination laws should only apply to the government, leaving the private realm to discriminate as it saw fit.

D'Souza's argument was a reversal of the "white man's burden." In the late nineteenth and early twentieth centuries, British and American colonizers believed that, because they had built a superior culture, they were duty bound to awaken nonwhite civilizations to the wonders of Christianity and capitalism (normally at the cost of those civilizations' material resources and sovereignty). But D'Souza stripped away the "burden," such as it was, arguing that it was up to Black Americans to lift themselves from what he saw as a bankrupt culture.

Just as Brimelow had leveraged his identity as an immigrant to write about immigration, D'Souza used his nonwhite identity as a shield against charges of racism. "As a 'person of color,'" he wrote in the introduction, "I enjoy an element of ethnic immunity that allows me to address topics with a frankness that would be impossible on the part of a white male." He acknowledged that his arguments would be useful to opponents of equal rights but concluded that was a price that had to be paid to tell the truth.[24]

And like Murray and Brimelow, he was handsomely rewarded. Taking on "taboo issues," as D'Souza described them, turned out to be a profitable project. And that particular blend used by all three books—pairing incendiary ideas about race with the appearance of scholarly rigor—turned out to be the perfect way to gain attention from the mainstream press and emerge as a star of the new post-Reagan right.

———

CHARLES MURRAY SETTLED into his seat in first class, champagne in hand and a *New York Times* reporter by his side. He was in a buoyant mood: off to Aspen to drink expensive wines at a wealthy friend's home, just as his new book, destined to be a best seller, was about to hit bookstores. Though his was not the only name on the cover, his coauthor's recent death meant Murray would get all the attention, good and bad, once it was published. The team at Free Press, headed by conservative publisher Adam Bellow, had carefully plotted the rollout. Vanishingly few advance copies were made available for review; instead, the American Enterprise Institute (AEI) paid to fly a carefully chosen group to Washington, DC, to be briefed by Murray on the book's contents.

With page after page of complex equations and carefully plotted charts, the book was, as Murray told the *Times* reporter from his window seat, "social science pornography." With that description, he had intended to underscore that the book was teeming with data and regression tables. But given that most pornography at the time was an expression of the fantasy life of white men, the description was more on the nose than Murray realized. A book promoting both racism and social Darwinism along with soft eugenics held a certain appeal for a subset of white readers.[25]

It was not the first time Murray had targeted those readers. When he pitched his 1984 book *Losing Ground* to publishers, he outlined his belief that it would sell well by tapping into a particular bloc of underserved readers. "A huge number of well-meaning whites fear that they are closet racists," he wrote in his proposal, "and this book tells them they are not. It's going to make them feel better about things they already think but do not know how to say."[26]

Though his ideas were allegedly so daring as to be nearly verboten, Murray had no trouble attracting sponsors for them. When he initially explored the argument for *Losing Ground* in a pamphlet he wrote for the Heritage Foundation, a donor read it and said it should be given a book-length treatment. Serious fund-raising—to the tune of $125,000—went to the project, setting Murray up at the Manhattan Institute, a conservative think tank, to write the book.[27]

The Manhattan Institute was less thrilled with his next project. When Murray signed on to write *The Bell Curve*, the think tank's leaders couldn't stomach the genetic component of his argument. They severed their relationship with Murray after learning he was writing the book, at which point the American Enterprise Institute scooped him up. Murray and Herrnstein went ahead with the project, knowing that if it was already shaking things up in the planning stages, the book was destined to make a splash when it landed.

Of course, it was one thing to court controversy and another to be cast out as an extremist. Here, Murray benefited greatly from the way the mainstream press treated *The Bell Curve*. One reviewer, Charles Lane, writing in the *New York Review of Books*, refused to pull his punches. He noted that the book relied on studies from white nationalist and eugenicist sources and that their conclusions shared a great deal with those sources. "Both sought to restore the scientific status of race, and to reintroduce eugenic thinking into the public policy debate." But in other coverage of the book, its sources and conclusions were rarely presented so baldly, and even when they were, they were bracketed by Murray's insistence that the book was not racist. This matters, because, while it did land on the best-seller list, most Americans would encounter *The Bell Curve* through articles like the sprawling, twelve-page story that appeared in *New York Times Magazine* the week the book came out: a look at Murray living the high life while calling for the end of welfare for the poor.[28]

Others would read about it in the *New Republic*, which devoted most of an issue to *The Bell Curve*, reinforcing the notion that controversy sold, even as it roiled the institutions that it touched. The decision to publish the excerpt triggered an explosive fight at the *New Republic*. Editor Andrew Sullivan had initially planned to simply run the excerpt as a cover story for the magazine. But that decision met with fierce resistance within the publication, leading to a lengthy series of rebuttals that ran alongside the excerpt. The editorial note that introduced the "Race & IQ" issue applauded the magazine's courage in running Murray and Herrnstein's work and denounced some of the internal objectors as illiberal. "If the TNR editors who authored some of the responses had had their way," the opening essay read, "the debate before you—and the arguments of those very editors—would never have seen the light of day."[29]

In addition to framing publication of *The Bell Curve* excerpt as a matter of free and open debate, the opening essay went one step further: it declared that the book's authors were not racist and that their findings were true. "A magazine should publish what is true. Sometimes the truth is intricate and ambiguous, which is why a debate may be needed to reveal the core of the matter." It also bought in to the notion that Herrnstein and Murray were offering up a hidden truth: something unspeakable but accurate. For magazines like the *New Republic*, spotlighting *The Bell Curve*, even though it caused significant disruption at the publication, had important upsides: it reinforced their brand as defenders of free speech and purveyors of dangerous—but necessary—ideas.[30]

While Murray seemed to have stumbled into the power of controversy, D'Souza had spent most of his early years trying to harness it. He learned to court controversy long before writing *The End of Racism*. His education as a right-wing controversialist started at Dartmouth College, where he joined the *Dartmouth Review*, a campus newspaper founded in 1980 by conservative students and supported by conservative activists and alumni (Pat Buchanan and Jack Kemp were two of its initial advisory board members). Closely linked to the *National Review*—the faculty advisor, Jeffrey Hart, was a senior editor at the magazine as well as an English professor at Dartmouth—the *Review* signaled to established conservative leaders that the next generation, coming of age during the

Reagan administration, would bring a new level of energy and style to the cause. Reagan himself applauded the *Review* as "an impressive paper."[31]

And what exactly did that new generation have to offer? The *Review* backed conservative policies and boosted the Reagan administration, but it mostly sniffed out—or stirred up—campus controversies, particularly ones that centered on race and gender. Soon after it launched, it became clear that the paper's house style aimed to maximize outrage. There was the time editors illustrated an interview with a member of the Klan with the image of a Black student hanging from a tree on the Dartmouth campus. And the time when *Review* staffers snuck out late one night and destroyed a shantytown erected on campus to protest apartheid in South Africa.[32]

One of its favorite topics was affirmative action. The *Review* staff regularly argued that affirmative action diluted the quality of students and the quality of classes at Dartmouth, driving the creation of what it labeled "victim studies": courses like Black studies, women's studies, and the like. Writing in 1981, D'Souza declared the "system of black favoritism" a failure. "Institutionalized advantage, such as affirmative action, encourages laziness and inefficiency, because there is no incentive to work hard—one is guaranteed of promotion and success," he wrote at a time when no Black person had ever headed up a Fortune 500 company. "The finesse demanded of other persons in society is not asked of a black, and being almost-good-enough has become a way of life." He argued that to succeed at Dartmouth, such students were shunted into easy courses taught by "that touchy-feely smorgasbord of homosexuals, sociologists, lesbians, and feminists" whose "idle rhetoric and shoddy scholarship have infected the minds of the blacks they woo."[33]

That article represented the *Review*'s formal mode, the register writers used when they were auditioning for a future stint at *National*

Review or the *Wall Street Journal*. But the paper made a similar argument a year later, when D'Souza was editor, that was much more the *Review*'s preferred style. "Dem white mo-fo be sayin' 'firmative action ain't no good fo' us, cause it be puttin' down ac-demic standards. Dey be spoutin' 'bout how 'firmative action be no hep to black folk 'cross da nation, on account we be not doin' too well wit da GPAs and sheet." That was the nearly unreadable opening of a piece titled "Dis Sho' Ain't No Jive, Bro," which ran in the *Review* in March 1982. When the expected outrage over the piece's racism erupted, D'Souza defended it as satire, though no one gave a clear answer as to what, exactly, was being satirized.[34]

"No Jive" got significant press coverage—the ensuing outrage led Jack Kemp to resign from the paper's advisory board—as did other controversies that popped up at the paper. In fact, the *Dartmouth Review* became something of a cultural touchstone. Not only was it featured in major newsmagazines like *Time* and *Newsweek*, plus most national newspapers, but the editors were featured on shows like *Donahue* and *Nightline*, making it quite the crossover hit. It became a model for a spate of conservative campus papers that emerged, well funded by the movement, in the late 1980s.[35]

D'Souza took note. In the offices of the *Review* he learned not only his conservatism but his theory of outrage. He claimed to have been radicalized by the opposition to the *Review*, going from a "moderating force" at the paper to one of its principal flamethrowers. Admitting years later that some of what he published as editor should not have made it into print, he insisted, "There was a purpose to this outrageous style. The *Review*'s radical tone is intended to challenge the etiquette which protects liberal orthodoxy and return taboos which are legitimate topics for argument to public debate." As he later put it, since American culture was thoroughly liberal, conservatives had "to undermine it, to thwart it, to destroy it at the root level." Conservatives in a liberal age had to be "philosophically conservative but temperamentally radical." "In other words," he wrote, "we had to become social guerillas." *Had to.* In D'Souza's recounting, the left made him do it.[36]

The style that D'Souza honed at Dartmouth was not embraced by the movement more broadly in the 1980s. Conservative leaders applauded the *Review* staff for causing trouble on campus, but they also saw their techniques as a product of youthful excess. D'Souza would work for much of the next decade to clean up his act, to earn a reputation as a serious writer and intellectual force. But with *The End of Racism*, he found that by bringing in some of that youthful provocation, he could get outsized attention—which in the years that followed, he seemed to crave more and more.

There was another cost to D'Souza's repackaged racism. In response to the publication of *The End of Racism*, two Black conservatives at AEI, Glenn Loury and Robert Woodson, resigned in protest. In a joint interview, they denounced D'Souza's book as "an anti-black pejorative" written in "an intemperate, irreverent, insulting way." Both men had previously argued that at least some inequality was driven by what they saw as "dysfunctional behavior" in Black communities, but D'Souza's screed landed differently. "We've been called Uncle Toms, which we are not," Loury said. "But to be silent in the face of this book, written by a conservative colleague, would make us Uncle Toms."[37]

The resignations were not the first sign that this turn toward scientific and cultural racism was driving a wedge between Black conservatives and the rest of the movement. Loury had already gone through a split with the neoconservative magazine *Commentary* after it refused to run his review of *The Bell Curve*. Now he would sever ties with AEI over *The End of Racism*. D'Souza and Murray would remain at the think tank for years, part of what one critic called AEI's "race desk"—which now had no Black conservatives. More than that, AEI had now rewarded the politics of outrage, making clear that it valued precisely the kind of controversy that led to Loury's and Woodson's resignations.[38]

For D'Souza, it was all upsides. His and Brimelow's and Murray's experiences served, for a conservative movement that had grown uncertain about how best to talk about race, as proof of concept for how to use controversy to gain stature and win big advances in the post-Reagan conservative movement.

CHAPTER EIGHT

POLITICALLY INCORRECT

Nineteen ninety-five was Laura Ingraham's year. You could find her everywhere. Settled in the driver's seat of her army-green Range Rover, zipping through Washington, DC, at sixty mph. Lounging in the back of a black limousine en route to the airport to make that evening's taping of *Politically Incorrect*. On the cover of *New York Times Magazine* in a leopard-print miniskirt, arms crossed and chin jutting up in a defiant pose. "It's getting a little crazy," she told a *Wall Street Journal* reporter writing a profile of her that fall, "but it's fun."[1]

Practically overnight, Ingraham had become one of the most sought-after conservative commentators in the country, the breakout star of a new group of right-wing women pundits. Young, telegenic professionals, they marketed themselves as next-generation conservatives: stylish, outrageous, media savvy, and steeped in pop culture. Though they shared many of the earlier generation's critiques of feminism, they presented themselves quite differently than an antifeminist activist like Phyllis Schlafly, who by that time was in her seventies. These women capitalized on an identity not as house-wives but as modern women who had reaped all the opportuni-ties second-wave feminism afforded while denouncing the politics of the movement. Those denunciations—necessary to make clear that, despite their professional ambitions, they were not closet fem-inists—often formed a core part of their public personas.

Though not yet old enough to vote in the 1980 election, Ingra-ham would emerge from the 1980s a committed Reaganite, even working for the administration for a while. After leaving the ad-ministration, she did not set her sights on holding public office or leveraging her law degree to aid the conservative cause. She spent a few years clerking for new Supreme Court justice Clarence Thomas and working at a DC law firm, then quit her job to become a full-time pundit, at just the moment when opportunities for political commentary—particularly cutting partisan commentary—were flourishing. By 1992, more than 60 percent of US households had cable, and new channels kept popping up to capture a slice of those subscribers. Not only did that lead to a rash of new cable news channels, but channels that seemed to have nothing to do with pol-itics, like MTV and Comedy Central, were edging their way into significant political coverage.[2]

While the 1990s marked a turning point for right-wing media, which flourished online and on air, places like the new cable channel Fox News were not the main breeding grounds for the new brand of conservative pundit. Like most up-and-coming stars of the right, Ingraham made her way into the spotlight as a right-wing voice in mainstream outlets. She was a regular on Bill Maher's comedy show *Politically Incorrect*, where she learned to blend politics with humor and outrage. She wrote occasional op-eds for the *New York Times* and worked as a pundit for CBS before being given her own show on the new cable network MSNBC in 1996. The style often credited to Fox News—the flashy graphics, punch-to-the-face punditry, and leggy blonde anchors—had been well-developed elsewhere first.

The political media landscape was being remade in the 1990s, as ideology, opinion, entertainment, and outrage became core components of the way politics was covered in nonconservative outlets—in outlets, in fact, that touted the ideas of objectivity and balance as central to their mission. The rise of right-wing pundits augured a new era of punditry, peopled by partisans who had little experience in journalism, politics, or the academy—whose only real expertise was their ability to score political points in a way that entertained and infuriated viewers.

Such punditry moved not just political programming but politics itself in a more inflammatory direction. Politicians who appeared on these shows tended to merge their talking points with this new, over-the-top rhetorical style, trotting out edgier and more extreme rhetoric that flowed back into Congress and the campaign trail. The end result was not just a more polarizing political media but a more partisan and destructive politics as well.

———

THOUGH SHE SEEMED like an overnight success, Ingraham had been laying the groundwork for a career in punditry for over a decade by the time she appeared on the cover of *New York Times Magazine*. Her career flowed from two main tributaries: the *Dartmouth Review* and the Independent Women's Forum (IWF). Those conservative institutions played a significant role in shaping the identity and style that would fuel her success in nonconservative outlets in the mid-1990s.

She arrived at Dartmouth in 1981, a few years after Dinesh D'Souza, and quickly fell in with him and the rest of the crew at the *Dartmouth Review*. Under his tutelage, she honed her ability to provoke liberals and snag headlines. She became editor of the *Review* after D'Souza graduated, practicing the same style of provocation publishing that had come to define the paper. As editor, she sent a reporter to secretly record a meeting of the Gay Students Association, publishing the names of board members and the private conversations of students who had not come out publicly. Apologizing for it more than a decade later, she described how the *Review* "adopted a purposefully outrageous tone—occasionally using, for example, the word 'sodomites' to describe campus gays."[3]

Nor was it just rhetoric: she opposed federal funding for AIDS research, believing it was "just part of a gay crusade for political affirmation and acceptance." (She changed her stance after watching her brother's partner die from AIDS.) That was an important connection: shock value may have been the defining characteristic of her tenure, but everything she did was tied to a deeper set of beliefs with policy implications.[4]

Those policy implications mattered, because after Dartmouth, she and D'Souza headed off to work for the Reagan administration. (They dated for several years; he dedicated the first edition of *Illiberal Education* to her.) After a stint in the Department of Education, she joined him in the White House working for Gary Bauer, a domestic policy advisor and emerging leader of the religious right. Then it was off to law school at the University of Virginia, where she tooled around town in a Honda bearing a license plate that read "FARRIGHT."[5]

For both D'Souza and Ingraham, 1991 would be a turning point in their careers. In July 1991, while D'Souza's *Illiberal Education* was still charting on the *New York Times* best-seller list, President George H. W. Bush nominated Clarence Thomas to the Supreme Court. During the confirmation hearings, Anita Hill, a lawyer who had worked for Thomas at the Department of Education and the Equal Employment Opportunity Commission, came forward to report that Thomas had sexually harassed her. The fight over Hill's explosive testimony thrust a new group of conservative women, formed to counter feminist opposition to Thomas, into the spotlight. They called themselves Women for Judge Thomas.[6]

Despite Hill's accusations, Thomas was confirmed, and a few years later, two things happened: Ingraham went to the Supreme Court to clerk for him, and Women for Judge Thomas became the Independent Women's Forum. That change came after the women, finding they had more than their support for Thomas in common, decided to broaden their mission and create an organization that would demonstrate that not all women were beholden to the feminist movement. The newly constituted organization would become the vehicle for Ingraham's national fame.

The Independent Women's Forum positioned itself as an alternative to both liberal feminism and socially conservative women's groups like Schlafly's Eagle Forum and the evangelical Christian group Concerned Women for America. Representatives of IWF regularly sparred with the National Organization for Women (NOW) and opposed legislation like the Violence Against Women Act and programs to increase women's representation in the workforce. But they also rejected the stuffy, midcentury housewife activism that the older socially conservative groups relied on. They tended to avoid issues closely associated with the religious right. For instance, the IWF did not take an explicit stance on abortion, favoring instead a different set of cultural issues, including gun rights and affirmative action. And while they joined the earlier conservative women's groups in idealizing motherhood and femininity, they talked about women's work as wives and mothers as a *choice* rather than the default.[7]

Though these antifeminist groups did not differ much in ideology or policy preference, stylistically IWF differed dramatically: the women representing the group self-consciously portrayed themselves as hip, sexy conservatives. That portrayal displayed real media savvy. Though the IWF had only around six hundred or so members by the mid-1990s, its representatives were *everywhere*: writing for the op-ed pages of the country's leading newspapers, yukking it up on entertainment shows like *Politically Incorrect*, and landing profiles on NPR and *60 Minutes*, in *Vanity Fair* and *The Village Voice*.[8]

Compared to NOW, IWF's membership was microscopic and its track record nonexistent. But in the mid-1990s, IWF got far more attention than NOW and, in stories about women's politics, was often represented as its conservative equivalent, which suggested IWF had a stature and influence far beyond what it had actually demonstrated. Journalists were fascinated by the seeming disconnect of women advocating against policies and programs designed to aid women. It's "the Talking Dog thing," explained IWF member Lisa Schiffren. "It's really hard to get articulate, Ivy League–educated, smart women who are really conservative."[9]

Of all the media-savvy members of this media-savvy organization, no one played the publicity game better than Ingraham. That *New York Times Magazine* cover launched her on a new career, one that took off so rapidly that a year after the cover appeared, she quit her job at a high-powered law firm to work full time in media. Antifeminism was the core of her brand. She dismissed the Violence Against Women Act as legislative pork that played on people's emotions with its "tear-jerker" name. She insisted that when women complained about their meager paychecks, it was not a call for pay equity but for lower taxes. She testified before Congress against sex-based preferences.[10]

She also pulled the same maneuver as D'Souza in his book *The End of Racism*, arguing that those opposed to equality were its real defenders. "Aside from being patronizing and simplistic," she wrote for the *New York Times*, "the idea that women are constantly thwarted by invisible barriers of sexism relegates them to permanent victim status. It also stands on its head the cause that true feminists originally championed: equal opportunity for all." In other words, antifeminists were the *real* feminists. It was the reverse-racism argument used by opponents of affirmative action, transported into the world of gender politics.[11]

A similar dynamic played out in the way Ingraham and other IWF members talked about issues like gun rights. Writing for the *Wall Street Journal* in 1996, Ingraham argued, "Smith & Wesson and the National Rifle Association are doing more to 'take back the night' than the National Organization for Women and Emily's List," a reference to the antirape marches that became commonplace on college campuses in the 1990s. She complained that women's rights groups had not celebrated when Marion Hammer was named president of the National Rifle Association (NRA), the first woman to hold the position in the organization's 125-year history. She also suggested that real feminists would support women arming themselves rather than relying on predominantly male police departments for protection.[12]

The article ended with the suggestion that some organization sponsor an "Annie Get Your Gun Permit" event to encourage women to obtain weapons. IWF did just that. On a warm fall morning in 1997, fifty-four women gathered at the Prince George's County Trap and Skeet Center in suburban Maryland. The group included women like Christine Hoff Sommers, author of *Who Stole Feminism?*, and Ann Coulter, decked out in jodhpurs and a Chanel bag, with an ammunition belt that kept slipping down her hips. Writing about the event for the *New Republic*, Hanna Rosin suggested that the women were engaging in "Chenoweth chic," a reference to Representative Helen Chenoweth. "As some ladies on the right have discovered," she wrote, "the great thing about Chenoweth chic is that it offers you a way to experience all the low-cost thrills of working-class life without actually having to move into a mobile home."[13]

As Coulter's Chanel bag and Ingraham's leopard skirt suggest, the women of IWF blended their antifeminist politics with an overtly feminine style: not the housedresses of an earlier era of activism but a self-consciously youthful appearance that leaned heavily on sex appeal. Lisa Schiffren, a former speechwriter for Dan Quayle, appeared on the cover of *New York Times Magazine* along with Ingraham; she too wore an animal-print skirt and dark top, though hers was a knee-length pencil skirt paired with a blazer. As one publicist who worked for a few IWF personalities explained, the women in the group understood "the need to be provocative, push buttons, be sexy."[14]

Provocative has two meanings: triggering outrage and triggering arousal. Right-wing personalities like D'Souza and Charles Murray relied solely on the first. But women on the right leveraged the full range of the word, knowing that by leaning into their sex appeal, they were upending expectations. Even in the post-Reagan era, conservatism had a staid, retrograde image, one reflected in style as well as politics. Because of the close association between the Republican Party and the religious right, the image of conservative women was even more prudish, embodied by activists who opposed revealing clothes, sex outside marriage, and suggestive songs and images.

The women of IWF flipped that image on its head. In addition to Ingraham and Coulter, there were women like Barbara Olson, a founder of IWF. She too was a lawyer—as chief counsel for House Republicans on the Oversight Committee, she led investigations into early Clinton scandals—and as a pundit she served as a vicious critic of both Bill and Hillary Clinton. The pollster Kellyanne Fitzpatrick also emerged as a pundit at this time: after working for Frank Luntz for a few years, she started her own polling firm in 1995 and supplemented that job with work as a popular cable commentator. As white women with blonde hair, bare legs, and a tendency to say the most shocking thing they could think of when in front of a microphone, these women embodied what observers dubbed "conservative chic."[15]

Given that it was their style that attracted attention, press coverage of Ingraham and her cohort unsurprisingly tended to focus on their appearance. That leopard-print skirt Ingraham wore made its way into nearly every profile written about her. Political journalists wrote lasciviously and dismissively about the women, using insulting descriptors like "pundettes" and "ignorant pixies." Coulter was described as a "conservative pin-up girl" in the *Hartford Courant.* "She's got the tight sweaters of a starlet, the long legs of a tennis star, the tumbling blond hair of a cheerleader and a hard-edged prosecutor's mind."[16]

Though the women of IWF tended to dismiss complaints about sexual harassment and sexism as encouraging women to see themselves as victims, they pushed back against their sexualization when it helped them score political points. When journalist Fred Barnes held up Ingraham as an example of the young pundits making the rounds on television without the requisite experience or knowledge, Ingraham offered a scattershot rebuttal that rested on her experience, her identity, and her attractiveness. "It's not just like I showed up blond and in a miniskirt and said, 'hire me!'" She had, she pointed out, clerked for the Supreme Court. "Those old white males don't speak to a lot of America—what does Fred Barnes know about my world? You don't hear male anchors and reporters being criticized for being too good-looking," she added, pivoting again. "No one wants to see Quasimodo up there."[17]

All that attention opened the door for new opportunities outside the narrow niche of conservative talk radio and low-reach television programming. Ingraham and her cohort weren't just covered by mainstream outlets—they worked for them. And the one place where they all had their turn in the spotlight wasn't a news channel but a comedy one.

———

LAURA INGRAHAM SETTLED into her seat as the cameras rolled, flashing a practiced smile as the evening's other guests strolled on stage. She was becoming something of a regular on *Politically Incorrect*, Bill Maher's show that blended comedy and politics and always tried to save a seat for a conservative. Maher liked the unexpected, so members of the IWF like Ingraham, Ann Coulter, Barbara Olson, and Kellyanne Fitzpatrick had become frequent guests, mingling with the show's mix of comedians, actors, journalist, and politicos. She sparred with Al Franken and Jon Stewart, Jay Leno and Zach Galifianakis (then an up-and-coming comedian). This was a new frontier in political entertainment, where celebrities weighed in on serious political topics and politicos cracked jokes (or tried to).[18]

When it launched in 1993, *Politically Incorrect* seemed unlikely to remake punditry in the United States. Siloed away on Comedy Central, a cable channel that had only debuted a few years earlier, *Politically Incorrect* quickly became the network's most popular show. But at the time, Comedy Central reached only about a third of US households, and at first the show had trouble drawing more than sixty thousand viewers. Within a few years, that number would swell to nearly three hundred thousand.[19]

The show tapped into a shift already underway in US political culture in the early 1990s. The line between entertainment and politics had been blurring for decades—Richard Nixon appeared on the sketch-comedy show *Laugh-In* way back in 1968—but by the early 1990s, cable had opened up a new world for presidential candidates: Pat Buchanan on *Crossfire*, Ross Perot on *Larry King Live*, Bill Clinton on *The Arsenio Hall Show* and MTV. But it wasn't just the candidates exploiting the shows; networks like MTV and Comedy Central were leveraging campaigns for influence and entertainment. Clinton's famous appearance on MTV, where he talked about everything from alcoholism to underwear, occurred during "Choose or Lose," part of a campaign to register twenty million young people during the 1992 election. Comedy Central, which had dipped its toe into political coverage with one of President Bush's State of the Union addresses, sent teams to both conventions as part of "Indecision '92," airing live comedy commentary for two hours each night. And while comedians anchored the coverage, they argued they were doing more than just entertaining. Mary Salter, who produced "Indecision '92," said Comedy Central was providing a public service, reporting on the conventions with a "raised-eyebrow approach" at a time when Americans had grown increasingly skeptical of the artifice of politics.[20]

The success of "Indecision '92" gave the fledgling network a boost. It also inspired Bill Maher, who had been one of the channel's correspondents covering the conventions. He had been itching to do a show that, as he put it, "made controversy funny." But when he looked at the three major broadcast networks' late-night shows, he saw a deep aversion to anything controversial—an accurate observation, given the networks' desire to appeal to as broad an audience as possible while offending no one. Maher didn't limit his criticism of bland programming to comedy shows, though. He also argued that political analysis had lost its edge, with too many people straight-jacketed by political correctness.[21]

So he set out to develop a show that would blend politics, comedy, and controversy: *The Tonight Show* meets *Crossfire*, or, as the show's developers talked about it in the press, "*The McLaughlin Group* on acid." *Politically Incorrect* reflected those hybrid origins in its structure: an opening monologue styled after Johnny Carson and a roundtable discussion copied straight from *The McLaughlin Group*. Like John McLaughlin, the crotchety host of the PBS show, Maher would throw out a topic for the group to seize on, chumming the waters with a few controversial thoughts of his own.[22]

In addition to these quasi-satirical origins, *Politically Incorrect* channeled a kind of stylistic populism, one that fit a show launched in the aftermath of the Perot campaign. The set was littered with broken Greek columns, a visual nod to the underlying theme of the show: democracy was broken—*everything* was broken—and the only way to begin rebuilding it was to cut through the bland blather of politics and seize on the most contentious issues. And while the guests were far from ordinary people, Maher argued there was a kind of populism of opinion in inviting actors and comedians to weigh in on politics. "The concept of this show is that we live in a democracy, so everyone's opinion is equal. If everyone has a vote, why shouldn't everyone have an opinion?"[23]

Comedy was an essential ingredient to the show's approach to controversy. Maher and his guests used it as a kind of shield, allowing them to say outrageous things and, if the blowback got too hot, shrug it off as just comedy. Maher regularly waffled on this question in the press, at times saying that his show had influence because it understood America better than the Beltway crowd, at other times playing down his influence ("Look, I'm not trying to be David Brinkley. It's a comedy show. A comedy show that uses controversial issues as its fodder"). He ended each monologue with the statement "It's all been satirized for your protection." The line sounded like just a jokey play on "sanitized," but coating controversy with comedy provided important protections for his guests—especially the noncomedians like Ingraham and Coulter, who relied more on outrage than humor to get a reaction from the audience. The show taught them that saying shocking things could be treated as a form of comedy instead of a serious political argument that required serious rebuttal.[24]

Maher provided another kind of cover as well, with the name *Politically Incorrect*. Though he described himself as a "reluctant conservative" (and voted for Bob Dole in 1996), he did not see being "politically incorrect" as a fundamentally conservative value. "To me, 'politically incorrect' means being honest," he said in a 1995 interview. That framing suggested that when the audience gasped at an offensive statement, it was because the comment had breached the bounds of propriety. And that was how outrageous, as well as racist and sexist, statements were treated on the show: as issues of *propriety*, not power, as true things people secretly believed, not false things they held onto as part of a social hierarchy.[25]

Adding to the show's transgressive reputation was its bawdiness: it was often sexually frank and sprinkled with profanities. Its home on cable put it out of the reach of network censors and meant it did not have to appeal to the mass audiences that free-to-air networks relied on. Being on cable may have limited the show's reach, but it did not stop it from becoming a phenomenon, one that would define Comedy Central's brand. But more than that, it left an imprint on American news media, even as its viewership hovered around a few hundred thousand. In 1996, the *New York Times* declared that *Politically Incorrect* was "almost single-handedly reviving political satire on television."[26]

Ingraham sharpened her skills through her appearances on *Politically Incorrect* and soon became a regular on shows like *Imus in
the Morning*, the shock-jock radio program simulcast on MSNBC,
and *The McLaughlin Group*. The appetite for this kind of programming was insatiable in the 1990s—so much so that after the 1996
election, *Politically Incorrect* ended its run on Comedy Central and
made a move to the big time: ABC's late-night lineup, with *Nightline* as its lead-in.

For *Politically Incorrect*, this would become a test of Maher's
theory that the broadcast networks were too wary of controversy.
But even before Maher made the leap to ABC, there were signs
that their wariness was on the wane; eager to tap into the new
style of punditry, CBS News had hired Ingraham to provide commentaries on the weekend news, rotating with former Democratic
senator Bill Bradley. The networks' tolerance for controversy was
clearly growing (though Maher and guests had to restrain their use
of swear words). With those slight amendments, *Politically Incorrect* attracted a massive new audience: in its first year, an average of
three million viewers were tuning in to the show.[27]

For Comedy Central, the loss of its flagship triggered a bit of
soul-searching. *Politically Incorrect* had been its biggest show and
as such had come to define the network as a channel dedicated
to more than just comedy—one that had become an increasingly
important part of political debate in the United States. Intent on
keeping that identity, corporate heads filled *Politically Incorrect*'s
time slot with a four-month-old show that they hoped could mature into something just as influential: *The Daily Show*, a satirical
take on nightly news.[28]

The glib, shock-jock approach to politics that talk radio and
Politically Incorrect made marketable would quickly transfer over
to cable news, especially when MSNBC and Fox News arrived on

the scene in 1996. The networks may have been created to compete with CNN, but *Politically Incorrect* was in their DNA.

———

IN THE SUMMER of 1993, while doing press for the debut of *Politically Incorrect*, Maher tried to explain the show's odd grab bag of guests. "To me, the first joke of the show is seeing an MTV deejay next to Roger Ailes—you'd never see those people together in real life." Ailes wasn't a name Maher just plucked out at random; he would be one of the panelists in the first season, there to spar with comedians and veejays in front of the show's crumbling Greek pillars.[29]

At the time, Ailes's main media role was as executive producer of Rush Limbaugh's television show. But he was about to embark on a new project, one that would lead, in 1996, to the founding of both Fox News and MSNBC. And while Fox News would carry the conservative brand, MSNBC would nurture the cable news careers of some of the most prominent right-wing figures of the 2000s and 2010s, from Laura Ingraham and Ann Coulter to Tucker Carlson and eventually Pat Buchanan.

Ailes's role in these networks began with a short-lived channel called America's Talking, one of NBC's efforts to branch into cable. He envisioned it as an all-talk television network, modeled after talk radio. That didn't mean he wanted to copy talk radio's conservatism—a show called *Pork*, about government waste, was the most conservative program on the network. Rather, he wanted to channel its populism (as well as its low production costs). He built that into the network's programming in two ways: by having interactive shows that allowed viewers to participate through phone calls, emails, and chatroom messages and by aiming programs at what Ailes called "the NASCAR audience," people in the middle of the

· country rather than on the coasts. The lineup included a morning
show with Steve Doocy, a love and life advice show featuring advice
columnist E. Jean Carroll, and an interview show hosted by Ailes
himself. The most political the network got was the prime-time
show *A-T in Depth* with Chris Matthews, former speechwriter for
Jimmy Carter, at the helm.[30]

America's Talking reached about ten million cable subscribers
when it first launched. It mixed bland, middlebrow programming
with the innovation of the internet, partnering with the online service provider Prodigy. The sets were styled to look like a coffeeshop,
inviting listeners in for a chat. But the shows needed constant reworking: Roger Ailes had dreamed up most of them, and most fell
flat when they were actually put into production. But Ailes kept at
it, trying to find some way to harness the electricity and popularity
of talk radio.[31]

America's Talking was not the only cable channel trying to tap
into the populist sentiment of the early 1990s. In fact, one network
was doing the same thing with an overtly conservative bent: National Empowerment Television (NET). Founded by Paul Weyrich, one of the leaders of the New Right, NET was an effort to
bring the New Right's populist, issue-oriented politics into the
1990s. *Newsweek* held that it was "the first of its kind in America—
an unabashedly ideological political-TV channel."[32]

NET, which first went live in late 1993, targeted the kind of
grassroots activists that Weyrich had sought to reach in the 1980s
through direct mail and local organizing. Yet the channel did not sell
itself as a right-wing alternative to CNN. Instead, it was pitched as
"must-watch television for public policy wonks and junkies"—or, as
the much-quoted tagline put it, "C-SPAN with attitude." Since that
crowd skewed older, NET also sought to attract younger viewers
with a program called *Youngbloods*, a roundtable of panelists in their

twenties. The standout of the show was Tom Fitton, who at the time worked at the right-wing media watchdog organization Accuracy in Media. The *Washington Post*, evaluating the show's entertainment value, declared him the star of *Youngbloods*, a pundit "whose charming sneer and venomous rhetoric keep the show from falling into the dreaded Policy Drone." Fitton underscored that analysis, saying, "I'm here to say what I think, as non-politically correctly as I can."[33]

But *Youngbloods* was an outlier on a network more oriented toward politics than entertainment. Most hosts were politicians or activists pressing their particular issues. Newt Gingrich hosted two shows on the network, one based on his video course on US history and one a call-in show about current events. Former Reagan attorney general Bill Barr also had a call-in show called *Crime and Punishment*, where he fielded complaints about the criminal justice system. Activist groups had their own programming as well: a pro-gun show called *On Target with the NRA*, a journalist-bashing show from Accuracy in Media called *The Other Side of the Story*, and an anti-immigrant show from the Federation for American Immigration Reform called *BorderLine*. That last show featured a number of white-nationalist activists, including Sam Francis, Peter Brimelow, and Jared Taylor.[34]

While NET claimed to be cutting-edge, stressing the network's interactive formats and confrontational attitude, it had a distinct public-access vibe, with poorly lit and plainly outfitted sets. The hosts, too, were not made for television, coming from the world of activism rather than journalism and entertainment. The network never had sufficient capital to be a real player: supported primarily by donations from conservative foundations, it had between $10 million and $25 million to fund its operations—not nothing, but far from the amount needed to compete with CNN or even C-SPAN, which had an annual operating budget of $15 million in the early 1990s, as well as something even more valuable: space in a cable company's lineup.[35]

One of the big stumbling blocks for the new cable networks was finding carriage, the industry term for space in the cable lineup. Though cable had dramatically expanded the number of channels on offer, space was not unlimited. So when executives went to cable companies, hat in hand, asking to become part of their already-full lineups, they were often turned away. Ultimately both NET and America's Talking floundered, unable to attract enough viewers to stay afloat. But their successors would transform the cable news landscape.[36]

Two new cable networks, MSNBC and Fox News, emerged from the demise of America's Talking. The route for MSNBC was more direct: unhappy with the channel's low ratings and wanting a property that could compete with CNN (which NBC executives had recently tried to purchase), NBC pulled the plug on America's Talking and replaced it with a new joint venture with Microsoft, MSNBC. They chose Andy Lack, president of NBC News, to head up programming for the channel. It was a choice with serious consequences: it left no role for Ailes at the new network, sending him running to Australian media mogul Rupert Murdoch, who had plans for his own cable news network after CNN rebuffed his efforts to buy it. Soon, two new twenty-four-hour cable news networks would be entering the market.[37]

MSNBC, which debuted in 1996, positioned itself as the news channel for Generation X, leaning into its tech roots. In its first year, the average age for contributors to the network was thirty-five, at a time when news programs, even those at competitor CNN, tended to feature older white men and some women who had spent their careers in journalism. Not so for the MSNBC contributors, who were plucked from a much wider array of backgrounds: activists, lawyers, consultants. And the analytical approach differed as well, being far more rooted in personal experience, emotional response, and combative sparring occasionally cut with humor. Nor was age the only consideration for the new network. MSNBC sought out conservative commentators, especially those that were young, hip, and controversial, like two of its early hires: Ingraham, who was given her own show on the network, and Ann Coulter, an acerbic young lawyer fueled by a deep-seated hatred of the Clintons that she channeled into quick-witted diatribes. The idea was more *Politically Incorrect* than *The McLaughlin Group*: less shouting, more wry commentary.[38]

Not everyone in the older generation was impressed. Robert Novak, who had been a regular on *The McLaughlin Group* and *Crossfire*, filling in during the periods that Pat Buchanan ran for president, said the new generation was good-looking but inexperienced. "Producers want to appeal to the X Generation—they're tired of the old geezers. But most of the young people don't know what they're talking about." Tom Brokaw was even more vicious about what he saw as the network's content-free blather. "It's kind of like marathon dancing. It's interesting that they can do it for so long, but it's not that fun to do it or watch it."[39]

And not many people were watching, at least not yet. Nor were they tuned in to the other new channel, Fox News, which launched a few months after MSNBC. Both networks wanted to take on CNN; both quickly realized how difficult it was to draw eyeballs. By 1997, when CNN averaged 578,000 viewers, Fox News drew 30,000 and MSNBC just 24,000. (The much-maligned *McLaughlin Group* averaged 4.5 million.)[40]

Despite the lack of viewers, the new cable news channels were doing important work in constructing a political media environment dominated by opinion, personality, and outrage. They marked a distinct evolution from CNN, which was struggling to find its own approach in the 1990s, as founder Ted Turner clung to straight news while audiences responded far more strongly to personality-driven programming. CNN had been founded on the idea that the news, not the newscaster, was the star. For years, Turner resisted investing heavily in set design and talent, even though his most highly rated shows in the 1980s and 1990s, *Larry King Live* and *Crossfire*, had evolved from talk radio. But Turner insisted that the network not be defined by those shows, that its identity be rooted in journalism, not opinion or celebrity.[41]

Fox News took the opposite tack. When founded in 1996, it flew the banner of objectivity: its slogan was "Fair and balanced," and its tagline was "We report, you decide." However, it leaned heavily on opinion, stacking its prime time with shouting heads like Bill O'Reilly and Sean Hannity who claimed to speak for white working-class men (though they had spent their careers in entertainment). It also quickly developed a reputation for its conservative tilt. That came in part from its founders: Ailes was a Republican operative and *Rush Limbaugh Show* producer; Murdoch was clearly right leaning but also had a strong attraction to power and disruption (he supported Pat Robertson in the 1988 Republican presidential primaries and voted for Ross Perot in 1992). But it was also because, while the network did hire some serious journalists and brought liberals on to act as sparring partners, its center of gravity was the right-wing personalities anchoring its biggest shows.[42]

It was not initially clear that Fox News's conservative bent was an asset. It lagged behind MSNBC in both ratings and carriage (Fox executives ultimately had to appeal to New York mayor Rudy Giuliani, who officiated Ailes's third wedding in 1998, to get access to the New York City market). MSNBC found it easy to negotiate with cable providers, often grabbing the slot that America's Talking had once held. It also had the cachet of its relationship to NBC, a broadcast network with a much longer track record than Fox.[43]

But Fox had its own advantages, foremost among them being Rupert Murdoch's deep pockets. Most cable providers paid networks in order to carry their programming. A network like CNN might get twenty-five cents per subscriber. Murdoch, desperate to get as wide coverage as possible, flipped the equation, offering to pay providers $10 per subscriber—a strategy that cost him hundreds of millions of dollars. But it worked, and the network soon had enough visibility to begin to build a base. It also had the benefit of novelty. The often explicitly conservative programming of shows like *The O'Reilly Factor* broke from both the more straightforward coverage and the right-left punditry of other networks. And Fox News had one other secret weapon. In 1996, a reporter named David Shuster reached out to an executive at Fox News to ask for a job. He explained that he had been working to uncover Clinton scandals, starting with Whitewater, since the summer of 1992—and he said the odds were fifty-fifty that Hillary Clinton was going to be indicted.[44]

That was all Roger Ailes needed to hear. A few weeks later, Shuster had a job. And for the next three years, he worked as the network's point person for every scandal, right through impeachment.

———

COMEDY CENTRAL, FOX News, and MSNBC all had small audiences in the mid-1990s, especially compared to the broadcast networks and CNN. But they revolutionized political journalism, introducing a new style of political entertainment that was rooted in outrage and partisan sparring. The turn toward entertainment introduced through shows like *Crossfire* and *The Rush Limbaugh Show* had now become institutionalized in the cable landscape. The

ability to narrowcast—to slice up the audience into niche groups—
had real consequences for the portrayal of politics on television.
It allowed channels like Comedy Central to experiment with new
styles of shows and networks like NET and Fox News to target
what they believed were underserved conservative audiences.

These new outlets also kick-started a style of inflammatory punditry that exerted disproportionate influence on American politics
at the time. CNN had long operated under the mantra "The news
is the star"; MSNBC and Fox News wanted the on-air talent to
star, to connect with audiences and tap into their discontents, to
foreground emotion. Even though Ailes insisted that Fox News
preferred facts over fame (a dig at the big names MSNBC had introduced to its lineup), the instant success of Bill O'Reilly's bluster-
ing, brawling show suggested that talk, not news, was the key to Fox
News's success.

That success was still a few years off. But the success of shows
like *Politically Incorrect* and the opinion-heavy lineups of the two
new cable news networks suggested the future of political programming on television would be rooted more in entertainment than
journalism, with profound consequences not only for news in the
United States but for politics as well. And one of those pioneering
pundits was about to blur the line between politics and entertainment even more as he launched his second bid for the White House.

CHAPTER NINE

PITCHFORK PAT

PAT BUCHANAN WAS WINNING.

Not like in 1992, when he considered his not-that-close second-place finish in New Hampshire a kind of moral victory. In 1996, he was *actually* winning, coming in first in the Alaska caucus, first in the Louisiana caucus, first in the New Hampshire primary. That, plus his close second-place finish in Iowa, meant he was the front-runner. And it was making Republican Party elites extremely nervous.

Nervous in part because Buchanan was winning even after they had started shifting their platform in his direction. As he rightly noted when he launched his second presidential campaign in March 1995, just a few months after Newt Gingrich became Speaker of the House, the party had moved toward many of his positions since his first run. "Four years ago," he told the crowd in Manchester, New Hampshire, "we came here to say 'no' to tax hikes and 'no' to quota bills, and now every Republican says 'no' to tax hikes and 'no' to quota bills and 'no' to affirmative action." Nor were taxes and affirmative action the only policies the party now rejected. Perhaps its most surprising, and most Buchanan-like, shift had been its rejection of immigration—a rejection that would only deepen as Buchanan racked up victories.[1]

It wasn't just the Republican Party moving in Buchanan's direction. The Clinton administration, while regularly clashing with Republicans in Congress, had also lurched to the right. The crime bill Bill Clinton signed in 1994 may have included gun regulations and protections for domestic violence, but it also lengthened prison sentences, expanded use of the death penalty, eliminated higher education funding for incarcerated people, and poured money into prisons and policing.

Near the end of his first term, Clinton signed a welfare-reform law that sharply limited assistance to low-income Americans, eliminating Aid to Families with Dependent Children and imposing work requirements and lifetime limits on welfare benefits. This wasn't just a matter of bending to Republicans; he had promised during the 1992 campaign to "end welfare as we know it." And not long after enacting welfare reform, he also signed the Defense of Marriage Act, which defined marriage as an institution limited to one man and one woman and allowed states to refuse to acknowledge same-sex marriages performed in other states.[2]

With the Democratic Party moving right, Republicans had greater incentive to move further right as well, to keep the differences between the two parties clear. Add in the extra incentive to adopt hard-line positions to please conservative media outlets and right-wing pundits, and it was no surprise that by 1996 most Republican candidates were well to the right of Ronald Reagan. But that presented another problem: moving that far right increasingly put the party out of step with the mainstream electorate. This was doubly a problem for Buchanan. Because even as Buchanan argued that his views had become mainstream, he could not escape the accusation that he was an extremist, one who invited far-right racists, nativists, and conspiracists into the party. Such accusations had been there in 1992 as well, but in 1996 they seemed to attract rather than repel Republican primary voters.

How the Republican Party responded to that dynamic—by trying first to co-opt, then to sideline Buchanan—showed a widening fissure between a base unwilling to compromise and a leadership that believed it had to tack to the center to win national elections. The lackluster Republican campaign suggested that there was something missing, that Buchanan, with his fervent followers and media-savvy campaign, had tapped into something necessary to win the presidency that the eventual nominee, Senator Bob Dole, did not. But with Buchanan unable to win the nomination and Dole unable to win the election, it was clear that the fissure was beginning to deflate the Republican Party's presidential hopes, even as it emboldened the party's base.

THE 1996 REPUBLICAN primary—the first wide-open primary since 1980—was packed with contenders hoping to be the first Republican president of the post–Cold War era. They had reason to be optimistic. Clinton had fallen short of a majority in 1992, after Ross Perot upended the race. No Democratic president had been elected to a second term since 1948. And the Republican wave of 1994 had been much larger than most midterm backlashes, large enough to convince Republicans they had a pretty good shot at winning back the White House.

The race attracted both those with previous experience in the presidential primaries, like Bob Dole and Pat Buchanan, and a bevy of newcomers who were eyeing a potential run: Steve Forbes, a magazine publisher running on a flat tax; Bob Dornan, a California actor turned congressman known for his over-the-top offensive statements; Phil Gramm, the Texas senator vying to be the Ronald Reagan of the race; and Colin Powell, the popular Gulf War general whom Republicans were desperate to draft as their nominee.

Powell and Gramm worried Buchanan most. Powell and Buchanan were polar opposites. Powell was a Black general who supported abortion rights, affirmative action, and gun control, but he had captured the public's imagination. Like Buchanan, he had never held elected office, and like Buchanan, he was a celebrity. Though he had worked in two administrations, serving as national security advisor under Reagan and chairman of the Joint Chiefs of Staff under George H. W. Bush, his political persona was, like Buchanan's, a media creation. But after months of dizzying speculation, Powell announced in November 1995 that he would not run.[3]

Which left the Reaganite Gramm to contend with. Like Reagan, Gramm had converted from Democrat to Republican, but not before cosponsoring a 1981 budget that would enact all of Reagan's economic priorities. A hardcore free trade conservative, he fought for deregulation, low taxes, and steep cuts to welfare programs. But his campaign never caught fire; a huge chunk of the party's conservative base wanted Buchanan, not a Reagan redux.[4]

That left a race primarily between Bob Dole, the brooding Senate majority leader who represented the party's conservative establishment, and Buchanan, who represented the conservative insurgency. When Gramm dropped out after a disappointing showing in Iowa, he immediately held a press conference to endorse Dole. And he made clear that Buchanan's extremist ties were why: "You don't see David Duke up here," he told reporters.[5]

Extremism became a focal point of Buchanan's campaign. It was something he could not shed, because his attractiveness to extremist groups was a feature, not a bug, of his politics. People liked him *because* he said outrageous things, because he flouted political norms, because he attacked a political establishment and social norms that they despised. But that extremism also limited his appeal.

His writing on immigration grew increasingly focused on race as the topic became a national political issue in 1994. Weighing in on Proposition 187, which he endorsed, he wrote that even the pro-187 boosters were missing the heart of the argument. It wasn't about the state's fiscal health or economic conditions. It was about "the deepest, most divisive issues of our time: ethnicity, nation, culture." What would it mean if the white majority were replaced by immigrants from Africa, Latin America, and Asia? Would native-born Americans lose control of their culture? Would the country fracture along ethnic lines? Buchanan mused about all these things, then called for a "timeout on immigration"—a moratorium—to ensure the assimilation of the immigrants already in the United States in an effort to preserve the dominant white culture.[6]

It was not the first time Buchanan had mused about the potential threat migration posed to US culture. In December 1991, he went on David Brinkley's ABC show to talk about immigration. He had already begun to separate from the rest of the Republican Party with his hard-line positions on the issue, including his call to build a "security fence" along the border between the United States and Mexico. But the scale of immigration and whether or not it was authorized were not his only concerns. "If we had to take a million immigrants in, say Zulus, next year, or Englishmen, and put them in

Virginia, what group would be easier to assimilate and would cause less problems for the people of Virginia?" His question pointed to his belief that white Europeans were more assimilable than Black southern Africans and that US immigration policy should reflect that in order to preserve US culture—arguments right in line with *Alien Nation* and *The End of Racism*.[7]

Still, it took a while for the extremism of Buchanan's campaign to penetrate press coverage. In one of several columns about the press's approach to Buchanan during that year's primaries, *Washington Post* columnist David Broder reflected on the pass Buchanan got from the press.

> He has been "Pat" to so many of us who have known him since he was a traveling valet and speechwriter for Richard Nixon in 1966—the combative but personally congenial guy who was writing columns, or doing TV or flacking for Nixon or Agnew or Reagan—that it's hard to imagine him as president or even presidential nominee. And there is an assumption that his views are too extreme to gain much support. The press has treated his campaign lightly, presuming that it is just an interlude before he goes back on CNN's "Crossfire" and the speaking circuit. That's a mistake. Like George Wallace, he has a deadly knack for finding the most divisive issues in American life, including race, and a growing skill in exploiting them.[8]

On the eve of the Iowa caucus, Broder again fretted that personal affection kept the press from fully reporting on Buchanan's growing support. "It spares him from critical examination of the way he has assembled a 'constituency of grievance' among those distraught with the economic and social conditions of the country." Joe Klein at *Newsweek* joined in on those concerns after Buchanan's victory in New Hampshire. "There are an awful lot of journalists who find what Buchanan says utterly abhorrent, but they have been giggling along with him," he wrote. "Part of every one of us is a theater critic, and he is appealing to that part."[9]

Like Peter Brimelow, Buchanan had been given, at least in some circles, the benefit of the doubt. It is no coincidence that the two men leading the charge about white culture and immigration were journalists—they were not dismissed as crackpots and kooks because they were *colleagues*. Their social and professional connections meant they were taken seriously, and their understanding of how journalism functioned, particularly the instinct to highlight contrarianism and "both sides," gave them a talent for framing their arguments in a way most likely to appeal to the journalistic centers of the day.

Brimelow had shown that, given space and soft coverage, those arguments about race and immigration could sell books. But could they win votes? That was Pat Buchanan's challenge in 1996.

He tackled it by reworking his political persona, completing a transformation he had begun when he first ran for president in 1992. Having watched how Perot challenged the North American Free Trade Agreement and big business, he elevated economic nationalism and populism to the fore of his campaign, sharpening his attacks on US corporations and free trade deals. During the early days of the campaign, he could be found speaking at a Harley-Davidson dealership in New Hampshire, telling the long-haired, tattooed men there that the economy wasn't working for them. "We've seen the real incomes of men who work with their hands, tools and

machines decline," he said. "The Dow Jones average went up about
20 percent in six months, the real income of American workers went
down 2.3 percent." The economy may have been booming, but the
wealth wasn't trickling down to American workers.[10] He attacked
fellow Republicans for embracing "the myth of the economic man,
that everything can be solved with tax cuts, balance the budget, get
the numbers rights, the problem is solved."[11]

How had the man who helped Reagan make the case for free
trade and immigration come to sound so different? In a January
1996 interview, he admitted that back in his Reagan days, he had
been "a free trader all the way" and hadn't cared much about immigration at all. Then Buchanan told the story of his uncle, who lived
in the Monongahela Valley in Pennsylvania, confronting him about
his views. "What are you doing this free trade stuff for?" his uncle
reportedly asked. "Go up to your mother's hometown, see what's
happening to our steel mills. Everything's shutting down up there."
It was Buchanan's road-to-Damascus story, a Rust Belt conversion
from free trader to economic nationalist. No such dramatics accompanied his conversion on immigration. He simply explained he'd
never paid much attention to it, and that had changed. "If you want
to keep this country one nation, we better have one language, one
common culture to which we all contribute."[12]

Those shifts brought Buchanan more in line with Perot voters,
who were an indispensable part of the coalition he had hoped to
build. All the candidates for president that year had their eye on
these voters, believing Perot had been the real spoiler in the 1992
race and his voters were the key to winning in 1996. In August 1995,
Perot's organization, United We Stand, held a conference in Dallas
attended by just about everyone planning to run for the Republican
nomination. Whereas other candidates offered punched-up stump
speeches, Buchanan had been carefully tailoring his attacks on in-

ternationalism for months for precisely this moment. Though he had been part of Republican politics since his twenties, he now positioned himself as a Perot-like figure outside the two-party system. "Politicians of both parties sold us out," he told the crowd. Nor was he shy about invoking the watchwords of right-wing conspiracies. "I want to say to all the globalists," he said during his speech, "when I raise my hand to take the oath of office, your new world order comes crashing down."[13]

Folded into this critique of internationalism—which he talked about in terms of "globalism" and the "new world order," phrases that carried a whiff of conspiracy—was his opposition to immigration. In May 1995, he appeared at a forum on immigration clutching a copy of Brimelow's just-published book, prepared to lay out his new, hard-line vision for immigration policy. He warned that Americans were in the midst of "an invasion of the country" that could be stopped in six months with the adoption of his restrictive new policies: a double security fence on the border, the end of birthright citizenship for children of undocumented immigrants, a beefed-up Border Patrol, and his newest addition, a five-year moratorium on immigration to the United States. He also included a call for English as the country's official language: "We have got to be one nation and one people again."[14]

All of these pronouncements forged a new Buchanan persona: Pitchfork Pat. Evoking the vision of a populist revolt, with the people picking up pitchforks and torches to overthrow the establishment, the pitchfork became the emblem of the Buchanan campaign. Enthusiastic supporters dragged pitchforks to rallies for Buchanan to sign, and he would pose with the unwieldly farm instruments, looking every inch the DC-born writer as he slipped a marker from his pinstriped suit to scrawl his signature along the wooden handle.

There was another, darker historical echo behind the nickname: "Pitchfork Ben" had been the nickname of Ben Tillman, who served as South Carolina's governor and then senator from the 1890s until he died in 1918. He claimed to speak for the farmers and mill workers of the state whom the governing elites were ignoring. His populism was deeply rooted in violent white supremacy: he led the Red Shirts, a white-supremacist paramilitary group, in their efforts to seize power in South Carolina in the 1870s. Later, as senator, he worked to disenfranchise all Black voters, called for lynchings, and encouraged a violent coup in Wilmington, North Carolina, in 1898. Quite a namesake for Pitchfork Pat.[15]

Picking up the pitchfork might have stirred populist fervor, but for Buchanan, like Tillman, that fervor was about racism as much as economic displacement. Given his fretting about an invasion of the country and his worries about a disappearing white culture, it is little wonder that far-right groups were attracted to Buchanan's campaign. Just as white-power groups had popped up at his border appearance four years earlier, now activists with white-supremacist ties were embedded in his campaign. One of the campaign's county chairs in Florida was ousted after reports surfaced that she was part of David Duke's National Association for the Advancement of White People. A South Carolina steering committee member got the boot for ties to Duke's 1992 campaign.[16]

But more significant were the people in his inner circle. Buchanan's friend Samuel Francis, who was fired as a columnist for the *Washington Times* in 1995 for speaking at a white-supremacist conference, served as an informal campaign advisor. In February 1996, just before the New Hampshire primary, the Center for Public Integrity revealed that Larry Pratt, founder of Gun Owners of America and one of four national cochairs for the Buchanan campaign, had spoken before white-power and militia groups in the early 1990s. His gun group had also donated to CAUSE, a legal organization whose name stood for the remaining areas of the world it had designated as truly white: Canada, Australia, the United Kingdom, South Africa, and Europe. Buchanan angrily defended Pratt from the charges, calling him a "very loyal supporter" and insisting he would not denounce him because "this campaign is about inclusiveness."[17]

Outside the official campaign structure, the far right was celebrating Buchanan's bid for the presidency. The Populist Party, which nominated Duke in 1988, decided that it would not nominate anyone for the 1996 race when it convened in fall 1995, because Buchanan was in the race. Militia members also applauded the campaign, seeing their own sense of rebelliousness reflected in Pitchfork Pat's positions, from the claims about embattled national sovereignty and border invasions to attacks on the United Nations and the "new world order." As Bob Fletcher, a leader of the Montana Militia who testified in the congressional hearings on the armed groups, put it, "Pat's general platform is absolutely verbatim with those things that we've been talking about."[18]

The blurred lines between the far right and the Buchanan movement worried some Republicans, who sensed the entire party could be tarred by association. Yet dissociating from Buchanan was a tricky thing. Party activists knew they would need his supporters to win in November. So, when the Dole campaign attacked Buchanan as an extremist after the New Hampshire primary, Ralph Reed cautioned them to back off. "Quit attacking him and calling him names," he said, worried about alienating the Buchanan brigade.[19]

He had good reason to worry. Buchanan supporters brought an alarming intensity to his rallies. "I don't just have support, I have a following," he told the *Washington Post* in March 1996, as his chances of winning the nomination were growing increasingly grim. The highs of February, when he had been dominating the race, had given way to a Dole rout in state after state—including South Carolina, where he'd hoped his southern roots and Jim Crow rhetoric would secure a victory. "I'm not going to let them down. And they know that. They sense that. They sense this is not just some politician who's come out here to get their votes and going through the motions. It is a very intense thing. They believe in me."[20]

They seemed to believe in him more the worse his odds got. As Dole racked up wins, Buchanan's rallies grew rowdier, with the crowds whooping at his attack lines and booing lustily whenever he ran through a catalog of enemies (everything from the Department of Education to the World Trade Organization). Vince Thompson, part of the Buchanan brigade, explained his support to the *Los Angeles Times* this way: "We're scared to say what we think some of the real problems are in this country for fear of being called a racist or extremist. Pat says it for us. He's giving the people a podium they can stand on. We may lose but this is how we feel, and it feels good to have our feelings aired." As if to leave no doubt as to the nature of Buchanan's appeal, Thompson added that Buchanan was "giving a voice to the silent majority—the white population that works too hard to have time to be politically active."[21]

That fervor worried Republican leaders, even after Buchanan suspended his campaign in late March. But as worried as they were about losing Buchanan's supporters in November, they were more worried that he would end up tarring the entire party as extremist. Memories of his dark, rousing speech at the 1992 convention stuck with Republican Party leaders, who would do anything to prevent a repeat performance. So this time, even though Buchanan won far more votes than he had four years earlier, the party refused him a platform at the convention. Their compromise: a video segment that would air out of prime time, which he promptly rejected.

Instead he held his own rally, a three-hour event called "The Man and the Movement: A Tribute to Patrick J. Buchanan." On the eve of the August convention in San Diego, fifteen hundred Buchanan supporters gathered to hear people like Oliver North and Phyllis Schlafly toast the man of the hour. Then he gave his own barn burner, an attack on the Republican establishment. He told those gathered they should set down their pitchforks for the next ten weeks so Republicans could defeat Clinton, and he celebrated that so much of the GOP platform echoed his own, even joking that he was planning to ask the Republican National Committee to pay royalties.[22]

But if party officials thought inching toward Buchanan would buy a lasting peace, they were sorely mistaken. Surveying the room of loyal supporters, he saw the future of the Republican Party. "Within this party, a new party is being born, even in this room tonight," he said. "God willing, we will be there at its birth and one day, the stone the builders rejected shall become the cornerstone."

WHILE BUCHANAN SOUGHT to shift the party hard right in 1996, Ralph Reed sought to soften the radical edges of the coalition he led. It was the perfect task for him, because by the mid-1990s, he had mastered the art of political compromise. Perhaps that's because, before heading up the Christian Coalition, he had been a political activist. Like Dinesh D'Souza, who was only a few months his senior, he cut his teeth at a college newspaper—in his case, the University of Georgia's *The Red and the Black*, where he wrote a column calling Mohandas Gandhi a "ninny" (he was ultimately fired not for the content of the article but for plagiarizing most of it from a piece in *Commentary*). That did little to slow his rise in the College Republicans, where in 1981 he would become, along with Grover Norquist and Jack Abramoff, part of the Triumvirate, the three leaders of the organization who would force it sharply to the right during the Reagan years.[23]

As a leader of the College Republicans, Reed learned to be a bomb thrower, relying on the same combination of trolling and hard-right politics that D'Souza and the Dartmouth conservatives did. He wrote a manual for the group that outlined how to pressure liberal professors and attack funding for gay-rights groups (including starting a "Bestiality Club" or "Straight People's Alliance"). Reed relished the fight, regularly scheming with the like-minded Norquist on how best to go to war, first with the moderates in the organization and then with the Democrats.[24]

Reed and Norquist may have remained a bonded pair if not for Reed's experience one night at Bullfeathers, a bar and restaurant in the Capitol Hill neighborhood. There, he suddenly decided to embrace religion, making a beeline for the nearest phone booth and rifling through the Yellow Pages to find the church in Camp Springs, Maryland, where he would answer the altar call the next morning. Now an evangelical and political organizer, he founded Students for America, a blandly named organization for conservative evangelical college students whom Reed helped usher into the Republican Party.[25]

A year later, Reed once again transformed, this time into a graduate student at Emory University, studying US history. He wrote a dissertation on nineteenth-century evangelical colleges, which, journalist Nina Easton observed, revealed him to be "a Christian evangelical eager to operate in a modern humanist world." And he would do that operating with a new organization he founded under Pat Robertson: the Christian Coalition.[26]

The coalition, which would become the dominant conservative religious organization of the 1990s (the Moral Majority dissolved in 1989), helped ensure that evangelical stances like across-the-line opposition to abortion would become a new litmus test for Republican politicians. Yet, at the same time, under Reed the organization worked to acclimate evangelical voters to the art of political compromise—something he signaled when he lobbied to omit the word "Christian" from the group's name, worried that it was too exclusive (Robertson overruled him). Reed himself was a compromise: he became the face of that coalition, a more mainstream alternative now that Robertson, no longer interested in running for president, had retreated to pump out conspiratorial tracts about the new world order.[27]

Reed hadn't lost his political bloodlust. As he began preparing the Coalition for the 1992 election, he envisioned himself as Lee Atwater. "Hardball, do whatever it takes, win at all costs. That is what I wanted to be," he explained later. He talked about politics as guerilla warfare, brutal and deadly. "It comes down to whether you want to be the British army in the Revolutionary War or the Viet Cong," he said, inexplicably comparing his movement to Vietnamese communists rather than American revolutionaries. "History tells us which tactic was more effective." That language would come to haunt him, and after 1992 he pivoted away from martial language, opting instead for a kind of compassionate conservatism.[28]

While boasting about the growing influence of evangelical voters in the Republican coalition, Reed worried that the movement was still too narrow. In an essay titled "Casting a Wider Net" that came out in the summer of 1993, he urged conservative evangelicals to move beyond opposition to abortion and gay rights to a broad "pro-family" agenda. Noting that 17 percent of people who identified as evangelicals voted for Perot in 1992, he argued that deficit reduction and tax relief were as much family-values issues as social issues were.[29]

That manifesto translated into support for the Contract with America, a document that pointedly excluded social issues. Reed smoothed that over with the Coalition, insisting that he had the ear of Newt Gingrich and the Christian right would have its day. To kick-start the shift toward Coalition priorities in advance of the 1996 election, he released his Contract with the American Family in 1995. Unveiled at a press conference held in a room just off the Senate chamber, a space arranged by Bob Dole, Reed was flanked by Newt Gingrich and Phil Gramm, a clear sign that he had the backing of the Republican Party for his agenda, which included a public-prayer amendment for the Constitution, a ban on late-term abortions, an end to funding for the National Endowment for the Arts, and tax deductions on retirement accounts for stay-at-home mothers. Each was carefully aimed to fit in with the work congressional Republicans were already doing, and Reed stressed that they were not make-or-break policies. "We are not here today to make threats. We are making no demands. We are issuing no ultimatums."[30]

The supremely conciliatory Reed would become a handy asset going into the 1996 election. Though he warned Republicans against calling Buchanan an extremist—he knew well that the Buchanan voters were a vital part of the conservative coalition—he was more of a Jack Kemp man. When Bob Dole won the nomination, he knew the evangelicals in his organization were far from pleased, having preferred a more conservative candidate like Gramm or Buchanan. But he also knew that if they abandoned Dole, the party could easily lose its hold on both houses of Congress. So he provided Dole cover as he tacked to the center in the general election, even arguing that there was wiggle room on the issue of abortion.

That wiggle room was particularly important because, aided by Buchanan's early success, Republican candidates were battling charges of extremism. Newt Gingrich was the face of much of this, thanks to the government shutdown, though the rise of talk radio and the Oklahoma City bombing had exacerbated the problem. Dole had tried combatting this. After his loss in the New Hampshire primary, he redefined himself as the more moderate, less dangerous option. "This is now a race between the mainstream and the extreme," he said the morning after his loss to Buchanan. "I know he appeals to the fears of people. I want to appeal to their hopes."[31]

The dour-faced Dole, who repeatedly flashed with anger on the campaign trail over things like wobbly microphones, had a hard time selling himself as a happy warrior for conservatism. He had an even harder time as he sought to move away from the party's base. He flip-flopped on repealing the assault weapons ban, on abortion, and on affirmative action, opposing them all in the primary and signaling he was open to them in the general. The National Rifle Association broke with the campaign, saying its members were "disappointed and disillusioned" with Dole. In a fit of frustration, one Republican official fumed, "We are demobilizing our party."[32]

But even as he disappointed conservatives, Dole found his move to the center repeatedly blocked by Bill Clinton, who kept shifting to the right. In 1996, Republicans in Congress struck a number of deals with the administration, not only piling up victories for Clinton as he ran for reelection but boxing Dole in. The 1996 immigration bill made that clear: Clinton's willingness to take a hard-line on undocumented migrants meant that Dole, to differentiate himself, grabbed onto an amendment barring undocumented children from using public schools—the same unconstitutional provision that had killed Proposition 187. Clinton vowed not to sign the bill if the amendment was approved, and congressional Republicans, eager for the win, dropped it. Clinton won, congressional Republicans won, and Bob Dole was left out in the cold.[33]

In fact, every time the right tried to force a contrast with Clinton, Clinton outmaneuvered them. Reed had decided that in the 1996 race, he would stay away from issues involving gay rights, worried about coming across as bigoted and hard-hearted. He had seen Buchanan hammered for comments he made in 1983 about the AIDS epidemic ("The poor homosexuals—they have declared war upon nature, and now nature is exacting an awful retribution") and understood that it would do nothing for the party's image to continue to attack gay men and women. Yet, when Hawaii began developing legislation recognizing same-sex marriages, Republicans in Congress moved to pass the Defense of Marriage Act, hoping to use gay rights as a wedge issue in the election.[34]

Reed quickly announced the Coalition's support. He was frank about the political calculations: "Once a bill goes to his desk, there's a better-than-even chance that the organized gay lobby will go into orbit and create a lot of problems for the President." Best-case scenario: Clinton vetoes the legislation, and his opponents paint him as a radical pro-gay politician. Worst-case: a risk-averse Clinton signs the legislation, and the new restrictions go forward. Clinton took the safer route, signing the bill in a late-night, closed-door ceremony. He wasn't about to give ground to the right, even if it meant angering his gay supporters.[35]

It turned out that Reed was being pushed to the right as well. He had drafted language in the platform that urged tolerance on issues like abortion, an effort to keep the party open to pro-choice Republicans (like, say, Colin Powell, one of the party's most popular figures) and signal to voters that the GOP was a big-tent party. But when the time came for the platform fight, antiabortion activists were on high alert. Reed felt good about the language he drafted, but he ran headlong into opposition from Bay Buchanan, Pat's sister and campaign manager. Even while other high-profile religious right activists, like Gary Bauer of the Family Research Council and Phyllis Schlafly of the Eagle Forum, were open to discussing the compromise, Bay Buchanan swept in and accused them of selling out. Fearful that the label might stick with their followers, they all caved. Reed went on to oppose the platform language he had authored.[36]

Reed's capitulation showed in microcosm the challenge looming for the party. To build national majorities, they would need to soften and broaden their platform; to keep their increasingly hard-line base satisfied, they would need to make it increasingly stringent.

Reed had no solution to this dilemma other than to stop focusing so much on national majorities. "Our movement has made the mistake in the past in focusing almost exclusively on the presidential race, to the detriment of our other interests," he told journalist Elizabeth Drew over hot-fudge sundaes in early 1996. "We do better not having the White House and having Congress than we do not having Congress and having the presidency." On the congressional level, the Coalition did not have to be so concerned about extremism; it was especially active in the reelection drive of Helen Chenoweth.[37]

Reed was on to something: the post-Reagan Republican Party was a congressional party. It was there that the party's oppositional identity cemented itself, there that "bipartisanship" became a dirty word, there that the big tent shriveled to include only True Believers. As the party tacked further right, Republicans could build majorities in Congress, but they were increasingly facing real challenges building them in presidential elections.

For Dole, those challenges were clear almost as soon as he had won the nomination. Trailing in the polls by double digits for most of the year, he hoped that a late-breaking scandal concerning fund-raising schemes at the Clinton White House would rescue his campaign. When it failed to close the gap, he exploded. "Where is the outrage?" he roared at a campaign rally a week before the election. He was furious that journalists were not going after Clinton as hard as he would like. "We've got to stop the liberal bias in this country. Don't read that stuff! Don't watch television! You make up your mind! Don't let them make up your mind for you!"[38]

But he also layered in a new, darker charge to explain what now looked like a certain loss. He charged Democrats with flooding the country with immigrants with criminal records to vote for Clinton. "We have all these new people coming into America, rushing through the immigration process," Mr. Dole said. "We find out that maybe as high as 10 percent are criminals. They want to get them ready for Election Day." He was not the first to make such charges. When Michael Huffington lost his race against Dianne Feinstein for one of California's Senate seats by more than 150,000 votes in 1994, he refused to concede, alleging overwhelming voter fraud in the form of mass noncitizen voting. Appearing on *Larry King Live* a few weeks after the race, he said his supporters would go door to door to quiz voters on their citizenship status. Proposition 187 supporters put together an ad hoc Voter Fraud Task Force to aid the effort.[39]

A Republican presidential candidate making that claim, however, resonated differently, especially when that person had been the Senate majority leader. Dole did not imply the sort of mass voter fraud that Huffington claimed, but by throwing suspicion on citizenship status and suggesting Democrats were attempting to rig the system with criminal immigrants, he was setting the stage for more dramatic claims down the line. Clinton won the election by significant margins, beating Dole by nearly nine points in the popular vote and 379 to 159 in the Electoral College. But in attacking the legitimacy of Clinton voters, Dole was once again seeding doubt about the legitimacy of Bill Clinton's presidency, a doubt the right would nurture in the coming months and years as they tried to delegitimize the president they could not defeat.

CHAPTER TEN

HIGH CRIMES

A CAREFUL OBSERVER, SURVEYING THE POLITICAL landscape at the start of 1997, could have reasonably concluded that the partisan fever that had wracked Washington since Newt Gingrich became Speaker was about to break. Bill Clinton had won reelection easily, and the Republicans had retained control of Congress, all after a burst of bipartisan legislating in the closing months of the election. Gingrich and Clinton discovered they could work together—they had even come to respect each other as intellects and policymakers. With Clinton continuing to move to the right and Gingrich eager to demonstrate he was an effective leader, the two were on track to establish a long-term partnership. After the election, they got straight to work on their next big project: privatizing Social Security. That plan, which revealed just how conservative Clinton was, even when he had no more elections to win, suggested that the era of big government really was over, just as he had promised in his 1996 State of the Union. For Gingrich, it was an ideal situation.[1]

There was even reason to believe that, after spending four years hyping scandals and two years investigating them, Republicans might be ready to call off hostilities. Not because the Clinton well had run dry, but because Gingrich, too, was facing serious ethics charges. The House Ethics Committee had been investigating charges that he had violated tax law, laundering political donations through a partisan college course he taught. The committee found that not only had he broken the law, but he had lied during his testimony. In the period from the election to the second inaugural, he struggled first to keep his speakership and then to battle back a censure vote. He managed to hold on to the Speaker's gavel, but the House voted 395 to 28 to reprimand Gingrich and fine him $300,000, making him the first Speaker ever punished for ethics violations. He was, at least temporarily, not in the mood to continue weaponizing ethics.[2]

At the same time, one of the leading right-wing writers pumping out anti-Clinton scandals seemed to have a sudden change of heart. David Brock, who had appeared on that *New York Times Magazine* cover alongside his good friend Laura Ingraham, wrote a piece for the *Weekly Standard* in January 1997 arguing that he, and the right more generally, had gone too far. In "My Scandalmongering Problem—and Ours," he reiterated his belief that the administration was wracked with wrongdoing and led by a man of poor character. But by larding real scandals with outlandish ones and focusing more on character than policy, Republicans had lost their way.[3]

"Scandals have been thought of as the best, maybe even the only, way of defining public character in an age seemingly without shame but with a hair-trigger mistrust and dislike of government," he wrote, explaining the political motivations behind right-wing attacks on Clinton. "But by placing too much emphasis on scandal and potential acts of criminality rather than on the ideological and political failings of our opponents, we have adopted the very tactics that we rightly deplored when liberals used them in an attempt to destroy the Reagan administration."

Though Brock continued to frame the right's scandalmongering as a tactic no different from those Democrats used, he nonetheless seemed perturbed by what was happening in conservative circles. In particular he recoiled at the right's embrace of outlandish conspiracies with no basis in reality. "Injecting hatred and phony charges into our politics is a pretty bad thing, no matter who is targeted. If this is what the conservative opposition to Clinton has devolved to, perhaps the question we should be asking is whether the character of some of Clinton's critics is really any better than the character of Clinton himself."

Several months later, Brock would include himself in that condemnation, splitting forcefully from the conservative movement in an essay in *Esquire* called "Confessions of a Right-Wing Hitman." But he was the exception. And he was quickly replaced by a new scandal merchant: Matt Drudge. Along with Drudge, the rest of the movement, including Gingrich, would soon be back in the thicket of scandalmongering, wedding it to Congress's power not only to investigate but to impeach.[4]

THROUGHOUT THE CLINTON presidency, the right was searching for a way to bring him down. Long before alighting on the scandal that would trigger impeachment, they began constructing a scandal infrastructure to continually call his legitimacy into question. That strategy helped to create a hyperpartisan environment even at a time when Clinton and congressional Republicans were finding a surprising amount of common ground. By the second term, the reliance on scandal not only ensured that Clinton would not be able to work with his Republican counterparts but also moved Republicans away from governing and toward investigation as an expression of raw political power—something deeply unpopular with voters and yet perfectly suited to the hungers of the grassroots right, the conservative publishing industry, and the new cable punditry programs.

That scandal machinery was already spinning up in the first year of Clinton's presidency. Its core was a monthly magazine called the *American Spectator*, edited by R. Emmett Tyrrell. It sat at the center of a web of anti-Clinton activists, Republican politicians, and conspiracy-minded media. Richard Mellon Scaife, whose vast fortune flowed throughout the conservative movement and Republican Party, funded the magazine's work. And the *American Spectator*'s main scandalmonger was David Brock.[5]

Brock had been part of the right's network of young conservatives since the 1980s, bouncing around places like the *Washington Times* and the Heritage Foundation before landing at the *American Spectator* in the early 1990s. A young gay man navigating a conservative movement vocally hostile to homosexuality, Brock carefully picked his way through the networks of the right, carving out a place for himself among what was known as the Third Generation, people like Dinesh D'Souza, Laura Ingraham, and Ann Coulter who had shaken off some of the fustiness of an earlier conservative generation.[6]

He won acceptance in the broader movement through his effectiveness as a weapon against the targets of the right. Before zeroing in on Clinton, he took on Anita Hill. In March 1992, he published a thirteen-page investigation of Hill in the *American Spectator*. He attempted to discredit her claims that she had been sexually harassed by Clarence Thomas by not only challenging her testimony but also sifting through the details of her personal life. Cobbling together rumor and innuendo, he declared Hill was "a bit nutty and a bit slutty." The article scored him a book contract for $120,000 with Adam Bellow at the Free Press (who also published D'Souza and Charles Murray).[7]

The book, pitched at a broader audience and shorn of descriptors like "nutty" and "slutty," received a pile of positive press from reviewers who assumed its contents were based on in-depth, fact-checked reporting. Lauded not only in the *Wall Street Journal* but the *New York Times, The Real Anita Hill* rocketed up the best-seller list (lagging a bit behind Rush Limbaugh's debut book, which had been out for a year but had yet to fall off the list). The book was treated as serious, literate, and *true*, even though *Wall Street Journal* reporters Jill Abramson and Jane Mayer would debunk many of its assertions in *Strange Justice* and Brock himself would eventually disavow it.[8]

At the time, though, *The Real Anita Hill* made Brock a star in right-wing circles. Smarting from the election loss six months earlier, conservatives saw in Brock's book a victory against the liberal establishment, the Democrats, and the feminist movement. He quickly established himself in right-wing networks and started looking for his next big story. Still a freelancer when he published his piece on Hill with the *American Spectator*, he was soon brought on as a full-time investigative reporter focused on the Clinton administration. As it became the go-to place for anti-Clinton stories, the *American Spectator* saw its readership balloon from 27,000 to 250,000.[9]

The 1992 campaign against Clinton had focused on character: accusations of draft dodging, pot smoking, and extramarital affairs, most famously one involving Gennifer Flowers, which Clinton denied at the time. (He would admit to it in a 1998 deposition.) But once he became president, the right needed more. Americans—at least, the forty-five million voters who had cast ballots for Clinton—appeared to have come to terms with his character. The right needed something more scandalous, something about not just character but corruption.

Enter Troopergate. Brock's next major investigation was a story for the *American Spectator* splashed across the cover under the banner "His Cheatin' Heart: David Brock in Little Rock." In it, Brock relayed the story he first heard from a lawyer in Arkansas named Cliff Jackson, whom the *Washington Post* described as Clinton's "worst friend" and "chief sniper." Jackson represented a group of Arkansas state police officers who provided protection for Bill Clinton while he was governor and now wanted to tell their stories about the new First Family.[10]

The story Brock told about the troopers did the work of connecting personal ambitions and appetites to public wrongdoing. All the pieces were there: tales of Clinton setting up secret rendezvous with women using state resources, detailed accounts of his sexual encounters, and the suggestion of a marriage of convenience in which Hillary Clinton played a foul-mouthed Lady Macbeth, "a shrewd and practical operator concerned primarily with personal political advancement," more invested in her husband's political success than he was.[11]

The portrait of the Clintons in Brock's piece would become a staple of right-wing attacks on the couple. But the Troopergate article also contained the seeds of another scandal that would haunt the Clinton administration. It included the story of a woman Clinton arranged to meet with and mentioned her first name: Paula.

Paula Jones would become a pivotal figure in the investigations into Bill Clinton, especially in the run-up to impeachment. But she was also a study in how right-wing media served as an incubator for anti-Clinton scandals. Jones alleged that, while she was a state employee attending a conference at a hotel in Little Rock in 1991, a state trooper approached her and invited her to meet with then governor Clinton in his hotel room. There, she said, he propositioned her and exposed himself. (He denied the encounter.)

Jones did not come forward with her story until after her name appeared in Brock's account. When she finally shared her story in February 1994, she chose the most partisan of venues: the annual Conservative Political Action Conference. There, flanked by Cliff Jackson and her husband, Jones announced that she was the "Paula" Brock had mentioned in his piece. But, she continued, the troopers' statement that she had sought Clinton out and hoped to remain in a relationship with him was incorrect; she insisted their interaction was nonconsensual.[12]

It was an explosive allegation, one that nonconservative journalists were understandably reluctant to engage, since it unfolded in the pages of a magazine looking to take Clinton down and at a conference where one speaker denounced him as "a sleazebag and a scumbag." Conservative outlets, though, were eager to promote Jones's story. She continued to speak to right-wing outlets, giving her first television interview on Reed Irvine's National Empowerment Television program, *The Other Side of the Story*. Soon after, she went on *The 700 Club*, the flagship show on Pat Robertson's Christian Broadcasting Network. Robertson first warned the largely evangelical viewership that the program was "something you might not want your children to watch," then brought out Jones, who gave a detailed account of Clinton exposing himself and asking her to "kiss it."[13]

The Jones story may have remained primarily an obsession of right-wing media. But then Jones filed a lawsuit against the president. With that blockbuster hook—a woman suing a sitting president for sexual harassment—mainstream outlets went all in on

Jones's story. She was featured across network news in the weeks that followed.

But even with that extensive coverage, her allegations had to compete with the dizzying swirl of other Clinton scandals unfolding at the same time. There were the mass firings at the White House travel office, which led to accusations that the Clintons, especially Hillary, were firing career government employees in order to make room for their friends. Both were eventually cleared of wrongdoing. There was also Whitewater, a failed real estate development deal first written about in the New York Times in the spring of 1992. The flurry of stories about the Clintons' finances made it difficult for the Jones story to get traction. While Brock's Troopergate story made the rounds, Attorney General Janet Reno was announcing the appointment of a special prosecutor to look into Whitewater; while Jones was preparing for her appearance on The 700 Club, Hillary Clinton was giving what the New York Times called "a highly un-usual news conference" to explain her investments and involvement with the Whitewater project.[14]

Whitewater, Troopergate, the travel office: these were the sto-ries, framed as scandals, that played out alongside policy battles like healthcare reform in the mainstream press. But sometimes, other, darker conspiracies would make their way into mainstream cov-erage, fanned by conservative media outlets and Republicans and gobbled up by a base hungry for increasingly shocking and salacious stories about the Clintons.

One such conspiracy theory involved the death of Vince Fos-ter, a longtime friend of the couple and colleague of Hillary Clin-ton at Rose Law Firm (he had lobbied for her to be hired as the firm's first female associate). Foster, who served in the administra-tion as deputy White House counsel, struggled with depression and anxiety after moving to Washington, DC. His family was still back in Arkansas, and after the firings at the travel office, he was suddenly an object of curiosity to reporters, especially at the *Wall Street Journal*, which had taken particular interest in fanning the flames of scandal already singeing the administration. On July 20, 1993, he drove to Fort Marcy Park in Virginia, where he died by suicide. Just forty-eight, he left behind a wife and three children.[15]

The death supercharged the conspiracies around the Clintons. Soon, right-wing media filled with insinuations that Foster had been murdered because he knew too much about the Clintons' misdeeds. It was a baseless conspiracy, repeatedly investigated by local police, the FBI, two congressional committees, and the special prosecutor. Yet it maintained so much traction on the right that it not only fueled a cottage industry of Foster conspiracy literature but also made its way into the offices of the Speaker and the independent counsel, Kenneth Starr, who replaced the special prosecutor. Both Rush Limbaugh and the *Wall Street Journal* promoted the conspiracy. Limbaugh repeatedly alleged that the suicide scene was staged and floated the idea that Foster was actually killed in an apartment owned by Hillary Clinton. In July 1995, Newt Gingrich told reporters he was "not convinced" that Foster's death was a suicide; over in the Senate, Bob Dole referred to it as an "alleged suicide."[16]

The conspiracy even made its way into the formal investigation of Clinton. Brett Kavanaugh, a young lawyer working for Starr, reinvestigated the suicide for three years as part of his work, helping to keep conspiracy theories about Foster's death alive.[17]

One of the people pressuring Kavanaugh to keep digging was Christopher Ruddy—a questionable person to have a direct line to the Starr investigation. Ruddy wrote anti-Clinton Whitewater stories for the *New York Post* in the first few years of the administration, before moving over to the Scaife-owned *Pittsburgh Tribune-Review*, where he focused more on his Foster conspiracies—so much, in fact, that in 1996 he published a collection of his articles under the title *Vince Foster: The Ruddy Investigation.* He followed that the next year with a book published by Adam Bellow at the Free Press, *The Strange Death of Vince Foster,* in which he concluded that "few 'facts' in the Foster case [were] not in serious dispute." He suggested that all the investigations into the case, including the Starr investigation, which he found wanting, had become part of a larger cover-up. (In 1998, with more funding from Scaife, Ruddy branched out on his own, starting a new media venture called Newsmax.)[18]

The Foster conspiracy was the one that most permeated mainstream outlets but far from the only one that circulated in right-wing circles. The Clinton body count conspiracy, a name popularized by a website that listed the names of the president and First Lady's purported victims, grew out of Foster's death. It served as a source for the conspiracy videos that became wildly popular on the right during the Clinton years. Some of the most popular were created by Larry Nichols, a longtime Clinton foe from Arkansas, and Pat Mastrisciana, who created films for fundamentalists on the evils of everything from evolution to gay people to Halloween. Jerry Falwell, the right-wing preacher who founded the now-defunct Moral Majority, distributed the films.[19]

The trio cut their teeth on the thirty-minute video *Circle of Power,* which detailed the "countless people who mysteriously died" after working with the Clintons, portraying a string of murders stretching from Arkansas to Washington. A segment hosted by Falwell added a salacious element: the claim that Hillary Clinton had been having an affair with Foster before he died. (Hillary Clinton's sex life—and her sexuality—were as much a part of these conspiracies as her husband's.)[20]

But the real moneymaker was the second video, *The Clinton Chronicles.* It opened with the claim "All information presented in this program is documented and true" (and a warning that it was only for mature audiences). Over nearly two hours, the video spun out every conceivable Clinton conspiracy: Bill Clinton lied about being a Rhodes scholar. He secretly conducted anti-American business in Moscow. He was part of an international cocaine smuggling ring in Arkansas. He got high on his own supply (in the governor's mansion, no less). The film also covered the trooper story, Whitewater, and Vince Foster's suicide, ultimately linking twenty-five deaths to the Clintons and calling that a "partial list." The video ended with an appeal from Representative William Dannemeyer, a Republican from Orange County who retired from the House in 1993 after a failed Senate bid. Dannemeyer not only endorsed the content of the video but called for Clinton's impeachment.[21]

The Clinton Chronicles was advertised in right-wing outlets like the newsweekly Human Events and in a half-hour infomercial on Falwell's syndicated television show, The Old-Time Gospel Hour. It initially retailed for $40 (plus shipping and handling) and, perhaps because of the high price tag, also was regularly pirated. By the mid-1990s, an estimated three hundred thousand copies of The Clinton Chronicles were in circulation.[22]

Nor were they only in circulation among the right-wing fringe. The Clinton Chronicles, which was sent to every member of Congress, had an ally in a sitting Republican member as well: Indiana representative Dan Burton. Burton, an ardent believer in the Foster conspiracy, reenacted his version of Foster's death in his backyard with a .38-caliber pistol and a melon, something he detailed in a speech on the House floor. He also welcomed Nichols to the Capitol and introduced him to other Republicans he suspected would be open to Nichols's salacious conspiracy theories.[23]

All those accusations and conspiracies swirling in the halls of Congress would have real consequences. Dannemeyer's call for impeachment may not have been taken up immediately, but before Clinton's first term came to a close, Republican members of Congress were already looking for ways—besides the ballot box—to remove him from office.

———

"MEET ANN COULTER, the constitutional lawyer turned journalist who finally puts the case for Bill Clinton's impeachment to bed."

The ad copy for the new book *High Crimes and Misdemeanors*, printed under the headline "Bill's Last Blonde?," did something unexpected: it made Coulter, queen of the shocking statement, a little uncomfortable. She understood why it read the way it did—"sex sells," she shrugged when a reporter asked about the ad campaign—but she didn't like it. Besides, it wasn't sex that moved copies of *High Crimes* when it came out in the fall of 1998—it was the promise that she had laid out the open-and-shut case for Clinton's removal from office, before an impeachment inquiry had even gotten underway in Washington. Given the lead time for the book and Coulter's own role in helping the independent counsel Ken Starr behind the scenes, it's fair to say that the world of conservative publishing played a critical role in the impeachment of Bill Clinton.[24]

The Clinton scandals made Coulter's career. She had been edging into the world of commentary for a few years, leaving her job in corporate law in 1995 to come to Washington and work for the Senate Judiciary Committee in the midst of the Republican revolution. She had come up through conservative ranks: she wrote for the right-wing campus newspaper as an undergrad at Cornell and was trained at the National Journalism Center, an organization that prepared conservatives for careers in media. Hired by MSNBC in 1996 as one of their young, brash conservatives, she traded her career in law for one in right-wing punditry, picking up a syndicated column in addition to her television work.[25]

As impeachment speculation accelerated, so did her on-camera presence. But she wasn't just writing columns and best-selling books about Clinton scandals and the need to remove the president. Behind the scenes, she was working on the Paula Jones case that made impeachment possible.

By 1997, the Jones team had begun working off the books with a handful of anti-Clinton lawyers, including Coulter and George Conway, an attorney who defended tobacco companies and was deeply embedded in DC's conservative social networks. Coulter and Conway played a significant role in making sure the Jones case stayed a live issue through late 1997 and early 1998, setting the stage for impeachment. When it looked like the Jones lawyers might settle their case against Clinton—a move that would eliminate the need for the president to sit for a deposition under oath and take one of the most important anti-Clinton stories out of the public sphere—Coulter and Conway reportedly scotched the deal by leaking descriptions of Clinton's genitals to the press, part of an effort to humiliate Clinton so that he would reject a settlement. And in January 1998, before news broke about Clinton and White House intern Monica Lewinsky, Coulter huddled in her apartment with Conway and another lawyer to copy the secret recordings of conversations between Lewinsky and Linda Tripp, tapes that would be used to set a perjury trap for the president. (Postimpeachment, Coulter would introduce Conway to fellow pundit Kellyanne Fitzpatrick, whom he would marry in 2001.)[26]

The Jones case was the second front in independent counsel Ken Starr's hunt for impeachable offenses. But even as the investigation went on, even when the news of the affair with Lewinsky broke, an impeachment inquiry in Congress was not a foregone conclusion. Though the idea had been bouncing around right-wing media in Clinton's first term and had trickled up to Congress early in his second, impeachment split the right. There were plenty of incentives for floating the idea: raising money off impeachment appeals, drawing the media spotlight, forcing the administration to spend time on investigations and lawsuits rather than enacting a second term agenda. But there were dangers as well: impeachment was not particularly popular, and Gingrich had things he wanted to get done with the administration, a goal that an impeachment inquiry would stymie by requiring Clinton to try to close ranks in the Democratic Party.[27]

Still, holding back impeachment was no easy feat. Support for impeachment had grown to a fever pitch in right-wing media after the 1996 election. "Listen to talk radio, surf the internet, read conservative editorials, and you'll notice that what were once underground murmurs about impeaching President Clinton are now an above-ground roar," wrote Laura Ingraham, who at the time opposed impeachment, in the *Washington Post*. It wasn't just that Republicans thought he should be removed from office. They also argued they were simply copying the politics of political investigation and personal destruction that the Democrats had pioneered in the Supreme Court hearings of Clarence Thomas and the extensive investigations into Iran-Contra. Impeachment was not only the right way to punish Clinton for his wrongdoing but only fair after the way Democrats had used their control of Congress.[28]

And the pro-impeachment crowd had some well-placed advocates in Congress. The far-right House caucus had already started beating the impeachment drum in the first term, with the Oversight Committee gathering information on potential impeachable offenses. Gingrich, trying to combat the party's obstructionist image as the 1996 elections approached, implored his members to stop using the word "impeachment" until after the election, with some success. But immediately after the election, the push was on. Dan Burton grabbed the gavel for the Oversight Committee (his Vince Foster conspiracies had no impact on his ability to move up the ranks in House leadership), and he vowed to pursue every sign of Clinton wrongdoing. In March 1997, Representative Bob Barr sent a letter to Representative Henry Hyde, head of the powerful House Judiciary Committee, asking him to begin an impeachment inquiry to explore "the alarming pattern of abuse of the political process by this White House." He returned to the issue in the fall, gathering seventeen Republican cosponsors, including Helen Chenoweth and Lindsey Graham, for a bill to initiate a preliminary impeachment proceeding.[29]

All this took place before the revelations that Clinton had lied about having a sexual relationship with Lewinsky. Once that news broke, Barr went a step further and called for Clinton to resign.

But if Barr was where House Republicans would end up by the end of the year, it took them a long time to get there. That was in part because Gingrich and other leaders were wary of going up against Clinton without bipartisan support, worried that it would play into the image of congressional Republicans as too partisan and obstructionist. The last time Gingrich and Clinton had faced off, during the government shutdown, Clinton had won handily. And poll numbers showed the public had little interest in impeachment—in fact, Clinton's approval ratings went *up* after the Lewinsky revelations, much to Gingrich's confusion.

Moderates and a skittish Speaker were not alone in trying to hold impeachment back. Ingraham, coming out against impeachment in late 1997, was convinced it would not succeed and would only be used to tar Republicans as "mean-spirited partisans." More than that, she saw it as a distraction from policy matters at a moment when Democrats seemed to be moving in a conservative direction. Channeling some of her friend David Brock's attitude, she wrote, "At a time when conservative ideas—from school choice to ending racial preferences—are catching on across the country, Republicans cannot afford to be sidetracked by Clinton bashing and impeachment gossip."[30]

Gingrich, pressed by both sides, waffled. In the months between the Lewinsky revelation in January 1998 and the release of the independent counsel's report on Clinton's impeachable offenses in September, he mostly stayed out of the spotlight, trying to calm his caucus behind the scenes. But at times the combative Gingrich would burst forth. Thrust in front of the fiercely partisan crowd at a GOPAC conference in the spring of 1998, he made the sort of speech that would become commonplace during impeachment. "What we have lived through for two and a half long years is the most systematic, deliberate obstruction of justice coverup in an effort to avoid the truth we have ever seen in American history," he thundered, dialing up the stakes as high as they would go. He insisted it was not about sex but about the rule of law. "This is the heart of America. This is what the Constitution means."[31]

But for the most part, Gingrich remained wary of impeachment. So much so that conservatives in the caucus complained that he was too focused on working with Clinton, too willing to compromise and shy away from the hard fights. Barr attacked him privately for his opposition to impeachment talk. "If Newt wasn't sitting so hard on this, we'd have 200 co-sponsors—not 20!" Furious with the Speaker's inconsistent impeachment message, House majority whip Tom DeLay set up his own war room to begin attacking the administration.[32]

But when finally faced with a choice between impeaching the president and censuring him—a compromise that would have

allowed Gingrich to declare victory and walk away—he simply
couldn't let Clinton win. He rejected not only a vote on censure
(which almost certainly would have passed with bipartisan support
from Democrats and moderate Republicans) but also the Democrats' offer of a narrow impeachment focused on the recommendations of the Starr report. Instead, he said they would tackle it all: a
wide-ranging impeachment inquiry would once again sort through
all the various scandals of the Clinton administration, even though
Starr had been unable to come up with anything other than Clinton's lie about his relationship with Lewinsky. When asked why he
pursued impeachment despite other, more popular options, Gingrich responded with an apt summation of the right's emerging
attitude toward power: "Because we can."[33]

THE FEAR THAT impeachment would wind up like the government shutdown—an unforced error by House Republicans that
would ultimately backfire—was warranted. Opinion polls warned
Republicans that they faced significant opposition heading into the
1998 midterms. But momentum seemed to be on their side: two
months before the election, Kenneth Starr released his salacious
report, detailing the sexual encounters between Clinton and Lewinsky (it read "like a bad Harlequin romance novel," Helen Kennedy wrote in the New York Daily News). A month after that, the
House launched its impeachment inquiry. And a month after *that*,
Americans voted in the midterm elections.[34]

Republicans were giddy about the midterms. Bill Clinton had
spent the last year mired in humiliating scandal, and while public sympathy seemed to be propping up his approval ratings, there
was no reason to believe that would benefit Democrats in Congress. Besides, the reelected president's party always lost seats in the

midterms. Gingrich guessed they'd pick up around twenty seats in the House, leaving him to command his biggest majority yet.[35]

Instead, he was handed the biggest midterm defeat for an opposition party since the Civil War era.

That resounding rebuke ended Newt Gingrich's career in Congress. He resigned as Speaker a few days after the election and announced he would leave Congress in January at the end of his term. It was a bitter resignation from a man who expected to hold power much longer. "I'm willing to lead but I'm not willing to preside over people who are cannibals," he said on a conference call to other Republican leaders, a reference to the even further-right wing of the party that was constantly challenging his leadership.[36]

In a way, it was good for Republicans that Gingrich would no longer be the face of impeachment: Not only was he deeply unpopular nationally, but a series of ethics violation on his record left Republicans open to charges of hypocrisy, since they had neither removed him from the speakership nor expelled him from Congress. He was also involved in an extramarital relationship of his own, with the woman who would become his third wife. Gingrich was hardly alone on that front, however: a parade of Republican representatives from Henry Hyde to Bob Barr to Helen Chenoweth to Dan Burton admitted to affairs in the months following the Lewinsky revelation. Even Bob Livingston, the Speaker-designate who took Gingrich's place, resigned abruptly after news broke of his own extramarital affairs. (His replacement, Dennis Hastert, would be the longest-serving Republican Speaker and was later imprisoned for illegal payments used to conceal a history of serial child molestation.)[37]

But though the drive to impeachment seemed to be shredding the party's leadership, Republicans continued to pursue it—despite its unpopularity, despite the damage it was doing to the party. They did so in part because it was popular with their base. Anti-Clinton rage had reached a fever pitch, fueled by years of anti-Clinton conspiracies, as well as a sense that Democrats had successfully weaponized impeachment, investigations, and scandal in Watergate, Iran-Contra, and the Supreme Court hearings of Clarence Thomas. Clinton's impeachment would be a glorious form of payback. Two-thirds of Republicans supported it, and activists pilloried anti-impeachment Republicans, threatening them with primary challenges.[38]

That support was bolstered by what Ingraham called "impeachment chic," the steady thrum of pro-impeachment propaganda coursing through conservative media. Limbaugh gloried in it, leveraging his listeners to pressure anti-impeachment Republicans like Connecticut's Chris Shays, who found himself at a town hall packed to the rafters after Limbaugh publicized the event; six thousand people had to be turned away once the room filled. The *American Spectator*, unsurprisingly, beat the impeachment drum as well. Its founder, Emmett Tyrrell, had a year earlier published *The Impeachment of William Jefferson Clinton*, a book imagining what such an event would look like. It got a boost when the desired impeachment became a reality.[39]

Impeachment chic was about more than just persuasion. Impeachment was a cash cow and, for some, a career maker. After Brock renounced his scandalmongering tactics and published an evenhanded book about Hillary Clinton, movement conservatives found their new go-to scandal source in Matt Drudge. Drudge started the Drudge Report, his news aggregation website, in 1995. He was well sourced enough to be the first to publish Jack Kemp's selection as Bob Dole's running mate in the 1996 race. But it was the news he broke in early 1998 that made him a household name. Taking advantage of his website's ability to instantly publish (and his lack of editorial oversight), he broke arguably the biggest story of the decade when he hit send on an item headlined "Blockbuster Report: 23-Year Old, Former White House Intern, Sex Relationship with President."[40]

Drudge had been well connected in conservative circles long before breaking the news of Clinton's affair. He bonded with Chris Ruddy over his anti-Clinton investigations, showing particular interest in the death of Vince Foster. Ann Coulter also quickly became a close friend and eventually his neighbor (though she wasn't his source for the Lewinsky news—that came from right-wing activist Lucianne Goldberg). And he became especially close with Laura Ingraham and David Brock. The pair hosted a party for Drudge in mid-1997 to introduce him to their circle: people like Andrew Sullivan, Tucker Carlson, George Conway, and journalist Elizabeth Drew. His work also brought him in contact with Andrew Breitbart, a young conservative who would help Drudge pump out a steady stream of content around the clock. His status as the Hot New Thing also caught the eye of Roger Ailes. Ailes had been considering him for a show on his fledgling network Fox News, something that became a reality a few months after the Lewinsky revelations.[41]

Fox News, like the other cable news outlets, thrived during impeachment. "It's been a sad moment for America," network vice president John Moody said, "a fine moment for Fox News." Fox News frequently hit new ratings highs, though it lagged behind both MSNBC and CNN. The network was also starting to find its place in the right-wing media ecosystem. As ratings slid postimpeachment (all three major cable news networks saw ratings plummet around 30 percent once impeachment wrapped), producers rooted around for new stories about the scandal. In March 1999, Fox picked up one of Drudge's stories—never confirmed—that the Clintons had returned from a ski trip early because of a nasty fight over Lewinsky, in which Hillary Clinton purportedly said, "I don't want to be in the same room with him, let alone the same bed." The story ultimately made its way to Rupert Murdoch's *New York Post*. The space between tabloid and news source had all but collapsed within right-wing media.[42]

For the pundits of the Independent Women's Forum, it was likewise high times. Not only were the antifeminist women delighted to skewer feminists for not standing behind Paula Jones and Monica Lewinsky, but the salacious material blended with constitutional questions was perfect for lawyers turned wisecracking pundits (Coulter, Ingraham, Fitzpatrick, and Barbara Olson all had JDs). Coulter in particular fortified her reputation as a scandalous, say-anything conservative. On MSNBC, she compared Hillary Clinton to a prostitute, while on *Politically Incorrect*, she slyly floated the notion that Bill Clinton had not just engaged in sexual harassment but committed rape. She would be repeatedly barred from MSNBC but then brought back again. Her statements may have been ridiculously offensive, but her shock-jock style was good for ratings. Fox News wasn't the only outlet where bad-for-America-good-for-us rang true.[43]

Back in Congress, that seemed to be the case as well. Impeachment was a bust, badly damaging the Republican Party and snuffing out the careers of several powerful party leaders. Clinton was impeached by the House by a vote of 258 to 176, with 31 Democrats joining every House Republican in voting yes. In the Senate, however, the Republicans fell well short of the necessary sixty-seven votes: all forty-five Democrats voted to acquit on both articles of impeachment, with ten Republicans joining to reject the perjury charge and five joining to vote against obstruction of justice. It was a verdict the public welcomed: only a third of Americans supported impeachment.

Impeachment may have failed, but many elected officials in the GOP understood that it was never just about removing Clinton from office. With a white-hot base and a quickly expanding conservative media ready to call out any sign of moderation or compromise, broadly unpopular policies and political maneuvers were becoming key to retaining office. If voting against impeachment earned you a flood of angry faxes and phone calls, followed by a primary challenge, suddenly voting for impeachment looked like the better option. Bad for the Republican Party, maybe, but good for the officeholder looking to stay in power.

That equation didn't hold true in every case. But impeachment showed that party dynamics were shifting in significant ways, decoupling from public opinion at the national level and becoming more reliant on partisan punditry and political entertainment. Whether those new dynamics would solidify depended quite a lot on what happened when Republicans controlled not just the Congress but—thanks to the Electoral College, the Supreme Court, and an astonishingly bad ballot design in Palm Beach County, Florida—the presidency as well.

CHAPTER ELEVEN

THE LAST REAGANITE

Twelve years after Ronald Reagan left office, his third term finally commenced. That's what a number of commentators concluded as they watched George W. Bush being sworn in on January 20, 2001, after a contentious, contested election decided by the Supreme Court just five weeks earlier. They returned to that parallel time and again in the years that followed. "George W. Reagan," one headline read. "Reagan's Son," read another. George H. W. Bush may have followed Ronald Reagan in office, but George W. Bush embodied his agenda. For conservatives, the father was the heretic; the son was the heir.[1]

The argument made a certain sort of sense. The younger Bush wore his West Texas folksiness more easily than his father, who spent his formative years in New England and never shed his blue-blooded mien. The younger Bush also seemed to embody a kind of optimism in his rhetoric that cut against the culture-wars pessimism of the 1990s. "Too often, on social issues, my party has painted an image of America slouching toward Gomorrah," he said on the campaign trail in 1999, intentionally tweaking the dour Robert Bork, author of the book *Slouching Toward Gomorrah*, who had lost a bruising Supreme Court nomination fight in 1986 and spent the years after as a think tank culture warrior. "But many of our problems—particularly education, crime and welfare dependence—are yielding to good sense and strength and idealism."[2]

In the end, many qualities linked Reagan and the new president: both were former governors of Sunbelt states, deeply conservative with a Manichean view of world politics and a deep belief in inerrant American exceptionalism. Policywise, too, they had much in common. Like Reagan, Bush pushed for free trade deals, more progressive immigration laws, deep tax cuts, and a belief that, in a choice between deficits and spending on military budgets and popular social programs, high deficits were the better option. And like Reagan, Bush attracted fierce opposition from within his own party, papered over by partisan loyalty and broad popularity. The right rallied around him in late 2000 in order to ratify his election, secured when the Supreme Court halted the recount in Florida. Following the terrorist attacks in September 2001, his approval ratings spiked to 90 percent and remained well above 50 percent during his first three years in office (with a second spike around the 2003 invasion of Iraq).

But while support for Reagan was rooted in his personality and politics, support for Bush was far more situational. The partisans of the 1990s were not ready to yield to calls for compassionate conservatism. They were not about to follow his appeals for immigration reform or his rhetorical distinction between Islam and terrorism. They were pleased to have the presidency but only lightly attached to the president.

During Bush's first term, few partisans sought to draw a bright line between themselves and the president. The centripetal force of the disputed election and the War on Terror kept them tightly bound. But by the second term, they were ready to break free, aligning with congressional Republicans and the party's base while rejecting the man whom his biographers dubbed "Reagan's disciple." With a Reaganite in the White House, it became clear that whatever affection they voiced for Reagan, by the start of the twenty-first century, a significant portion of the right was finished with Reaganism.[3]

PAT BUCHANAN WAS in the wilderness. His strong showing in the 1996 presidential primaries should have given him more power in the party, a bigger stage, and recognition of the role he played in shifting Republican politics. But he was shut out of the convention, treated like an unwelcome interloper. It was not his last presidential bid, but 1996 would mark the last time he ran for the Republican nomination. In October 1999, he left the Republican Party.[4]

He had hinted at the break in the months prior. In an interview on Fox News that August, Sean Hannity had asked Buchanan if he was contemplating jumping ship for Ross Perot's Reform Party. Buchanan, playing to their shared Irish-Catholic roots, responded, "Let me admit, Father Hannity, I have engaged in impure thoughts about possibly running for another party. But no one has consummated any act." He gave the Republican Party one last look that month, at the Iowa Straw Poll. There, he gave a speech attacking the North American Free Trade Agreement (NAFTA), the World Trade Organization (WTO), and the decision to grant China most-favored-nation status. His biggest applause line, though, came near the end, when he said that if he were elected, his first act would be to place Bill Clinton under arrest.[5]

But his fifth-place finish in the poll made clear what he already knew: his time in the GOP was over. He ran instead for the Reform

Party, believing that it gave him his best chance to remain a player in a race that was shaping up to be a battle between Bush, who seemed to have the backing of the entire party establishment, and Vice President Al Gore, Bill Clinton's heir apparent. On foreign policy, Bush had taken positions not so different from Buchanan's: he pledged to do no nation-building, to reduce military spending, and to denuclearize. But there the similarities ended. Bush leaned heavily on Latino outreach, attacking English-only laws and tapping his nephew to give a bilingual speech about compassionate conservatism during the convention. He sought deep tax cuts focused on the wealthy and more federal oversight and spending on education. And he spoke about compassionate conservatism in a way that could not be more distinct from Buchanan's cutting culture-wars anger.

For his part, Buchanan sought to forge a left-right coalition opposing global trade. He'd laid out his ideas on economic nationalism in his 1998 book *The Great Betrayal*, the first of a trilogy that would outline his thoughts on trade protections, isolationism, and the decline of white America. He even headed to Seattle for the WTO protests, a scene that should have made clear how challenging it would be to unite the anti-WTO left and the Buchananites. The raucous band of anarchists, environmentalists, and labor activists protesting economic globalization may have wanted some of the same things as Buchanan, but culturally they were a world apart.[6]

It was support not from the left but from the far right that once again shaped his campaign. In the month between the Iowa Straw Poll and his resignation from the GOP, the second book in Buchanan's trilogy hit bookstores. *A Republic, Not an Empire* laid out his vision for foreign policy. The United States, he argued, had ceded too much of its sovereignty, had gotten too entangled in military and peacekeeping missions headed up by the United Nations or the North Atlantic Treaty Organization. US troops served in Europe and Asia, and US dollars flowed across the globe through foreign aid and trade deficits.[7]

Nothing new there: that had been Buchanan's approach to foreign policy for some time. But he also used the book to render judgment on the history of US intervention abroad and came down particularly hard on the decision to go to war with Nazi Germany. He heaped praise on the America First Committee, insisting that it had done its best to prevent Nazis and antisemites from joining its ranks. At the same time, he touted the leadership of Charles Lindbergh, a prominent America Firster, without ever mentioning Lindbergh's corrosive antisemitism. The book sparked renewed attention to Buchanan's antisemitism and defense of Nazi soldiers, as well as his broader ties to the far right.

The two other men vying for the Reform Party presidential nomination, both entertainers turned politicians, immediately leveraged those attacks. Jesse Ventura, the pro wrestler serving as Minnesota governor, held Buchanan in disdain. He toyed with a run of his own, but newly ensconced in the governor's seat, he opted instead to promote another candidate whom he knew through professional wrestling: Donald Trump. Trump, who announced his candidacy on *Larry King Live*, ran on a mishmash of issues, from lowering taxes, to repealing NAFTA, to implementing universal health care, to reforming campaign-finance laws. When he attacked Buchanan, he denounced him as a "Hitler lover" who would only attract the "really staunch right wacko vote. . . . I guess he's an anti-Semite," Trump said. "He doesn't like the blacks. He doesn't like the gays. It's just incredible that anybody could embrace this guy." (When asked if he had read *A Republic, Not an Empire*, Trump hedged, "I've seen the phrases we're dealing with.")[8]

Neither Ventura nor Trump could stop Buchanan. He won the nomination, Ventura and Trump left the Reform Party, and

Buchanan limped to the finish line in November, winning fewer than five hundred thousand votes, for a fourth-place finish behind Green Party candidate Ralph Nader. His campaign would have been entirely forgettable were it not for two things. First, his running mate, Ezola Foster, a former member of the John Birch Society, was the first Black woman to appear on a federally funded presidential ticket. And second, he won 3,407 votes in Palm Beach County, Florida, due to a poorly designed ballot. That ballot, which made it easy for those intending to vote for Democratic candidate Al Gore to accidentally vote for Buchanan, helped tip Florida to Bush in the official count, delivering him the presidency.[9]

The failed Reform Party run ended Pat Buchanan's presidential hopes. What started as an effort to transform the Republican Party led to his exile from it, and he had no desire to try to turn the Reform Party into a viable political vehicle. After leaving *Crossfire* for a third time in order to run for president, he had also worn out his welcome at CNN, which declined to bring him back after the election. At the end of November, as Gore and Bush were battling in the courts, Buchanan was left without much to do. "I haven't made any decisions," he told a reporter. "I'm going to take it easy and spend some time off doing a little writing, which I like to do. I have a few ideas for books."[10]

But semiretirement was not in the cards. Less than a year later, as he watched passenger jets slam into the World Trade Center, Buchanan zeroed in on a new danger. Though he agreed with the need for revenge, he placed blame for the attacks on US intervention in the Middle East and warned against a widening war. He had little confidence that he could prevent it, though, with Bush surrounded by hawkish advisers and already licensed by Congress to counterattack. "What took place last Tuesday was an atrocity," he wrote in the week after the attack. "What is coming may qualify as tragedy."[11]

FOR THE PARTISANS of the 1990s, the terror attacks accelerated a change already underway. Many of them had made their names by opposing the Clinton administration, and it was unclear how they would adapt to being pundits for the party in power. There was no shortage of opportunities—in the years between 2000 and 2002, right-wing talk radio exploded in popularity, and the cable news networks continued to pump out new shows and fresh faces. But all that churn meant some shows would fail. Even the brightest stars dimmed near the end of the 1990s: Drudge's television and radio shows were snuffed before the 2000s rolled around. Laura Ingraham's low ratings led to her MSNBC show's cancellation in 2000.

The terror attacks had a profound impact on this already-shifting media environment, as news appetites changed and the range of tolerable opinions narrowed. Media observers noted the demise of the "blonde pundit"—people like Ingraham, Ann Coulter, and Kellyanne Fitzpatrick—who had dominated cable television in the Clinton era. Phil Griffin, an executive producer who at the time headed up prime-time programming for MSNBC, explained the pivot away from the style of the 1990s (and away from on-camera opportunities for women): "Those blondes had their field day prior to the 2000 election," he said. But the terror attacks changed that. "We want people who are working in government, who know the Taliban, who have expertise in the military. Even if they're a bunch of fat old men. You can be a fat old man if you've got something to say and you've got expertise."[12]

The statement, rooted in sexism, spoke to both the type of women MSNBC hired in the 1990s and the way it envisioned expertise. Nor was the problem limited to MSNBC: studies showed that after the 9/11 attacks, the number of women guests on the Sunday news shows plummeted by 39 percent—and they had only represented 11 percent of guests *before* the attacks. Print wasn't any better: 92 percent of the opinion pieces in the *New York Times*, *Washington Post*, and *USA Today* in the month after the attacks were written by men.[13]

The constrained politics of the War on Terror era also shook up the media landscape. The team at *Politically Incorrect* had been personally affected by the attack: Barbara Olson had been aboard American Airlines Flight 77, en route to Los Angeles for a taping of the show that night, when hijackers wrested control of the plane and crashed it into the Pentagon, killing everyone aboard. When the show returned, Maher left a seat empty for Olson. One of the other seats was filled by Dinesh D'Souza, who had not shed his contrarian, outrage-generating politics in the aftermath of the attacks. "One of the themes we hear constantly is that the people who did this are cowards. Not true," he told Maher. He went on to describe the hijackers as courageous, willing to give their lives for their cause. "Exactly," Maher agreed. "But also, we have been the cowards, lobbing cruise missiles from 2,000 miles away. That's cowardly. Staying in the airplane when it hits the building, say what you want about it, it's not cowardly. You're right."[14]

In all the years he had hosted *Politically Incorrect*, Maher had managed not to make anyone particularly angry. But he had not anticipated how abruptly the atmosphere had changed in the six days since the attack. Advertisers yanked their sponsorship, and a few affiliates refused to air the show. The Bush administration even singled Maher out. Press secretary Ari Fleischer, asked about the comments, told reporters, "It's a terrible thing to say," then added that Americans "need to watch what they say, watch what they do. This is not a time for remarks like that. There never is."[15]

Several months later, with the show still struggling to regain advertisers, ABC canceled *Politically Incorrect.*

Others would run into similar problems. In the aftermath of the attacks, Ann Coulter, then a columnist for *National Review*, lashed out, writing, "We should invade their countries, kill their leaders and convert them to Christianity." (The quote would later appear on T-shirts at right-wing events.) The magazine's editors killed a follow-up rant about "swarthy males." She then went on *Politically Incorrect* to complain about censorship, at which point her employment with *National Review* ended. Though clearly stung, Coulter brushed it off, boasting to the *Washington Post*, "Frankly, I'm getting a lot of great publicity."[16]

Buchanan, too, would feel the lash of postattack restrictions. Halfway through Bush's first term, Buchanan emerged as the nucleus of the anti-Bush right. Forcefully opposed to immigration and fiercely protective of whiteness, furious about the US interventions in Afghanistan and Iraq and pessimistic about the nation's future, he built his new media presence around his opposition to the new administration. First there was his new book, the third in his trilogy, published in January 2002, titled *The Death of the West.* Characteristically negative, the volume fretted that white birthrates were falling as nonwhite immigration rose, while the mores of the 1960s revolution in culture and politics were moving the United States away from traditional Christian values. Bush, he believed, had yet to rise to the challenge that presented. "In the 2000 election, the Republican ticket ran away from the issues of race, culture, and life, assuming, correctly, that the hostility to and even detestation of Clinton would bring social conservatives home," Buchanan wrote.

But, he continued, "no matter what compassionate conservatives' may wish, the culture war and racial conflict are not going away."[17]

Later that year, Buchanan launched a new magazine, the *American Conservative*, to promote the anti-Bush, paleoconservative line. He started the venture with Greek magnate Taki Theodoracopulos and former *New York Post* editor Scott McConnell. "The movement has been hijacked," he said by way of explanation, "and turned into a globalist, interventionist, open-borders ideology, which is not the conservative movement I grew up with." His goal was to wrest it back. He took that message to a broader audience on MSNBC, which snatched him up in early 2002 for a show called *Buchanan & Press*, which revived the *Crossfire* format with liberal commentator Bill Press. The show was canceled in 2003, in part because the hosts, who were supposed to be combatants, both opposed the war in Iraq, the central issue of the day. (MSNBC made a concerted effort in 2003 to hire pro-war pundits, since its biggest names all opposed the intervention.)[18]

If the ranks of partisans were temporarily culled in the early days of the War on Terror, other parts of the conservative ecosystem thrived in the newly martial atmosphere. Sean Hannity, who had become a more popular right-wing pundit after he joined the fledgling Fox News network, made his national radio debut on September 10, 2001. The timing of his syndication infused both his radio and television shows with a sense of mission. Fox News also soared in the ratings, passing CNN for the first time in January 2002. Viewers seemed to respond to the network's overtly jingoistic turn, particularly during the prime-time hours. All the cable networks were festooned with flags and wall-to-wall war coverage. But Fox dialed up the bloodlust. Anchor John Gibson lobbied for military tribunals, mocking the idea of courtroom trials like those used after the 1993 World Trade Center bombing. Geraldo Rivera, the network's new gun-toting war correspondent on the ground in Afghanistan, mused about shooting Osama bin Laden himself. Off air, Roger Ailes sent a note to Bush's senior advisor, Karl Rove, laying out his advice for the administration, one reflected on the network itself: "The only thing the American people won't forgive you for is under-reaching."[19]

The War on Terror provided a clear set of enemies abroad, but partisans on the right also saw it as a chance to define enemies at home. Without the Clintons to take aim at, they began developing broadsides against liberals, tying them not only to cultural decay and national decline but to terrorism and war as well. Hannity came out with back-to-back best sellers: *Let Freedom Ring: Winning the War of Liberty over Liberalism* and *Deliver Us from Evil: Defeating Terrorism, Despotism, and Liberalism*. Laura Ingraham, whose nationally syndicated radio show launched in early 2001, published *Shut Up and Sing: How Elites from Hollywood, Politics, and the UN Are Subverting America*. The title referenced the Dixie Chicks, whose lead singer's negative comments about Bush triggered a massive boycott of the group in the United States. Coulter came out with *Treason: Liberal Treachery from the Cold War to the War on Terrorism* (one of five antiliberal books she published between 2002 and 2007), radio host Michael Savage published *The Enemy Within: Saving America from the Liberal Assault on Our Schools, Faith, and Military*, and Michelle Malkin offered *Unhinged: Exposing Liberals Gone Wild*.[20]

The apotheosis of this liberals-are-the-real-enemy genre came in 2007, with Dinesh D'Souza's *The Enemy at Home: The Cultural Left and Its Responsibility for 9/11*. The title and subtitle were bald declarations of his thesis: "The cultural left is responsible for 9/11."

He rejected the argument that terrorists hated Americans for their freedoms and argued instead that they hated Americans—rightfully—for liberals' licentiousness and decadence. Conservatives hated those things too. Which gave D'Souza an idea: "American conservatives should join the Muslims and others in condemning the global moral degeneracy that is produced by liberal values" like "separation of church and state, feminism, and the idea of the working woman."[21]

This was vulgar trolling, rooted not in a set of beliefs—D'Souza had argued precisely the opposite in his 2002 book, *What's So Great About America*—but in a vicious antiliberalism precisely calculated to provoke as much outrage as possible. It hit the mark a little too well, generating piles of contemptuous reviews from conservatives as well as others. D'Souza bristled at being so easily dismissed, writing a seven-thousand-word rebuttal to his conservative critics in *National Review*, one that repeatedly asserted his seriousness and expertise. But in reality, D'Souza had been shedding his intellectual pretenses for some times, as he sought a broader market for his work. *The Enemy at Home* served as a turning point in his career. He had tapped into a rich and enriching vein of antiliberalism and learned that he did not need to spend quite so much time making his books seem erudite and respectable: he could go straight for that vein, and as long as his audience found his arguments appealing, it didn't really matter that they made him a laughingstock among intellectuals.[22]

These books, almost all of which became instant best sellers, showed a right-wing media apparatus zeroing in on the most active and excitable parts of the base. And liberals were far from their only target.

"THERE ARE LEGITIMATE questions about whether or not this was a self-inflicted wound."

Michelle Malkin slipped the comment in as another guest on *Hardball* spoke, but host Chris Matthews immediately latched onto it. The accusation that John Kerry had shot himself to win a purple heart was new to him, though it had been rattling around the right-wing fever swamps for months. Matthews pressed and pressed Malkin, who retreated to say that she couldn't definitively say Kerry had shot himself, but someone needed to get to the bottom of it. In fact, she said in an affronted tone, "I wish you would ask these questions instead of me."[23]

Matthews cut the segment off, leaving Malkin fuming. MSNBC had booked her for two segments, one on the Swift Boat controversy being promoted by right-wing groups and one on her new book, *In Defense of Internment*. She was happy to pitch in on the election-season conspiracy, but she had been far more interested in talking about the book. For the past several years she had been carefully plotting a path to the right of Bush—she had no desire to be seen as his operative.

Malkin, the daughter of Philippine immigrants, started her career as a right-wing journalist. Like Ingraham, Coulter, and D'Souza, she wrote for a right-wing newspaper while a student at Oberlin College. In this case, the paper was started by her future husband, Jesse Malkin. Her first article was an attack on the school's affirmative action programs, a popular target of campus conservatives. She quickly developed a style similar to Coulter's: caustic and outrageous, just as mean but somehow sharper because it was seldom cut with humor.[24]

By the start of the Bush administration, she had zeroed in on immigration as the key issue for Republican politics, making her book-writing debut with an anti-immigration tract called *Invasion*.

But it was her book applauding Japanese internment—written, notably, by an Asian American—that made her truly famous. She buttressed her book writing with extensive blogging, publishing on both the white nationalist website VDARE and her immensely popular personal blog, MichelleMalkin.com. In her blogging and book writing, she leveraged her identity as the daughter of Asian immigrants, which she used as a defensive shield against accusations of bigotry. Her views placed her decidedly to the right of Bush on anti-immigration and anti-Muslim politics.[25]

When it came to anti-Muslim sentiment, the space to the right of Bush was mostly rhetorical. In the aftermath of the terror attacks, he had made a point to differentiate between Islam and terrorism. "The war against terrorism is not a war against Muslims, nor is it a war against Arabs," he said in the days after the attacks, as hate crimes against Muslims peaked. But that tolerance seldom extended to policy. The Bush administration would use the Patriot Act and a new array of homeland security powers to profile Muslim travelers, infiltrate mosques, and invade and bomb Muslim-majority countries. It would also oversee and defend war crimes in the prosecution of the Iraq and Afghanistan Wars, including prisoner abuse at the Abu Ghraib prison in Iraq, the torture of suspected terrorists, and the indefinite detention of people held at facilities in Guantánamo Bay.[26]

But his rhetoric still set him apart at a moment when anti-Muslim sentiment was on the rise on the right. Many believed Bush was not going far enough, that he needed to put the entire force of the US military behind the invasions and more explicitly target not just terrorists but Muslims. Coulter called for forced conversions; Malkin called for racial profiling; radio host Michael Savage called for the eradication of one hundred million Muslims. On a call-in show, Tucker Carlson called the people of Iraq "semi-literate primitive monkeys." He went on to say that if a presidential candidate just admitted to being a bigot who hates "lunatic Muslims" and vowed "to kill as many of them as I can if you elect me," he would win in a landslide. "I'd vote for you if you said that," Carlson added. Anti-Muslim blogs proliferated in the early 2000s, including *Little Green Footballs*, a militant site that cheered on the War on Terror, and *Atlas Shrugs*, a site led by far-right activist Pamela Gellar, who spearheaded efforts to block a Muslim community center near Ground Zero in Manhattan.[27]

While the differences between the grassroots right and the administration on Islam largely turned on language, their differences on immigration were rooted in both policy and philosophy. For most Americans, immigration, which had been an explosive issue in the mid-1990s, had largely receded from their list of top political concerns. But for right-wing partisans, mass immigration, and what it meant for the white majority in the United States, remained a top issue. And while Buchanan's *Death of the West* reiterated the arguments of the 1990s, Malkin showed what the debates of the 2000s could look like, when immigration was slotted into a national security framework.

That itself did not set her wholly at odds with the administration. The creation of the new Department of Homeland Security involved a wholesale reorganization of the federal immigration agencies, now housed in the new department. Institutionally, immigration was now part of the national security apparatus, which ensured that ideas like border security would be prioritized, while migrant protections and services became second-tier responsibilities.

Beyond that, however, the restrictionist right had little in common with the Bush administration's approach to immigration. Malkin's first book, which had come out in 2002, laid out what Bush-critical politics looked like in a post-9/11 atmosphere. *Invasion: How*

America Still Welcomes Terrorists, Criminals, and Other Foreign Menaces to Our Shores only hinted at its main subject. Though it opened with the 2001 hijackings, terrorism was not the main subject. *Invasion* was instead a broadside against immigration. Malkin readily attacked Bush on the issue. "Unfortunately," she said at an event promoting *Invasion*, "the Bush Administration remains far more concerned with appeasing Mexican President Vicente Fox than it is with protecting American men and women who are at the border on our front lines."[28]

Malkin was far from the only one uncomfortable with the Bush administration's liberal approach to immigration reform. Coulter had focused on immigration law when she worked in Congress in the mid-1990s and began to hit it even harder in the 2000s. So did Laura Ingraham, who emerged as a leading critic of the administration in the fight over reform in the second term.

Nor were these objections limited to media figures. Immigration cleaved the conservative coalition, pitting the pro-business *Wall Street Journal* against the New Right *Washington Times*, the libertarian Cato Institute against the hard-line nativist Center for Immigration Studies. Those divisions meant that Bush might have a path to reform, but it likely would require bipartisan legislation ardently opposed by some in his own party. Yet Bush was optimistic. It had been fifteen years since the last comprehensive immigration reform legislation, and so much needed fixing. He was already working on bipartisan education reform. Bipartisan immigration reform might not be that heavy a lift. On September 6, 2001, he met with Mexican president Vicente Fox and announced plans to work together on immigration.[29]

The terror attacks five days later not only scuttled those immediate plans but short-circuited work on immigration reform for nearly two years. By summer 2003, the timing once again felt right.

A contingent of Republicans from Arizona—Representatives Jim Kolbe and Jeff Flake and Senator John McCain—began to develop the architecture of a massive immigration overhaul.[30]

The backlash to their plans was immediate and intense. Right-wing media vibrated with cries of "amnesty." When the Arizona legislators returned home for summer recess, their town halls were packed with protesters. Proponents of an initiative called Protect Arizona Now, which would require voters and those who used state services to submit proof of citizenship, argued "the spineless" congressional delegation was out of touch with what Arizonans wanted. Restrictionists in Congress introduced the Clear Law Enforcement for Criminal Alien Removal Act, which would allow state and local law enforcement to enforce immigration laws and would penalize states that did not. The legislation attracted 112 cosponsors, 105 of them Republican. A Republican was also responsible for the Mass Immigration Reduction Act, a piece of proposed legislation to introduce an immigration moratorium that would be in effect until immigration levels dropped to ten thousand a year, a quota that could only be increased if Congress and the president agreed that doing so would not affect native-born laborers.[31]

That bill, first introduced in 2001 and lauded by the Federation for American Immigration Reform, was written by Tom Tancredo. Tancredo's tenure in office had been defined by his opposition to immigration. He had cut his teeth as an activist in the 1970s on campaigns against bilingual education. He served a stint as a regional director of the Department of Education under Reagan, where his primary accomplishment was slashing the staff by two-thirds. Elected to the House from Colorado in 1998, he established the Congressional Immigration Reform Congress, a group of legislators who supported stronger immigration restrictions. Its numbers swelled from fifteen to sixty-nine between 2001 and 2003, a sign that the restrictionist wing of the Republican Party had gained significant strength in the space of time understood by McCain and his allies as relatively quiet for immigration.[32]

The *Financial Times* assessed Tancredo as the "political heir" to Pat Buchanan for his claims that migrants brought crime and drugs to the United States and threatened "Western values." He also constantly bragged that he had made himself a thorn in the administration's side, boasting that Karl Rove had told him "never to darken the White House door again." And while Tancredo remained a backbencher during his decade in Congress, he still wielded influence. A Denver newspaper noted that he was on Fox News so often, "he's practically a regular contributor."[33]

With Democrats out of power, the immigration fight played out within the Republican Party. The intraparty warfare helped hone a new argument for the partisans who supported restriction: they were fighting not just liberals but a conservative elite that valued corporate interests and global capital over the interests of Americans. It was a familiar argument—Pat Buchanan had returned to it again and again in the 1990s and made it the core of his 2000 Reform Party run. But it was now spreading among right-wing Republicans. Laura Ingraham's 2003 book *Shut Up and Sing*, a broadside against elites in the United States, attacked not only liberals but "elitist Respectable Republicans." Channeling the arguments of the New Right, she sneered at those Republicans "who look down on socially conservative, middle-class Americans as being too radical and hard-edged" while seeking out bipartisan deals with Democrats.[34]

Even as she occasionally lumped Bush in with those "Respectable Republicans," Ingraham nonetheless curbed her charges against the president. It was, after all, 2003, and she had written the book to denounce a singer who had criticized George W. Bush. While Bush certainly had his detractors on the right, in those days they trod carefully. He was simply too popular.

But almost as soon as he was reelected, that would change, sending the conservative crack-up into overdrive.

———

THE SCRATCHING AT the door had been going on for a while, a low-level distraction as the president tried to persuade the five radio talk show hosts gathered around him. Bush finally stood up and opened the door, allowing Barney, his black Scottish terrier, to trot into the Oval Office. It was a moment of relief from the heavy topics at hand: war, immigration, scandal. Unpleasant as it was, though, Bush kept at it. He had to win over the group of hosts, which included Laura Ingraham and Sean Hannity, who had been hammering the administration and the Republican Party in advance of the midterm election, now less than two months away.[35]

Bush could no longer count on his popularity to bind the conservative base to his administration. His approval ratings had spent most of 2006 in the thirties and showed little sign of rebounding. The party was not faring much better, weighed down by endless congressional scandals: House Majority Leader Tom DeLay had resigned from leadership after being indicted for money laundering and criminal conspiracy (his conviction would be overturned on appeal); activists Ralph Reed and Grover Norquist had been caught up in a lobbying scandal that engulfed a number of conservative activists, including Republicans in Congress and the White House; Republican representative Mark Foley resigned following revelations that he had sent sexually explicit messages to congressional pages; Republican representative Duke Cunningham went from Congress to prison for accepting $2.4 million in bribes. The charge that the Republican Party had fostered a culture of corruption in its twelve years in power was difficult to refute.[36]

No longer constrained by the sky-high popularity Bush enjoyed in his first term, conservatives were more openly hostile to many of his policies. Tucker Carlson had turned against the war by 2004, inching his way closer to his transformation into the second coming of Pat Buchanan. Laura Ingraham and other radio hosts quashed Bush's nomination of Harriet Miers to the Supreme Court in 2005, insisting to their listeners that she was both unqualified and an unknown quantity, a wild card on the Court when they needed a committed conservative. And conservative Republicans, backed by pundits like Ingraham, Hannity, and Lou Dobbs, joined Democrats in blocking Bush's deal with a Dubai-based company to manage six US ports.[37]

So Bush knew he needed to win the right back. In addition to those in that Oval Office meeting, he met separately with Rush Limbaugh, who required a special kind of solicitousness. Limbaugh had shown he was willing to throw punches at the administration, hitting Bush hard in 2004 about growing deficits. "This may be compassionate," he told his audience, "but it is not 'conservatism' at all." Casting a wider net, the White House invited more than forty right-wing hosts to broadcast from the North Lawn a few weeks before the midterm election, making senior officials, including Vice President Dick Cheney, available for interviews.[38]

The charm offensive worked, for a while. Those who attended the Oval Office meeting, impressed with the president's warmth and passion, urged their listeners to give the GOP their support. Limbaugh lobbied his audience to vote Republican, bringing on Senator Mitch McConnell and White House press secretary Tony Snow (a former Fox News host) to lay out the dire consequences of a Democratic victory. But no one adopted the role of party apparatchik more eagerly than Sean Hannity. He went out on the campaign trail to rally Republicans, stumping from Arizona to Pennsylvania on behalf of conservative candidates. He brought incumbents in close races onto his show to boost their support. He railed against moderates—which for him now included conservatives like John McCain and Lindsey Graham—but insisted that power was more important than purity: if moderates were necessary to secure a Republican majority, then that's who they would have to support to keep the Speaker's gavel out of the hands of House Minority Leader Nancy Pelosi, a California representative who had been serving in the House for nearly three decades.[39]

The effort to hold the House in 2006 failed. Democrats picked up five seats in the Senate and thirty-one in the House, giving them control of both chambers. The era of united Republican governance was over.

Bush's opportunity to pass immigration reform was over as well, though he didn't yet know it. He geared up to make a big push on immigration, once again soliciting right-wing talk show hosts in the hopes of winning over their support. But by focusing exclusively on radio, the administration missed a reservoir of deep discontent: right-wing blogs. Furious about the immigration bill making its way through the Senate in 2007, the right-wing blogosphere devolved into what CNN called "a full-scale revolt against the Bush administration." Michelle Malkin called the bill "a White House betrayal," while Hugh Hewitt, then primarily a blogger, deemed it "a disaster." Another popular right-wing blog, *Ace of Spades HQ*, called on the "embarrassingly dimwitted" president to resign.[40]

Bush pushed back, a sign of how important the immigration reform bill was to him. Using the same rhetorical with-us-or-against-us framework he had used for the War on Terror, he slammed his opponents as people who "don't want to do what's right for America."

"If you want to scare the American people, what you say is the bill's an amnesty bill," he said at a speech in southeastern Georgia. "That's empty political rhetoric trying to frighten our citizens."[41]

The restrictionists were apoplectic. They had stood by Bush even as his poll numbers sank, trying to buoy the Republican Party that was sinking alongside the president. No longer. They would mostly continue to stand by him as he prosecuted his wars abroad, particularly as he geared up for the surge in Afghanistan. "As for the rest of it, they are looking for ways to reshape the party agenda going into the next election," conservative blogger Ed Morrisey said of his cohort. "That's a nice way of saying they are going to consider him irrelevant."[42]

Having lost the support of his conservative base, Bush faced another serious crisis as his presidency limped to an end. In September 2008, the US economy suddenly collapsed. As the housing market slowed, the many high-risk mortgages that had kept it artificially inflated suddenly came due. And when those mortgages failed, so did the mortgage-backed securities, and their derivatives, that had superheated the finance industry. The American financial system was honeycombed with fraudulent financial instruments, leading to the collapse of major investment banks. The stock market would lose 50 percent of its value before it started to recover in early 2009.[43]

The financial collapse crippled what remained of the Bush presidency. By late September, the administration and congressional leaders had hammered out a deal for the government to buy up the faulty mortgage-backed securities (rightly called "toxic assets") in an effort to pull the economy out of free fall and prevent the collapse of the rest of the banking system. But it turned out the right-wing rebellion against the Bush administration was still underway. When the rescue legislation went to the House, two-thirds of the Republican caucus voted against it. The next day, the stock market plunged 777 points, the largest one-day drop in history. A few days later, a number of spooked representatives switched their votes, passing the Emergency Economic Stabilization Act. By October 2008, Bush's approval ratings were hovering in the mid-twenties, a little lower than his father's lowest point.[44]

And that is how the reign of Reagan's disciple ended: with him regarded as far more like his father than his idol.

And what did this mean for Reaganism? Bush embraced free markets and deep tax cuts and left office in the midst of a financial collapse and the worst recession in nearly a century. He embraced a good-versus-evil foreign policy and left the country mired in what would be the two longest wars in its history. He embraced open immigration and left his party sliced in two, more restrictionist than it had been in decades. He talked about conservatism with a heart, compassionate and optimistic, and oversaw a regime of torture abroad and neglect at home, with images from Abu Ghraib and a flooded New Orleans the most indelible of his presidency.

If this was Reaganism, the country, and the conservative movement, were ready to move on.

CHAPTER TWELVE

THE TRIUMPH OF PITCHFORK POLITICS

W HO IS THE MAIN PERSON YOU THINK SPEAKS for the Republican Party today?" Gallup posed that question in May 2009, a bleak moment for the GOP. Barack Obama had won the presidency and brought with him substantial majorities in the House and Senate. There was no natural leader for the party in any branch of government. Ronald Reagan was dead; George W. Bush had slunk back to Texas. The Republican minority leaders, Representative John Boehner and Senator Mitch McConnell, had only held their positions for a few years and were hardly household names, despite their long tenures in Congress. So, perhaps unsurprisingly, the person who topped the list— after "no one"—was Rush Limbaugh.[1]

Limbaugh snagged the top spot in part because of his longevity: in 2008, he celebrated twenty years as a nationally syndicated host. He also remained profitably popular, having just inked an eight-year, $400 million contract (a significant pay raise from his last eight-year contract, worth $285 million). As such, he had become untouchable. When Michael Steele, the new chair of the Republican National Committee and the first Black person to hold the position, criticized Limbaugh as an entertainer who relied on "incendiary" and "ugly" rhetoric, the blowback was so intense that Steele was forced to apologize. The party remained just as deferential to the talk show host as it had back in 1992.[2]

But Limbaugh also topped the poll because of his implacable opposition to the Obama administration. A few days before Obama's inauguration, Limbaugh told his audience that the *Wall Street Journal* had approached him to provide a four-hundred-word essay on his hopes for the new administration. "I don't need 400 words," he scoffed. "I need four: I hope he fails."[3] It was a blunt, pessimistic assessment, delivered in the midst of a national crisis, that shocked and worried some on the right. Even as Republican leaders were plotting to obstruct every piece of legislation backed by the new administration, they saw no upside in saying it out loud.

Yet "I hope he fails" became the governing ethos of the Republican Party and the conservative movement during the Obama years. It was the one idea that could hold a deeply divided party together, especially given the growing antipathy some on the right nursed for Republican leaders and the new conservative establishment. Those antiestablishment conservatives would present themselves as heterodox populists and yet remained yoked to the GOP. Republican leaders, in turn, found they couldn't purge the party's antiestablishment wing; nor could they effectively negotiate with its members. As a result, the party reorganized around antiliberalism and, in particular, intractable opposition to Barack Obama.

THE PRESIDENCY OF Barack Obama was illegitimate. A faction on the right had drawn that conclusion even before Obama took office. His disqualifications were legion. He was a foreigner. He was Muslim. He was anti-American. He was in league with liberal groups that had stolen the election. A heady mix of conspiracies and calumnies rattled through right-wing media, grassroots organizations, statehouses, and Congress during the early Obama administration. And on the cutting edge of those conspiracies was Lou Dobbs.

Dobbs, an intense, jowly man with a thin helmet of reddish-blond hair fading into gray, had been at CNN since its launch in 1980. He started at the network with a business show, *Moneyline*, part of an emerging genre of financial entertainment. In that first iteration, he was a classic Reaganite: pro free markets, pro unregulated capital. His show was a love letter to corporations and finance capitalism. But when he returned to CNN in 2001 after a brief spat with the network president, he remade himself into what the *New York Times* called a "pinstriped populist." His new creed shone through not only on his show, retitled *Lou Dobbs Tonight* to allow for more wide-ranging commentary, but also in his best-selling (and laboriously subtitled) books, *Exporting America: Why Corporate Greed Is Shipping American Jobs Overseas* and *War on the Middle Class: How the Government, Big Business, and Special Interest Groups Are Waging War on the American Dream and How to Fight Back*.[4]

The new Lou Dobbs laid out his worldview in the titles of his show segments: "Broken Borders," "Homeland Insecurity," "War on the Middle Class," "Exporting America," and "The Best Government Money Can Buy." Dobbs was a right-wing pundit, but he had dubbed himself "Mr. Independent," in part for his willingness to break with the Republican Party on issues like immigration reform and tax cuts. He presented himself as the defender of American workers, arguing that they were the "true victims of corporate America's lust for cheap labor."

As he explained to a journalist at the *New Yorker*, he was promoting not just a set of populist policies but a particular approach to media that he identified as both nonobjective and nonpartisan. "What you won't see on our broadcast is 'fair and balanced journalism.' You will not see 'objective journalism.' The truth is not 'fair and balanced.' There is a nonpartisan, independent reality that doesn't give a damn, frankly, what two Democrats and two Republicans think about anything or say about anything."[5]

That made his show an increasingly uncomfortable fit at CNN. By the mid-2000s, CNN was trying to differentiate itself from its competitors. Fox News was the overtly conservative news network, and MSNBC was starting to tilt left, so CNN worked to brand itself as something in the middle: sometimes the home of straightforward news, at other times the voice of "the people," however that was conceived. The new direction augured poorly for partisan sparring and opinion programming. In 2005, the network canceled *Crossfire*, which Tucker Carlson had cohosted since 2001, for *The Situation Room*, a more straightforward news program. That left *Lou Dobbs Tonight* as the network's most opinionated—and most conservative—show.[6]

When Barack Obama arrived on the scene, Dobbs shifted from attacking the Bush administration to questioning Obama's legitimacy. One of his first targets, shared across right-wing media, was the Association of Community Organizations for Reform Now (ACORN). Among its many programs focused on aiding low-income households, ACORN worked on voter registration. The Obama campaign contracted with an ACORN subsidiary to work on get-out-the-vote efforts during the primaries. The right alleged the community activist group had been the center of a voter-fraud campaign to swing the election to Obama, an allegation Dobbs repeated regularly on his show. Though there was no evidence of fraudulently cast ballots (most of the issues revolved around voter registration forms, and it had been ACORN that called attention to those issues, as required by law), ACORN remained a right-wing bogeyman, kept around to insinuate that something nefarious had happened in the 2008 election, which Obama won by some ten million votes.[7]

The ACORN pseudoscandal was the entering wedge for right-wing arguments about voter fraud. Fueled by a new generation of right-wing scandalmongers—including James O'Keefe, whose selectively and deceptively edited videos would be at the center of a number of Obama-era stories—and amplified in nonconservative outlets, the ACORN attacks had profound consequences: the organization lost so many contracts that it ultimately folded in 2010. And the episode laid the groundwork for a torrent of new voter-suppression laws passed when Republicans took over state governments in the 2010 elections. Struggling to win majorities of voters, Republicans began looking for ways to exclude them instead.[8]

ACORN, though, was just a seedling of a scandal compared to the mighty oak of birtherism. In the summer of 2009, Lou Dobbs's show became the most prominent platform for the racist conspiracy theory that argued Obama was not born in the United States. He flogged the theory repeatedly on his radio show, where he hosted Alan Keyes, who had run against Obama for the Senate in 2004, and Orly Taitz, the "queen bee" of birtherism. While he tended to save his most conspiratorial content for his radio program, his focus on birtherism seeped into his CNN show. Soon the network that imagined itself as the all-news alternative to the other partisan outlets had become the platform for the country's most prominent birther.[9]

Dobbs may have been the most visible birther, but the conspiracy spread rapidly on the right, thanks to a preexisting conspiracy infrastructure erected during the Clinton administration. Free Republic, the message board that first gave life to the birther conspiracy, launched in 1996. Its traffic surged during the Whitewater investigation and the Clinton sex scandal and impeachment, thanks in large part to frequent links on the Drudge Report. The site even sponsored a "March for Justice," held on the National Mall in October 1998, to support the Clinton impeachment. Several thousand people showed up to listen to Representative Bob Barr, Clinton conspiracist Gary Aldridge, Alan Keyes, Ann Coulter, and an Arkansas trooper who told the crowd that Hillary Clinton had been having an affair with Vince Foster.[10]

WorldNetDaily, a must-visit website for birther conspiracists in the early years of the Obama presidency, followed a similar trajectory from Clinton to Obama. Its founder, Joseph Farah, the ghostwriter for Rush Limbaugh's second book, was also a cofounder of the Western Journalism Center, which funded Chris Ruddy's investigations into Vince Foster's suicide (Farah was a major proponent of the Foster-was-murdered conspiracy). Jerome Corsi, a columnist at WorldNetDaily, had entered the national spotlight as coauthor of the book *Unfit for Command*, an error-laden (and best-selling) book attacking then Democratic presidential nominee John Kerry's service in Vietnam. Corsi would contribute to the hundreds of articles on WorldNetDaily questioning Obama's birthplace, as well as write two best-selling conspiratorial books about Obama, *The Obama Nation*, published during the 2008 campaign, and *Where's the Birth Certificate?* Birtherism was big money for the site, whose traffic doubled once Obama took office; according to Farah, it was on track to make $10 million during the first year of the Obama presidency.[11]

Most Americans were not tuned in to sites like Free Republic or WorldNetDaily. But the conspiracies passed through porous borders to people like Bob Barr in Congress and Lou Dobbs on CNN.

Uncomfortable with the conspiracies Dobbs was spreading, CNN finally intervened. In July 2009, after gathering research about Obama's birth certificate and other supporting documents from CNN reporters, network president Jon Klein sent an email to staffers on Dobbs's show, asking them to cite the research on air. "It seems this story is dead," he told the staffers, making clear that CNN no longer backed birther content. But as protective as Klein was of CNN's reputation, he turned out to be more protective of his relationship with Dobbs. In an interview a few days later, Klein backpedaled, creating a carve-out for Dobbs. "He's got more than 30 years as a television journalist, and I trust him, as I trust all our reporters and anchors, to exercise their judgment as various stories evolve." He went on to say that if there were future news pegs for stories about Obama's birthplace, then the issue might warrant more coverage.[12]

The problem with that stance, however, was that there was *always* a news hook. The grass roots were saturated with the birther conspiracy, which rattled around on right-wing message boards and in the comment sections of conservative blogs. Sites like WorldNetDaily kept its front page clogged with items about Obama's religion, citizenship, and loyalties. Polling companies regularly checked to see just how rampant belief in the birther conspiracy was in the Republican Party. A reserve major in the US Army reversed his voluntary deployment to Afghanistan, arguing his orders were not valid since the president was not a citizen. Each of these moments served as a hook for more birther coverage.[13]

Dobbs pushed back hard against criticism from inside and outside the network. He argued that Obama's birthplace was a question of genuine controversy. He emphasized that he personally believed Obama had been born in Hawaii and was a US citizen; at the same time he claimed that the president was not being fully transparent. When Dobbs asked, "Where's the birth certificate?" he explained, he was "just asking questions." And wasn't that what journalists were supposed to do?[14]

"Just asking questions"—especially when those questions suggested there was something illegitimate about Obama's election—was hardly a neutral act. Giving voice to conspiracists who argued the first Black president was secretly an anti-American immigrant fit with Dobbs's nativist politics. Between segments on the birth certificate, he continued to rant about undocumented migrants, arguing that they were disease-ridden invaders who were taking jobs from native-born Americans. In September 2009, he did a live broadcast of his radio show from a conference for the virulently anti-immigrant Federation for American Immigration Reform.

The combination of birtherism and his vociferous anti-immigrant rhetoric triggered a "Drop Dobbs" campaign organized by civil rights groups, Latino organizations, liberal activists, and Media Matters, a media-watchdog organization founded by recent convert David Brock to track right-wing outlets. In November 2009, CNN finally did drop Dobbs, saying that his advocacy style no longer fit with the network's decision to double down on news.

Rumors swirled that Dobbs would join Fox News, a network more in line with his political preferences, and that soon came to pass as Dobbs launched a new show on the Fox Business Network. In making the transition from CNN to Fox News, he joined other conservative cast-offs who landed at Fox at the start of the Obama era. Tucker Carlson, who had been snatched up by MSNBC in 2005 after CNN let him go, had his low-rated show canceled in early 2008. He stayed at MSNBC to provide election coverage, but

in early 2009 he made the jump to Fox News as a regular contributor. And Glenn Beck, who had found surprising success at CNN
Headline News, announced just before the 2008 election that he
would be joining Fox News as well.

All of these pundits presented themselves as iconoclasts, not
loyal to a single party, unwilling to toe the conservative movement
line. Yet, as CNN and MSNBC grew less comfortable with the
incendiary right-wing pundits in their ranks, and as Fox News
sought to poach the proven ratings stars on the right, these partisans found themselves lashed to the conservative news network,
speaking more directly to a right-wing base as they lost their reach
beyond it. In that sense, they were right in line with shifts in the
Republican Party, which was about to be swept up by a movement
that empowered an activist base and moved the party even further
from the center of US politics.

———

"IT WAS JUST a little over a year ago that House Speaker Nancy
Pelosi said the tea parties are AstroTurf." Boos echoed across the
room after Lou Dobbs delivered the line, and he flashed a veneer-
filled smile at the twenty-eight hundred tea partiers packed into the
Greater Richmond Convention Center.

"Kiss my AstroTurf!" shouted a woman from somewhere near
the back, causing Dobbs and the crowd to burst into laughter. After
taking a long drink of water, he responded, "As Steve Bannon said,
patriots do fire back!"[15]

Bannon, looking schlubby in a worn pullover, smiled from the
sidelines. As the organizer of the two-day event for Virginia tea
partiers, he had arranged to have Dobbs speak, part of his broader
push to get Dobbs to run for president in 2012. It might seem like a
long shot—a former TV host with no political experience who had

promoted racist conspiracies and was fiercely anti-immigrant—but
Bannon saw potential in "Mr. Independent." Dobbs's lack of experience would be a selling point to a movement that saw both Democrats and the Republican establishment as the enemy and imbibed
a steady diet of conspiracy theories and extreme rhetoric. Dobbs
seemed like just the man to harness that energy.[16]

And Dobbs was open to the idea. When he announced on air
that he was leaving CNN, he signaled that he might have a bigger job in mind. "Some leaders in media, politics and business have
been urging me to go beyond the role here at CNN," he said, "and
to engage in constructive problem-solving, as well as to contribute
positively to a better understanding of the great issues of our day." A
few weeks later, he told Fred Thompson, a former actor turned senator turned radio talk show host, that he was considering a run. He
repeated that line in an interview with GQ in April 2010, published
just before he was slated to appear at a Tax Day Tea Party rally in
New York City, introduced again by Bannon. The tea party rallies
were a testing ground for Dobbs for president (or maybe Dobbs for
Senate—he was keeping his options open).[17]

But Dobbs had some major obstacles to overcome if he was going to win over the tea party purists. There were the hypocritical but
potentially forgivable stories, like the revelation in The Nation that
he hired undocumented workers to work on his property. Dobbs
simply denied it, ignoring the evidence the reporters had amassed.
Then there were the flip-flops that littered his record, particularly
on protectionism. He assured GQ that he had always been for the
North American Free Trade Agreement (NAFTA)—"I was there
before Clinton, for Chrissakes!"—but he had spent years attacking
the trade agreement on his show.[18]

Nothing damaged Dobbs's potential candidacy more, though,
than his shift on immigration. Dobbs seemed to believe that he

would need Latino voters and a more tolerant position on immigration to run for office. After leaving CNN, he stopped using the phrase "illegal alien." He began reaching out to Latino groups and privately brainstorming with members of Congress to see if they could reach some compromise on immigration reform. He then went on Telemundo and declared that he supported a path to citizenship. His most fervent supporters quickly disappeared. Even the creators of LouDobbsForPresident.org dumped him. "I would not vote for him for dog catcher now," one wrote.[19]

He would not be the last Republican candidate to run aground on that issue.

By the time his show on Fox Business launched in March 2011, it was clear that Dobbs had opted for political entertainment over electoral politics. But he and Bannon had zeroed in on a tectonic shift happening within the Republican Party and the conservative movement, one that would create a market for unconventional candidates while feeding a new strain of radicalism and antiestablishment politics in the GOP: the tea party.

If there was a formal beginning to the tea party, it took place on cable news. In mid-February 2009, President Obama announced a plan to aid millions of homeowners at risk of foreclosure as a result of the financial crisis. Hearing news of this plan, Rick Santelli, an on-air reporter for the business channel CNBC, exploded. Broadcasting from the floor of the Chicago Mercantile Exchange, he ranted about having to "subsidize the losers' mortgages." Turning to the crowd of traders on the floor, he shouted, "This is America! How many of you people want to pay for your neighbor's mortgage that has an extra bathroom and can't pay their bills?" Boos rang out across the trading floor.[20]

It was a perverse reversal of populism: stock market traders portraying themselves as the victims of homeowners who had been sold predatory mortgages. But when Santelli suggested launching a new tea party, his rant went viral. The symbolic power of the tea party, with its ties to revolutionary America and a people rising up against a distant, uncaring ruling class, spread across the conservative movement. By April, hundreds of Tax Day Tea Parties, promoted by Fox News and headlined by conservative media personalities, had sprung up across the country. And this was not a one-day event: local tea party groups combined with new Republican organizations like FreedomWorks and Americans for Prosperity to provide an activist infrastructure that kept right-wing voters engaged as the movement's focus shifted from homeowner relief to bank bailouts to the Affordable Care Act (ACA). Though many of the smaller organizations were founded to support the new activism, groups like FreedomWorks and Americans for Prosperity had been around since the Bush years, supported by wealthy industrialists like Charles and David Koch and repackaged to suit the new spirit of the tea party.[21]

Sarah Palin, the Alaska governor who had served as John McCain's running mate in 2008, emerged as one of the tea party's leading lights. Oscillating between quippy and snarling, she was an instant media star. Incurious and unprepared, she constantly fumbled on the campaign trail. But the more criticism she received for her lack of knowledge and nonsensical statements, the closer the right clung to her, insisting that the negative press was a result of liberal media bias. After resigning as governor of Alaska in July 2009, she quickly took her place as a tea party leader, becoming a commentator on Fox News and speaking at the first tea party convention in 2010.

The tea party was not a third party, though it was often confused for one. Instead, it was an intraparty revolt, a protest against the party establishment as well as a way of organizing the right-wing backlash to the election of the first Black president.

The two were, in a way, connected. At the end of the Bush administration, the party's right-wingers had grown discontented. They were especially upset with the nomination of John McCain, a rock-solid conservative who had nonetheless engaged in compromise and bipartisanship, supporting immigration reform, working with Ted Kennedy on the patients' bill of rights, and voting for cap-and-trade and against oil drilling in the Arctic National Wildlife Refuge. In 2008, Joseph Farah of WorldNetDaily captured the right-wing case against McCain in his book *None of the Above: Why 2008 Is the Year to Cast the Ultimate Protest Vote*. In it, he argued that McCain was a pro-immigration globalist—"Barack Obama lite"— and the Republican Party had become just a weaker version of the Democratic Party. It was hardly a novel argument—movement conservatives had been making some form of the Republicans-are-Democrats-in-disguise argument since the 1950s. But the Republican Party of the 1950s was a far more liberal party. The post-Reagan, post–Newt Gingrich Republican Party was deeply conservative—just no longer conservative enough.[22]

A testing ground for Republican squishiness was how strongly, and how bitterly, one opposed Barack Obama. To match the response of the party's base, politicians would need to reflect the emotions gripping it. And those emotions were cranked all the way up. Fear rippled through the grass roots. As soon as Obama was elected, gun sales skyrocketed. A run on ammunition, fed by fears that the Obama administration would soon tax bullets, triggered a shortage that sent prices through the roof. The number of militias in the United States, on the decline since the late 1990s, exploded. Two months after Obama's inauguration, a former staffer for Representative Ron Paul founded the Oath Keepers, a far-right militia that drew its membership from veterans and law enforcement officers.[23]

It wasn't just that the right believed Obama was a gun-grabber (they'd argued that about Clinton as well). They also saw him as foreign, un-American. Birtherism was part of that, but so were the claims that Obama was Marxist, a Muslim, a radical. Those beliefs, prevalent among the base, were also widespread in right-wing media and politics. In 2010, Newt Gingrich suggested that "the most accurate, predictive model" for Obama was "Kenyan, anticolonial" thinking. He claimed that, in presenting himself as a reasonable, moderate politician committed to bipartisanship, Obama had "played a wonderful con, as a result of which he is now president." (Gingrich later called Obama "the most successful food stamp president in American history," balancing his claims of Obama's foreignness with a label more rooted in domestic racism.)[24]

Gingrich's comments came in response to a cover story in *Forbes* by Dinesh D'Souza, drawn from his new book *The Roots of Obama's Rage*. That book, deemed "ideological birtherism" by conservative Daniel Larison, argued that Obama's hatred for the United States stemmed from his absent father's Kenyan anticolonialism. Badly misreading—or more likely, not reading at all—Obama's memoir *Dreams from My Father*, D'Souza argued that Obama saw his father as "an inspirational hero," from whom he derived his rage against colonial powers, including the United States, for their history of oppressing nonwhite peoples.[25]

Both D'Souza and Glenn Beck, who attributed Obama's politics to his "deep-seated hatred of white people," leveraged their conspiratorial anti-Obama content into media empires. D'Souza refashioned *The Roots of Obama's Rage* into a political documentary titled *2016: Obama's America*, released just in time for the 2012 election. The tagline—"Love him or hate him, you don't know him"—revealed what would become D'Souza's trademark, one that Beck also used to great effect: the claim that he was revealing something dark and hidden about liberals and Democrats, that he was exposing events and ideas that were not only previously unknown but deliberately kept out of the public domain. The approach was remarkably effective: *2016: Obama's America* became the second-highest grossing political documentary of all time.[26]

Obama's "rage," his "deep-seated hatred": these were deeply emotional descriptors and quite at odds with the even-keeled president, whose placid demeanor, measured tones, and careful rhetoric had earned him the nickname "No-Drama Obama." But attributing deeply negative emotions to Obama was critical to a movement that fed off its own deeply negative emotions: fear, anger, revulsion, and loathing. It is no coincidence that the leading voice of the tea party was Glenn Beck or that right-wing pundits like Mark Levin and Michael Savage, with their hostile, biting personas, thrived during the Obama years. Though journalist Dave Weigel rightly noted that the radio and television personalities most linked to the tea party were those who stressed the Constitution and founding documents, they were also the most pessimistic and emotional voices as well, an odd combination of lawyerly exegesis and teary catharsis.

Beck was a particularly central figure to the tea party. His radio show, which entered national syndication in 2002, stood out from other right-wing shows because it married a morning-zoo zaniness with an apocalyptic political analysis. He spoke openly to his audience about his struggles with drug addiction, alcoholism, and mental illness and regularly burst into tears on both his radio and television shows. He also detailed his survivalism, stockpiling food and weapons and sharing his belief that the end-time was near. His shows were conspiracy smorgasbords, particularly his television show, where he used his ever-present chalkboards—old-fashioned slates, covered in pictures and scribbled words, that he would roll out in the middle of his show—to trace the web of dark powers that conspired to take away Americans' freedoms.

Beck had begun to define himself as a bit of a maverick, less tied to the Republican Party than Rush Limbaugh or Sean Hannity. On air, he was heavily critical of the Republican Party, stressing that he was a conservative and that the party had lost its way. Which is not to say he was always opposed to the Bush administration, even at its most unpopular; when the administration pushed for a $700 billion bailout of the financial industry in the midst of the global financial crisis, Beck threw his support behind Bush. "I think the bailout is the right thing to do," he said on his CNN show. "The $700 billion that you're hearing about now is not only, I believe, necessary, it is also not nearly enough, and all of the weasels in Washington know it."[27]

The election of Barack Obama catapulted Beck to national fame. His new Fox News show debuted the day before Obama's inauguration, a deliberate decision that signaled he would be a leader of the opposition (even though polls still gave Rush Limbaugh that title). Though the show would be marketed as postpartisan—"I'm tired of left and right!" he said in the promo ads—he almost immediately began using the broadcast to compare Obama to dictators like Adolf Hitler and Joseph Stalin. Two weeks into the Obama administration, he warned his audience, "We are really, truly stepping beyond socialism, and we're starting to look at fascism." That message was wildly popular: by the end of its first month on air, his 5 p.m. show was pulling in 2.2 million viewers, doubling the time slot's previous ratings.[28]

Nor was Beck content with sticking to media. Less than two months into the Obama presidency, Beck launched the 9/12 Project. He named it that, he explained, "to bring us all back to the place we were on September 12, 2001. The day after America was attacked we were not obsessed with Red States, Blue States or political parties.

We were united as Americans." He did not say, of course, that it was shock and fear that united the country, fear that was weaponized against Muslims, used to hem in civil liberties, and mobilized to invade two countries.[29]

Beck had hoped the 9/12 Project would be the hub of anti-Obama activism, but the tea party eclipsed it. The call to rally on Tax Day, April 15, coming just a month after Beck tied his fortunes to September 12, was a case of events overriding plans. He initially opposed the Tax Day rallies, arguing they would come too soon, that higher taxes hadn't hit yet, but no one listened. So he gave in, anchoring Fox News coverage of the rallies from the Alamo in a symbolic bit of stagecraft. Nor was he alone in anchoring both a television show and a rally: Fox News anchors were leading tea party protests across the country, spurring the network to brand the rallies the FNC [Fox News Channel] Tax Day Tea Parties.

That branding turned out to be a real problem, because at the time a sizable contingent at the network was still invested in the appearance of journalistic distance from the burgeoning movement. So as the 9/12 rally date approached, Fox executives made clear that while Beck could cover the event, he could not headline it.

Still, the spirit of Beck prevailed: in the sea of people gathered at the Lincoln Memorial, flapping banners read, "Beck/Palin 2012."

THE TEA PARTY was not just about rallies and radio shows. It was also about elections. And there, the movement's antiestablishment streak would have profound consequences for the Republican Party.

That's because, when it came to electoral politics, the tea party was entirely a Republican affair. Though many tea partiers insisted they were *not* Republicans but conservatives, they were pretty certain the only party open to their politics was the GOP. As a result, they went after the Republican establishment, focusing their energy on the party primaries rather than the general elections. They didn't need a perfect record in the general election if they managed to take out high-profile incumbents who didn't fit with the tea party vision, a vision that was less about ideology—the GOP was almost uniformly conservative by 2010—and more about political absolutism. A Republican politician guilty of compromise was inviting a primary challenge.

Republican leaders were already on board with that absolutism (if not eager to see incumbents primaried). In separate meetings before Obama's inauguration, House and Senate leaders held secret meetings to plot a strategy of absolute obstruction. Faced with a stimulus bill to help resuscitate the imploding economy, House whip Eric Cantor drew a line in the sand, insisting that no Republicans vote for the bill in any form. Obama could not be allowed to tout it as bipartisan. When the Democratic chair of the House Appropriations Committee reached out to negotiate, his Republican counterpart turned him down, saying, "I'm sorry, but leadership tells us we can't play."[30]

And they didn't. No House Republican voted for stimulus, and only three Senate Republicans did. Only three House Republicans and three Senate Republicans voted for the Dodd-Frank financial reform bill. And the keystone policy of the Obama administration, the Affordable Care Act, modeled after Republican legislation in Massachusetts, attracted only one GOP vote from either chamber. (It also spawned a raft of conspiracy theories of its own, including "death panels," a conspiracy invented by Palin that said the elderly and children born with disabilities would have to be evaluated by a government panel before receiving life-saving care.) Yet even that strict discipline could not protect more moderate incumbents. Tea party candidates knocked off incumbents and party-backed candidates across the country, with mixed final results. Rand Paul of Kentucky, Mike Lee of Utah, and Marco Rubio of Florida all made their way to the Senate after defeating party favorites in the primary.[31]

But another tranche of tea party Senate candidates in Colorado, Delaware, and Nevada showed that flame-throwing political amateurs came with liabilities. Take Christine O'Donnell of Delaware, a media-savvy religious conservative who surged past former governor Mike Castle to unexpectedly win the Republican nomination. O'Donnell had spent the 1990s in media relations for groups like the Christian Coalition and Concerned Women for America, before starting her own group, the Savior's Alliance for Lifting the Truth. She embraced hardcore fundamentalist views, denying evolution, arguing that the earth was only around six thousand years old, and opposing masturbation and sex outside marriage.[32]

These beliefs, espoused by a woman in her twenties in the 1990s, caught the eye of a number of outlets. MTV featured her in its *Sex in the 90s* series, and she became a regular on *Politically Incorrect*, where Bill Maher approached her with a kind of anthropological curiosity, lightly shaded with disdain. Those appearances would be the source of the most humiliating part of her campaign, when a clip from *Politically Incorrect*, in which she admitted to "dabbling in witchcraft" when younger, led her to cut a political ad that started with her awkwardly addressing the camera to say, "I am not a witch." O'Donnell lost badly, as did her counterparts in Colorado and Delaware, leading many commentators to muse that the tea party had perhaps not been entirely beneficial to the Republican Party. While the Republican Party had swamped the election, picking up sixty-eight seats, the most in more than sixty years, Democrats retained a narrow hold on the Senate. Those three lost tea party seats stung.[33]

Yet, for the tea party, even the losses were a kind of win. The vote had been down to a Democrat or a hard-right Republican: no chance of a moderate Republican holding those seats. They may not have the majorities, but they were pulling the party even further to the right.

Even with those losses, Republican voters had delivered Democrats a shellacking, in Obama's words. Buoyed by that success, Republican leaders had their plan of action going forward. Soon-to-be House Speaker John Boehner said of Obama's agenda, "We're going to do everything—and I mean everything we can do—to kill it, stop it, slow it down, whatever we can." And Senate Minority Leader Mitch McConnell planned to do the same. "The single most important thing we want to achieve is for President Obama to be a one-term president." That continued obstruction served two purposes: it presented the GOP as an implacable, united front against the Democrats, and it helped squelch the growing divisions within the GOP caucus. The tea party members brooked no compromise; fortunately, that was the leadership's strategy as well.[34]

But that could only hold together for so long. The 2012 Republican presidential primary—a wide-open race that attracted a large and volatile field—put the tensions in the party on center stage. Mitt Romney, former governor of Massachusetts, was the odds-on favorite. But for tea partiers, he was anathema. It wasn't a question of his conservatism—in 2008 he had been the conservative alternative to John McCain—but he was ill-suited for tea party politics. He'd spent his career in finance capital, supported the 2008 bank bailout, and, worst of all, been the architect of Romneycare, the Massachusetts healthcare policy that had become the template for the Affordable Care Act. Even though he seized the anti-Obama line early on, opposing the auto industry rescue and calling the ACA "an unconscionable abuse of power," he had "establishment Republican" written all over him.[35]

That created an opening for challengers. Those vying to be the Romney alternative, ranging from tea partier Michele Bachmann to former Pennsylvania senator Rick Santorum to former Speaker Newt Gingrich, all attacked Romney from his right, depicting him as the choice of the Republican establishment. But then they went further, introducing a novel argument about the establishment: challengers Gingrich and Santorum accused Fox News of being part of that establishment, propping up Romney instead of backing the true conservative candidate. Gingrich lashed out at Fox for "bias" and "distortion," while Santorum grumbled that Romney had an unfair advantage: "He has Fox News shilling for him every day."[36]

That innovation signaled not only how deep the antiestablishment turn ran but also how conservative the party had become. For decades, the right had fought to gain a toehold in the Republican Party, then a majority share. Now, though, the party was entirely conservative, with no real moderates left (since even the moderates—those with even temperaments and a willingness to compromise here and there—were devoted conservatives). To rail against the establishment meant railing against fellow conservatives, shifting further to the right, into the wilds of a Buchanan-esque politics.

Those new dynamics were on full display after Romney lost the election. The Growth and Opportunity Project, universally known as the 2012 Republican autopsy, painted a path forward for the GOP: reach out to minority voters, soften the rhetoric on immigration, make clear women are welcome in the party. It was the responsible Republican statement of how to widen the party's base—and the partisans wanted no part of it. When onetime tea party darling Marco Rubio pushed for immigration reform in 2013, he went from being a 2016 favorite to a noncontender overnight. Right-wing hosts

like Hannity and Limbaugh, who briefly boosted immigration reform, quickly dropped it when it became clear their listeners wanted
nothing to do with it. Though Boehner tried to navigate a deal, it
quickly became apparent that he could not bring along the tea partiers in his caucus, and the reforms died in the House. Republicans
continued to flex their investigatory powers, ginning up conspiracies
that they then spent millions to investigate, but by 2014 the party
had given up on governance. Boehner, irritated by repeated attempts
by the tea party caucus to overthrow him as Speaker, gave up. The
man who had devoted the final years of his career to obstructing the
Obama administration had been so successfully obstructed himself
that he resigned his speakership and left the House.

THE CANDIDATES STOOD in a scrum beneath a life-size model
of *Air Force One*. They were gathered at the Reagan Library for the
second debate of the 2016 Republican primaries, and what better
place to stage that debate than the Simi Valley shrine to the former
president? Throughout the debate, candidates glued themselves to
the GOP icon. Senator Marco Rubio said that Reagan had inspired
him to enter public service. Governor John Kasich pointed to the
image of *Air Force One* behind him and said that he'd once flown
with Reagan on that plane: "His goals, and mine, are pretty much
the same." Governor Jeb Bush compared his immigration plan to
Reagan's, saying he was following the same "hopeful, optimistic approach." Scott Walker, Rand Paul, Mike Huckabee, Ted Cruz, Ben
Carson, Chris Christie: they all found a way to tie themselves to
their idol.[37]

Donald Trump did not. Though he was the candidate with
the fewest ties to the conservative movement and the Republican
Party—he switched parties easily and often and had only returned

to the GOP four years earlier—he felt no compulsion to mention Reagan or tie himself to Reagan's record. Instead, he talked about raising taxing on hedge fund managers and sharply limiting immigration—not as a rebuke to Reagan but without any reference to Reagan at all.

Trump understood something the debate moderators and other candidates did not: the age of Reagan was over. It had been over for a long time.

If Trump was channeling anyone, it was Pat Buchanan. Of course, Trump didn't mention him at the debate either. But from his "America First" slogan, to his opposition to the North Atlantic Treaty Organization, to his call for tariffs, to his hard-line, hard-nosed, racist attacks on immigration, he had recreated the Buchanan agenda with relatively few updates. (Buchanan had run on his opposition to the first Iraq War and Trump was running on his claimed opposition to the second, but other than that, they were in sync.) Both men had relied on media platforms to shape their political personas, and both left outside observers—and some Republican insiders—worried about a turn toward fascism in the party.

Like the right-wing pundits of the 1990s, Trump also knew how to get coverage in the mainstream press by leaning into the outrageous. Every incendiary comment bought him more airtime and column inches. He dominated the news from the moment he entered the campaign. What's more, he knew it was as good for the media outlets as it was for him. His campaign was ratings gold, and the press was soon addicted to covering it, commenting on it, and condemning it, a cycle that kept both their coffers filled. Though Trump already understood this dynamic, CBS president Les Moonves confirmed it in early 2016. "Man, who would have expected the ride we're all having right now? . . . The money's rolling in and this is fun," he crowed. "It may not be good for America, but it's damn good for CBS."[38]

Not only did Trump's path to the nomination run through the politics of the 1990s, but the people who had built that new politics quickly spotted something attractive in the Trump campaign. Ann Coulter endorsed him almost as soon as he entered the race, applauding his opposition to immigration. Rush Limbaugh and Laura Ingraham both climbed aboard the Trump train early, reminding their audiences that the outrage in the media over Trump's shocking statements was a sign that he was hitting his mark. "There's a percentage of the population that is totally fed up with the political class, including the media. And they have wanted things said to people and about people [from] the people they've been voting for [for] years and they haven't heard it," Limbaugh said, translating Trump for his audience. "Even when he's not on message or when he's not on issues, he comes across as somebody that says things they would like to say, things they have wanted to say, things they have hoped other people would say."[39]

Buchanan, too, saw Trump as a contender—and as an heir to his own political campaign. The difference, he told the *Washington Post* in early 2016, was that the dangers he pointed to in the 1990s had come to fruition. He'd warned about trade deals and immigration and affirmative action; he'd railed against political correctness and weak Republican elites. But at the time, the true costs of those policies had not yet matured. "What's different today is that the returns are in, the results are known," he said. "Everyone sees clearly now the de-industrialization of America, the cost in blood and treasure from decade-long wars in Afghanistan and Iraq, and the pervasive presence of illegal immigrants. What I saw at the San Diego border 25 years ago, everyone sees now on cable TV. And not just a few communities but almost every community is experiencing the social impact."[40]

Buchanan's diagnosis was debatable—Trump's support was predicated more on race than class—but enough had changed in political culture to transform a candidate like Trump from unimaginable into a credible choice.

Few people in the Reagan Library in the fall of 2015—including Donald Trump—believed Trump would be president two years later. Yes, he had quickly risen to the top of the polls and stayed there, but just as 2012 had seen the rise and fall of a string of improbable candidates, the Trump bubble would soon surely burst.

They didn't realize that the ground had already shifted—had been shifting for a quarter century—and they were only now beginning to catch up. The trip to Simi Valley was just the final stop in a long good-bye.

Acknowledgments

I T IS A STRANGE THING TO SIT DOWN, MORE THAN A YEAR and a half into a global pandemic, and map out the network of people it takes to bring a book like this to life. Webs of friendships, professional relationships, and intellectual communities now nearly two decades in the making went into this book, but for the last eighteen months, they have been held together by the force of Zoom calls and text threads and Twitter DMs, rather than fortified by the constant in-person connections of conferences, coffee dates, and late-night hangout sessions of previous years.

And yet, though most of these words were written in a period when the word "virtual" modified nearly every interaction I had, the dramatic isolation of the pandemic has reinforced how important these relationships are. Books are very rarely solitary ventures, even during lockdowns.

First, this book would not have been possible without the support of the Center for C-SPAN Scholarship & Engagement at Purdue University, where I was a fellow in residence during the spring of 2019, as well as the support of my colleagues at the Obama Presidency Oral History Project at Columbia University's Interdisciplinary Center for Innovative Theory and Empirics since I joined in fall 2019.

It also could not have come into being without my agent, Lisa Adams of the Garamond Agency, who has been a thoughtful and engaged collaborator, nursing this book from a germ of an idea into a full-fledged manuscript. My editor at Basic, Brian Distelberg, has been indispensable, sharpening both my thinking and my writing. Michael Kaler at Basic has likewise been a sharp-eyed reader and editorial assistant.

I have benefited greatly from being part of a number of intersecting scholarly communities. Kathryn Cramer Brownell and Leah Wright Rigueur, who cofounded the "Remaking American Political History" conference with me in 2019, are two of the most generous, hardworking scholars I know. Natalia Petrzela and Neil J. Young regularly prodded me to see the world differently in our weekly podcast sessions and gargantuan group texts. At *This Day in Esoteric Political History*, Jody Avirgan, Kellie Carter Jackson, Jacob Feldman, and Brittani Brown regularly reminded me that history is, at its heart, about people and their stories. And I owe special thanks to two talented historians (and my very dear friends), Elizabeth Ingleson and Will Hitchcock, who, along with Katie Brownell and Neil Young, read and commented on versions of the manuscript.

I have been fortunate to have a writing group that continued through the pandemic; my thanks to Matt Connelly, Jim Goodman, David Greenberg, Jim Ledbetter, Dahlia Lithwick, Michael Massing, Natalia Petrzela, Claire Potter, and Jim Traub for their attentive reading and warm camaraderie. Over the years I have also been in conversation with a number of brilliant political historians. They are too many to name, but special thanks to Brian Balogh, Kathleen Belew, Gerry Cadava, Charlie Edel, Carly Goodman, Ray Haberski, Heather Hendershot, Sarah Milov, Margaret O'Mara, Brian Rosenwald, and Oscar Winberg.

I've been working through these ideas for years in podcasts, columns, and conversations with reporters, all of which has helped clarify my thinking. My thanks to Jane Carr at CNN, Aaron Retica at the *New York Times*, Christopher Shea at *Vox*, Angus Holland at the *Melbourne Age*, Robert Schlesinger at *U.S. News & World Report*, and Mike Madden and Adam Kushner at the *Washington Post*. I'm also grateful to Ezra Klein at *The Ezra Klein Show*, Matthew Sitman and Sam Adler-Bell at *Know Your Enemy*, and Ray Haberski and Andrew Hartman at *Trotsky & the Wild Orchids*. My conversations with Jeremy W. Peters at the *New York Times* and David Folkenflik at NPR have also helped me think through the implications of this history for contemporary politics.

For most of the past two years, my family has been scattered across the country, unable to meet, celebrate, mourn, and reconnect. Yet, through it all, my mom has been a constant support, as she has been throughout my life. This book is dedicated to her.

Notes

INTRODUCTION: THE PUZZLE OF THE PARTISANS

1. The literature on the Cold War conservative movement is vast, but recent works on the institutional nature of Cold War conservatism include Kim Phillips-Fein, *Invisible Hands: The Businessmen's Crusade Against the New Deal* (New York: Norton, 2010); Jason M. Stahl, *Right Moves: The Conservative Think Tank in American Political Culture Since 1945* (Chapel Hill: University of North Carolina Press, 2016); Neil J. Young, *We Gather Together: The Religious Right and the Problem of Interfaith Politics* (New York: Oxford University Press, 2016); Nicole Hemmer, *Messengers of the Right: Conservative Media and the Transformation of American Politics* (Philadelphia: University of Pennsylvania Press, 2016); Julian Zelizer, *Burning Down the House: Newt Gingrich and the Rise of the New Republican Party* (New York: Penguin, 2020). Excellent new work is being done on the extreme right and its embeddedness in the conservative movement. See, for instance, Kathleen Belew, *Bring the War Home: The White Power Movement and Paramilitary America* (Cambridge, MA: Harvard University Press, 2018); John S. Huntington, *The Far-Right Vanguard: The Radical Roots of Modern Conservatism* (Philadelphia: University of Pennsylvania Press, 2021); Edward H. Miller, *Nut Country: Right-Wing Dallas*

and the Birth of the Southern Strategy (Chicago: University of Chicago Press, 2015).

2. On the Old Right, see, for instance, Paul V. Murphy, *The Rebuke of History: The Southern Agrarians and American Conservative Thought* (Chapel Hill: University of North Carolina Press, 2001); George Hawley, *Right-Wing Critics of American Conservatism* (Lawrence: University of Kansas Press, 2016).

3. On the mid-twentieth-century parties and their transformation, see, for instance, Leah Wright Rigueur, *The Loneliness of the Black Republican: Pragmatic Politics and the Pursuit of Power* (Princeton, NJ: Princeton University Press, 2015); Geraldo L. Cadava, *The Hispanic Republican: The Shaping of an American Political Identity, from Nixon to Trump* (New York: Ecco, 2020); Geoffrey M. Kabaservice, *Rule and Ruin: The Downfall of Moderation and the Destruction of the Republican Party, from Eisenhower to the Tea Party* (New York: Oxford University Press, 2012); Kari Frederickson, *The Dixiecrat Revolt and the End of the Solid South, 1932–1968* (Chapel Hill: University of North Carolina Press, 2001).

4. Sam M. Jones, "From Washington Straight," *National Review*, November 19, 1955, 2. For a detailed history of Taft and Eisenhower's fight, see Michael D. Bowen, *The Roots of Modern Conservatism: Dewey, Taft, and the Battle for the Soul of the Republican Party* (Chapel Hill: University of North Carolina Press, 2011).

5. On Goldwater and the conservative movement, see, for instance, Rick Perlstein, *Before the Storm: Barry Goldwater and the Unmaking of the American Consensus* (New York: Hill and Wang, 2001); Elizabeth Tandy Shermer, ed., *Barry Goldwater and the Remaking of the American Political Landscape* (Tucson: University of Arizona Press, 2013); John William Middendorf, *A Glorious Disaster: Barry Goldwater's Presidential Campaign and the Origins of the Conservative Movement* (New York: Basic Books, 2006).

6. On conservatives and Nixon, see Sarah Katherine Mergel, *Conservative Intellectuals and Richard Nixon: Rethinking the Rise of the Right* (New York: Palgrave Macmillan, 2010).

7. Hemmer, *Messengers of the Right*, chap. 11.

8. "Clinton, Trump Supporters Have Starkly Different Views of a Changing Nation," Pew Research, August 18, 2016, www.pewresearch.org /politics/2016/08/18/5-issues-and-the-2016-campaign; R. J. Reinhart, "Republicans More Positive on U.S. Relations with Russia," *Gallup*, July 13,

2018, https://news.gallup.com/poll/237137/republicans-positive-relations -russia.aspx; Nathaniel Rakich and Dhrumil Mehta, "Is Trump Fueling Republicans' Concerns About NATO, or Echoing Them?," *FiveThirtyEight*, July 13, 2018, https://fivethirtyeight.com/features/is-trump -fueling-republicans-concerns-about-nato-or-echoing-them.

CHAPTER 1: THE REVOLUTION

1. "Reagan Victory Speech," C-SPAN, November 4, 1980, www.c-span .org/video/?418300-1/reagan-victory-speech.

2. On the New Deal order, see Romain Huret, Nelson Lichtenstein, and Jean-Christian Vinel, "The New Deal: A Lost Golden Age?," in *Capitalism Contested: The New Deal and Its Legacies*, ed. Romain Huret, Nelson Lichtenstein, and Jean-Christian Vinel (Philadelphia: University of Pennsylvania Press, 2020), 1–16.

3. Kathryn Cramer Brownell, *Showbiz Politics: Hollywood in American Political Life* (Chapel Hill: University of North Carolina Press, 2014), 106–107; Seth Rosenfeld, "Reagan's Personal Spying Machine," *New York Times*, September 12, 2012, 4.

4. Congress, House of Representatives, Committee on Un-American Activities, *Hearings Regarding the Communist Infiltration of the Motion Picture Industry: Hearings Before the United States House Committee on Un-American Activities, Eightieth Congress, First Session, on Oct. 20–24, 27–30, 1947* (Washington, DC: Government Printing Office, 1947).

5. William F. Buckley Jr. and L. Brent Bozell, *McCarthy and His Enemies: The Record and Its Meaning* (Chicago: Regnery Publishing, 1954); Ronald Reagan, *Where's the Rest of Me?* (New York: Duell, Sloan, and Pearce, 1965), 139.

6. Thomas W. Evans, *The Education of Ronald Reagan: The General Electric Years and the Untold Story of His Conversion to Conservatism* (New York: Columbia University Press, 2006), chaps. 3–5.

7. Evans, *Education of Ronald Reagan*, 84, 159, 164.

8. Robert Mann, *Becoming Ronald Reagan: The Rise of a Conservative Icon* (Lincoln, NE: Potomac Books, 2019), 192.

9. Charles Mohrs, "Goldwater Asks A-Arms for NATO," *New York Times*, August 26, 1964, 1.

10. Evans, *Education of Ronald Reagan*, 164–170.

11. Evans, *Education of Ronald Reagan*, 169; Ronald Reagan, *Speaking My Mind: Selected Speeches* (New York: Simon & Schuster, 2004), 22–36.

12. Carl Greenberg, "Reagan Announces He's Candidate for Governor," *Los Angeles Times*, January 5, 1966, 3.

13. Reagan gubernatorial campaign ad, "Ronald Reagan and 'a Need for Action!' (04 Jan 1966)," video uploaded to YouTube by Kevin Heine on October 18, 2011, www.youtube.com/watch?v=nvMPFP470i0.

14. Ian Haney-López, *Dog Whistle Politics: How Coded Racial Appeals Have Reinvented Racism and Wrecked the Middle Class* (New York: Oxford University Press, 2014), chap. 3.

15. On the origins of the New Right, see Marcus M. Witcher, *Getting Right with Reagan: The Struggle for True Conservatism, 1980–2016* (Lawrence: University Press of Kansas, 2019), chap. 3.

16. Nick Thimmesch, "The Grass-Roots Dollar Chase—Ready on the Right," *New York*, June 9, 1975, 58–63.

17. Witcher, *Getting Right with Reagan*, 53–54.

18. Richard West, "Prop. 6 Dangerous, Reagan Believes," *Los Angeles Times*, September 23, 1978, A26; Witcher, *Getting Right with Reagan*, 54–55.

19. Hemmer, *Messengers of the Right*, 254.

20. "President Jimmy Carter Concession Speech," C-SPAN, November 4, 1980, www.c-span.org/video/?418299-1/president-jimmy-carter-concession-speech.

21. Reagan, *Speaking My Mind*, 59–66.

22. Witcher, *Getting Right with Reagan*, 21–25.

23. Haney-López, *Dog Whistle Politics*, 70.

24. Terry H. Anderson, *The Pursuit of Fairness: A History of Affirmative Action* (New York: Oxford University Press, 2004), 177–179. Ari Berman, *Give Us the Ballot! The Modern Struggle for Voting Rights in America* (New York: Farrar, Straus and Giroux, 2015), 139–142; Anderson, *Pursuit of Fairness*, 177.

25. Haney-López, *Dog Whistle Politics*, 58–59.

26. Lou Cannon, "Reagan's Ranch a Retreat, Tax Shelter—and Security Risk," *Washington Post*, July 8, 1980, A2; Molly Michelmore, *Tax and Spend: The Welfare State, Tax Politics, and the Limits of American Liberalism* (Philadelphia: University of Pennsylvania Press, 2012), 148; W. Elliott Brownlee and C. Eugene Steuerle, "Taxation," in *The Reagan Presidency: Pragmatic Politics and Its Legacies* (Lawrence: University Press of Kansas, 2003), 161–168.

27. "Transcript of Reagan's Speech on Soviet-American Relations," *New York Times*, January 17, 1984, A8. For more on the post-1983 pivot, see Beth A. Fischer, *The Myth of Triumphalism: Rethinking President Reagan's Cold War Legacy* (Lexington: University Press of Kentucky, 2020), 27–34; Stanley Meisler, "Reagan Recants 'Evil Empire' Description," *Los Angeles Times*, June 1, 1988.

28. Fred R. Conrad, "Reagan, Entering Presidency Race, Calls for North American 'Accord,'" *New York Times*, November 14, 1979, A1; Alan Richman, "2 Nations Are Cool to Reagan Plan," *New York Times*, November 15, 1979, B16.

29. Benjamin Francis-Fallon, *The Rise of the Latino Vote: A History* (Cambridge, MA: Harvard University Press, 2019), 363.

30. Carl J. Bon Tempo, *Americans at the Gate: The United States and Refugees During the Cold War* (Princeton, NJ: Princeton University Press, 2008), chap. 7.

31. "Reagan Remarks at Naturalization Ceremonies for New United States Citizens in Detroit, Michigan," Ronald Reagan Presidential Library and Museum, October 1, 1984, www.reaganlibrary.gov/archives/speech/remarks-naturalization-ceremonies-new-united-states-citizens-detroit-michigan-0.

32. Bill McAllister, "HUD's 'Stealth Secretary,'" *Washington Post*, January 24, 1987, A1.

33. Rigueur, *Loneliness of the Black Republican*, 269; Francis-Fallon, *The Rise of the Latino Vote*, 365; Marisa Chappell, "Reagan's 'Gender Gap' and the Limits of Free Market Feminism," *Journal of Policy History* 24, no. 1 (January 2012): 115–134.

34. Doug Rossinow, *The Reagan Era: A History of the 1980s* (New York: Columbia University Press, 2015), 91–93.

35. Rossinow, *The Reagan Era*, 52.

36. Dan Jacobson, "Stockman Says Reaganism Lacks 'Intellectual Content,'" August 23, 1986, 9.

CHAPTER 2: THE APOSTATE

1. Margaret Garrard Warner, "Bush Battles the 'Wimp Factor,'" *Newsweek*, October 19, 1987.

2. Viguerie quoted in Daniel K. Williams, *God's Own Party: The Making of the Christian Right* (New York: Oxford University Press, 2010), 197; "Has Reagan Deserted the Conservatives?," *Conservative Digest*, July 1982.

3. Williams, *God's Own Party*, 200–202; Witcher, *Getting Right with Reagan*, 76–81.

4. "Whip of a Different Stripe," *Christian Science Monitor*, March 24, 1989, 2.

5. Witcher, *Getting Right with Reagan*, 136.

6. Sidney Blumenthal, "The Politics of Resentment," *Washington Post*, February 1, 1987.

7. Pat Buchanan, "A Budget Summit Is Long Overdue, Mr. President," *Human Events*, August 6, 1988, 17, 22; *Wall Street Journal* quoted in Witcher, *Getting Right with Reagan*, 161; Pat Buchanan, "The Reagan Administration and the Politics of Placation," *Human Events*, June 5, 1982, 4, 6.

8. Buchanan, "How History Passed Us By," *National Review*, September 16, 1988, 34–35.

9. Thomas B. Edsall, "Robertson Takes Half Step into the Presidential Arena," *Washington Post*, September 9, 1986, A1; Dudley Clendinen, "The Electoral Evangelism of Pat Robertson," *New York Times*, September 21, 1986, E4.

10. On Pat Robertson's early career, see Alec Foege, *The Empire God Built: Inside Pat Robertson's Media Machine* (New York: Wiley & Sons, 1996); Pat Robertson, *Shout It from the Housetops!* (Plainfield, NJ: Logos International, 1972).

11. Foege, *Empire God Built*, 88–90.

12. Williams, *God's Own Party*, 161; Foege, *Empire God Built*, 101.

13. Williams, *God's Own Party*, 171.

14. Williams, *God's Own Party*, chap. 9.

15. "Robertson Announcement," C-SPAN, October 2, 1987, www.c-span.org/video/?3191-1/robertson-announcement.

16. John Ellement, "Tracking Robertson on AIDS," *Boston Globe*, December 26, 1987, 3; Cathleen Decker, "Robertson Tailors His Message to Audiences," *Los Angeles Times*, November 23, 1987, 6.

17. Sidney Blumenthal, "For the GOP's Moderates, a Time of Hope," *Washington Post*, October 12, 1988, D1.

18. John Robert Greene, *The Presidency of George H. W. Bush*, 2nd ed. (Lawrence: University Press of Kansas, 2015), 34–35.

19. Steven V. Roberts, "Bush Intensifies Debate on Pledge, Asking Why It So Upsets Dukakis," *New York Times*, April 25, 1988, A1; David Nyhan, "Bush, Quayle Take the Low Road," *Boston Globe*, September 18, 1988, 89.

20. Greene, *The Presidency of George H. W. Bush*, 45–47.

21. Wynton C. Hall, "Economically Speaking: George Bush and the Price of Perception," in *The Rhetorical Presidency of George H. W. Bush*, ed. Martin J. Medhurst (College Station: Texas A&M University Press, 2006), 171–196.

22. David Shribman, "GOP's Right Wing, Bitter over Bush's Triumph, Debates Whether to Support Him in November," *Wall Street Journal*, April 26, 1988, 72.

23. Greene, *The Presidency of George H. W. Bush*, 77.

24. Richard Bernstein, "The Rising Hegemony of the Politically Correct," *New York Times*, October 28, 1990, E1. Also see Andrew Hartman, *A War for the Soul of America: A History of the Culture Wars* (Chicago: University of Chicago Press, 2015), 242–243; Harold K. Bush Jr., "A Brief History of PC, with Annotated Bibliography," *American Studies International* 33, no. 1 (April 1995): 42–64.

25. William Neikirk, "Bush on Diversity," *Chicago Tribune*, May 12, 1991, C1; Maureen Dowd, "Bush Sees Threat to Flow of Ideas on U.S. Campuses," *New York Times*, May 5, 1991, 1.

26. Greene, *The Presidency of George H. W. Bush*, chap. 11.

27. Don Phillips and Tom Kenworthy, "Gingrich Elected House GOP Whip," *Washington Post*, March 23, 1989, A1; Rowland Evans and Robert Novak, "No Bush Revolution," *Washington Post*, March 1, 1989, A23.

28. Bob Woodward, "Debut of a Power Player," *Washington Post*, December 25, 2011, A1.

29. Woodward, "Debut of a Power Player."

30. Neal Devins, "Reagan Redux: Civil Rights Under Bush," *Notre Dame Law Review* 68 (1993): 955–1001; Roger Clegg, "A Brief Legislative History of the 1991 Civil Rights Act," *Louisiana Law Review* 54, no. 6 (July 1994): 1459–1471.

31. Ann Devroy, "President Signs Civil Rights Bill," *Washington Post*, November 22, 1991, A1.

32. See Hartman, *A War for the Soul of America*, chap. 6, esp. 190–198.

33. David Lauter, "Bush's Decisions Are Being Shaped by WWII Lessons," *Los Angeles Times*, August 19, 1990, A8; Robert Shogan, "Gulf War Rallies Conservatives Behind Bush," *Los Angeles Times*, February 13, 1991, A12.

34. Pat Robertson, *The New World Order* (Dallas, TX: Word Publishers, 1991).

35. Pat Buchanan, "Requiem for a Patriot," *American Conservative*, March 2011, 15; Ben Wildavsky, "Going Nativist?," *National Journal*, May 27, 1995, 1278.

36. E. J. Dionne Jr., "Conservatives Denounce President," *Washington Post*, January 8, 1991, A4; "Fortune Favors the Brave," *National Review*, December 16, 1991, 14–16.

CHAPTER 3: THE POPULISTS

1. For Buchanan campaign speech in Manchester, New Hampshire, see "New Hampshire Primary," C-SPAN, February 18, 1992, www.c-span.org/video/?24477-1/hampshire-primary.

2. Timothy Stanley, *The Crusader: The Life and Tumultuous Times of Pat Buchanan* (New York: Thomas Dunne Books, 2012), 171.

3. Steven A. Holmes, "Buchanan Knows Tricks of the Trade," *New York Times*, March 20, 1992, A22.

4. Joseph B. White, "Populist Billionaire's Feet of Clay," *Wall Street Journal*, May 21, 1990, A10.

5. Stanley, *The Crusader*, 32–38.

6. Hemmer, *Messengers of the Right*, 201–210.

7. Stanley, *The Crusader*, 11, 24–25.

8. Stanley, *The Crusader*, 60–64.

9. Steve Kornacki, *The Red and the Blue: The 1990s and the Birth of Political Tribalism* (New York: Ecco, 2018), 150; Michael O'Connor, *Ted Turner: A Biography* (Santa Barbara, CA: Greenwood, 2010), 131; Aljean Harmetz, "Cable TV, Buoyed by Popularity, Looks to Future," *New York Times*, May 4, 1982, C16.

10. John B. Judis, *William F. Buckley, Jr., Patron Saint of the Conservatives* (New York: Simon & Schuster, 1988), 290–293; Hemmer, *Messengers of the Right*, 223.

11. Sidney Blumenthal, "Pat Buchanan and the Great Right Hope," *Washington Post*, January 8, 1987, C1.

12. Pat Buchanan, *Right from the Beginning* (Boston: Little Brown, 1988), 4; John Carmody, "The TV Column," *Washington Post*, February 6, 1985, C9.

13. "President Reagan's Remarks at Pat Buchanan's Farewell Party on February 24, 1987," video posted to YouTube by Reagan Library, September 28, 2017, www.youtube.com/watch?v=zZQzRBO1s6s.

14. Stephen Chapman, "Pat Buchanan: An Enemy of Liberty," *Chicago Tribune*, December 12, 1991, 27.

15. Pat Buchanan, "Democracy Worship Has Emerged as the New Idolatry," *Times Leader* (Wilkes-Barre, PA), January 13, 1991, 5C.

16. E. J. Dionne Jr., "Buchanan Challenges Bush with 'America First' Call," *Washington Post*, December 11, 1991, A1.

17. Dionne, "Buchanan Challenges Bush with 'America First' Call."

18. Details of the press conference are from Sebastian Rotella, "Migrants Hear Buchanan Pitch a Tighter Border," *Los Angeles Times*, May 13, 1992, SDB1.

19. On Metzger's background, see Belew, *Bring the War Home*, 59–60.

20. John Dillin, "Buchanan Zeroes In on 'Illegals,'" *Christian Science Monitor*, May 15, 1992, 2; "Buchanan: Jail Those Who Stay Homeless," *Chicago Tribune*, December 24, 1991, NW4; Steven A. Holmes, "White House Hopes to Trip Buchanan on His Paper Trail," *New York Times*, March 1, 1992, 1.

21. John Harwood, "Buchanan Issues His Verdict on Los Angeles Riots," *Wall Street Journal*, May 5, 1992, A22.

22. Ronald J. Ostrow, "William Barr: A 'Caretaker' Attorney General Proves Agenda-Setting Conservative," *Los Angeles Times*, June 21, 1992, M3; Ronald Brownstein, "Buchanan Links Border Problem to Riots That Gripped Los Angeles," *Los Angeles Times*, May 14, 1992, A4.

23. Michael Zatarain, *David Duke: Evolution of a Klansman* (Gretna, LA: Pelican, 1990), 194–199.

24. Lawrence N. Powell, *Troubled Memory: Anne Levy, the Holocaust, and David Duke's Louisiana* (Chapel Hill: University of North Carolina Press, 2000), chap. 14.

25. Frances Frank Marcus, "Victorious Duke Spars with Republican Chairman," *Baltimore Sun*, February 20, 1989, 1A.

26. Pat Buchanan, "Old Klansman, New Republican," *News Leader* (Staunton, VA), March 9, 1989, A4.

27. Buchanan, "Old Klansman, New Republican."

28. Lally Weymouth, "Buchanan: Throwing a Hard Right at Bush," *Washington Post*, December 22, 1991, C1.

29. Buchanan even reached out to original members of the America First Committee to get their support. See Henry Regnery to Buchanan, October 16, 1991, Box 120, Folder B, Henry Regnery Papers, Hoover Institution, Palo Alto, California.

30. Stanley, *The Crusader*, 176–177; "Buchanan Campaign Rally," C-SPAN, February 29, 1992, www.c-span.org/video/?24755-1/buchanan -campaign-rally.

31. Stanley, *The Crusader*, 136–137.

32. William F. Buckley Jr., "In Search of Anti-Semitism," *National Review*, December 30, 1991, 20–62.

33. Jacob Weisberg, "The Heresies of Pat Buchanan," *New Republic*, October 22, 1990, 22–27; "Buchanan Campaign Speech," C-SPAN, May 13, 1992, www.c-span.org/video/?26086-1/buchanan-campaign-speech; Cadava, *Hispanic Republican*, 294–296.

34. Paul Richter, "Perot Seen as Freestyle Mr. Fixit," *Los Angeles Times*, May 15, 1992, A1.

35. Thomas B. Rosenstiel, "The Talk Is About New Media," *Los Angeles Times*, May 23, 1992, A1.

36. Peter Applebome, "Perot, the 'Simple' Billionaire, Says Voters Can Force His Presidential Bid," *New York Times*, March 29, 1992, 1.

37. Rosenstiel, "The Talk Is About New Media."

38. Ronald B. Rapoport and Walter J. Stone, *Three's a Crowd: The Dynamic of Third Parties, Ross Perot, and Republican Resurgence* (Ann Arbor: University of Michigan Press, 2008).

39. Ronald Brownstein, "Both Parties Favored Perot, Exit Poll Finds," *Los Angeles Times*, June 3, 1992, A1.

40. Joe Klein, "Rescue Fantasy," *New York*, May 18, 1992, 22–27.

41. Samuel Francis, *Beautiful Losers: Essays on the Failure of American Conservatism* (Columbia: University of Missouri, 1994), 60–78; Samuel Francis, "From Household to Nation," *Chronicles* (March 1996): 12–16; Pat Buchanan, "Hope from Mars," *Pittsburgh Post-Gazette*, March 7, 1994, B3.

42. E. J. Dionne Jr., "This Season's Political Mavericks See Perot's Rise as Validation," *Washington Post*, May 31, 1992, A16.

43. Doron P. Levin, "Billionaire in Texas Is Attracting Calls to Run, and $5 Donations," *New York Times*, March 7, 1992, 11; Rapoport and Stone, *Three's a Crowd*, 62.

CHAPTER 4: REAGAN'S HEIR

1. Lois Romano, "The Reliable Source," *Washington Post*, August 19, 1992, B3; Newt Gingrich, "Republican National Convention Address,"

C-SPAN, August 18, 1992, www.c-span.org/video/?31300-1/republican
-national-convention-address.

2. John B. Judis, "Voice from the Right," *Washington Post*, September 5,
1993, 2.

3. Henry Allen, "Media to the Left! Media to the Right! Rush Limbaugh,
on the Republicans' Wavelength," *Washington Post*, August 20, 1992, C1.

4. David Zizzo, "Radio Talk Show Host Finds Spotlight," *Daily Oklaho-
man*, August 19, 1992, 121.

5. Romano, "The Reliable Source."

6. "Sad: George Will Hopes Hillary Landslide Will Emancipate GOP
from Talk Radio," *The Rush Limbaugh Show*, November 2, 2016, www
.rushlimbaugh.com/daily/2016/11/02/sad_george_will_hopes_hillary
_landslide_will_emancipate_gop_from_talk_radio.

7. Ed Bark, "Backstage Power," *Chicago Tribune*, April 29, 1992, E4.

8. "EIB Sparks Conservatism Debate," *The Rush Limbaugh Show*, January 17, 2008, www.rushlimbaugh.com/daily/2008/01/17/eib_sparks
_conservatism_debate; Stanley, *The Crusader*, 80.

9. See Bob Grant's *Let's Be Heard* (New York: Pocket Books, 1996);
Philip Gourevitch, "Dial Hate," *New York*, October 24, 1994, 28–34; Randy
Bobbitt, *Us Against Them: The Political Culture of Talk Radio* (Lanham, MD:
Lexington Books, 2010), 42–45.

10. Zev Chafets, *Rush Limbaugh: An Army of One* (New York: Sentinel,
2010), 36–37.

11. Chafets, *Rush Limbaugh*, 41.

12. Chafets, *Rush Limbaugh*, 41.

13. Roger Catlin, "The Talk of Radio," *Hartford Courant*, March 8,
1991, C1.

14. Brian Rosenwald, *Talk Radio's America: How an Industry Took Over
a Political Party That Took Over the United States* (Cambridge, MA: Harvard
University Press, 2019), 26–27; Chafets, *Rush Limbaugh*, 69.

15. Allen, "Media to the Left!"

16. Hemmer, *Messengers of the Right*, 261.

17. David Montgomery, "Room with a View," *Washington Post*, September 23, 1993, D1; Nita Lelyveld, "Dining with 'Dittoheads,'" *Chicago Tribune*, October 5, 1993, 2.

18. Chafets, *Rush Limbaugh*, 57, 64.

19. James Fallows, "Talent on Loan from the GOP," *The Atlantic*, May
1994, 133–138.

20. Lloyd Grove, "The Image Shaker," *Washington Post,* June 20, 1988, B1.

21. Rosenwald, *Talk Radio's America,* 42–43; "Barbara Bush: A Grand Old Dame She Was," *The Rush Limbaugh Show,* April 18, 2018, www .rushlimbaugh.com/daily/2018/04/18/barbara-bush-grand-old-dame.

22. Roland Evans and Robert Novak, "Bush's Problem," *Washington Post,* May 20, 1992.

23. Chafets, *Rush Limbaugh,* 58.

24. Ernest Leiser, "The Little Network That Could," *New York Times,* March 30, 1988, 30–38; Charles L. Ponce de Leon, *That's the Way It Is: A History of Television News in America* (Chicago: University of Chicago Press, 2015), 188. Pat Buchanan, who came on as a guest when working for the Reagan administration, guest-hosted during his stretches at the network.

25. Brownell, *Showbiz Politics,* 225–229.

26. Joan Didion, "Eye on the Prize," *New York Review of Books,* September 24, 1992, 57–66.

27. Larry King, *Anything Goes! What I Learned from Pundits, Politicians, and Presidents* (New York: Warner, 2000).

28. "Quayle Campaign Appearance," *The Rush Limbaugh Show,* recorded for C-SPAN, July 7, 1992, www.c-span.org/video/?27000-1/quayle -campaign-appearance; Michael Wines, "Bush Says Economy Not as Bad as People Think," *New York Times,* September 22, 1992, A25; James Gerstenzang, "Bush Hits Hard on Clinton's Draft Record," *Los Angeles Times,* September 22, 1992, A1.

29. Charles Walston, "Center's Limo Offers Voters a Taste of Gingrich Lifestyle," *Atlanta Constitution,* October 24, 1992, 26.

30. Rosenstiel, "The Talk Is About New Media."

31. Simon Maloy, "Limbaugh's Unrivaled Influence on Republican Politics," Media Matters for America, March 13, 2012, www.mediamatters .org/rush-limbaugh/limbaughs-unrivaled-influence-republican-politics. The Reagan letter was dated December 11, 1992.

32. James Bowman, "The Leader of the Opposition," *National Review,* September 6, 1993, 44–52.

33. Chafets, *Rush Limbaugh,* 54–56; "Are Liberal Vulnerabilities Now Apparent?," Hoover Institution Archives, September 16, 1992, https://digital collections.hoover.org/objects/7134.

34. Paul D. Colford, "Talk's Cheap in the City," *Newsday,* September 1, 1993, 89.

CHAPTER 5: THE OTHER LEADER OF THE OPPOSITION

1. Steven A. Holmes, "True Believers Rejoice in Babylon," *New York Times,* January 5, 1995, A1.

2. "What Conservatives Think About Ronald Reagan," *Policy Review* (winter 1984): 16.

3. Elizabeth Williamson, "Gingrich's College Records Show Professor Hatching Big Plans," *Wall Street Journal,* January 18, 2012, A6.

4. "Not with a Bang," *National Review,* November 30, 1992, 14.

5. Kornacki, *Red and the Blue,* 215.

6. Rowland Evans and Robert Novak, "From Blue Jeans to Blue Suits," *Washington Post,* January 25, 1993, A17; Rosenwald, *Talk Radio's America,* 57–59.

7. Marian Meyers, "Defining Homosexuality: News Coverage of the 'Repeal the Ban' Controversy," *Discourse & Society* 5, no. 3 (1994): 321–344.

8. Jack Anderson and Michael Binstein, "Republicans for Perot," *Washington Post,* June 27, 1993, C7; Kornacki, *Red and the Blue,* 169; Rapoport and Stone, *Three's a Crowd,* 64–67.

9. Richard Blow, "The Clinton Plan to Control Perot," *Mother Jones* (January/February 1994): 22–25.

10. Gerald F. Seib, "NAFTA Vote Holds a Political Test for the GOP, Too," *Wall Street Journal,* November 3, 1993, A24.

11. Jill Dutt and Susan Page, "Trading Arguments," *Newsday,* November 10, 1993, 1; Gwen Ifill, "Clinton Extends an Unusual Offer to Republicans on the Pact," *New York Times,* November 13, 1993, A10.

12. Rapoport and Stone, *Three's a Crowd,* 148–149.

13. Peter H. Stone, "Man with a Message," *National Journal,* April 19, 1997.

14. Thomas B. Rosenstiel, "Gingrich's Plan for Power 10 Years in the Making," *Los Angeles Times,* December 19, 1994, A1.

15. Newt Gingrich, "Language: A Key Mechanism of Control," GOPAC, 1990; Michael Oreskes, "For G.O.P. Arsenal, 133 Words to Fire," *New York Times,* September 9, 1990, A30; Stone, "Man with a Message."

16. Kevin Merida and Thomas B. Edsall, "Perot's Ex-Pollster in the Limelight at GOP Retreat," *Washington Post,* March 1, 1993, A7.

17. Steven M. Gillon, *The Pact: Bill Clinton, Newt Gingrich, and the Rivalry That Defined a Generation* (New York: Oxford University Press, 2008), 123–135.

18. Rapoport and Stone, *Three's a Crowd*, 152.

19. Frank I. Luntz, *Words That Work: It's Not What You Say, It's What People Hear* (New York: Hyperion, 2007), 151.

20. George F. Bishop, *The Illusion of Public Opinion: Fact and Artifact in American Public Opinion Polls* (Lanham, MD: Rowman & Littlefield, 2005), 144–146; Michael Traugott and Elizabeth C. Powers, "Did Public Opinion Support the Contract with America?," in *Election Polls, the News Media, and Democracy*, ed. Paul J. Lavrakas (New York: Chatham House, 2000), 93–110.

21. Richard Morin, "Famous for 15 Minutes," *Washington Post*, August 28, 2000.

22. Traugott and Powers, "Did Public Opinion Support the Contract with America?," 106; "Pollster Admits Fudging Popularity of 'Contract,'" *Chicago Tribune*, November 12, 1995, 15; Stone, "Man with a Message."

23. Rapoport and Stone, *Three's a Crowd*, 150–163.

24. Rosenwald, *Talk Radio's America*, 74–75; Robin Toner, "Election Jitters in Limbaughland," *New York Times*, November 3, 1994, A29.

25. Charles Watson, "Center's Limo Offers Voters a Taste of Gingrich Lifestyle," *Atlanta Constitution*, October 24, 1992, 26.

26. Hemmer, *Messengers of the Right*, 113–126.

27. Hemmer, *Messengers of the Right*, 258–260.

28. Toner, "Election Jitters in Limbaughland."

29. Zelizer, *Burning Down the House*.

30. Christopher Drew, "Religious Right Phone Banks Put Lobby Reform on Hold," *Chicago Tribune*, October 7, 1994, 1.

31. John Harwood and Phil Kuntz, "Gingrich Tactic to Derail Lobbying Reform Shows His Skill at Rousing Conservative Opinion Makers," *Wall Street Journal*, October 5, 1994, A18; Rosenwald, *Talk Radio's America*, 64–67.

32. Maureen Dowd, "Vengeful Glee (and Sweetness) at Gingrich's Victory Party," *New York Times*, November 9, 1994, B2.

33. Linda Killian, *The Freshmen: What Happened to the Republican Revolution?* (Boulder, CO: Westview Press, 1998), 25–26; Kevin Merida and Kenneth J. Cooper, "New Heritage Emerges at Orientation," *Washington Post*, December 10, 1994. There were rumors that one or two of the Democrats had registered but no evidence that they attended.

34. Melissa Healy, "Lunch Opens Briefing for D.C. Neophytes," *Los Angeles Times*, December 9, 1994, A46.

35. Katharine Q. Seelye, "Republicans Get a Pep Talk from Rush Limbaugh," December 12, 1994, A16; "Republican Freshman Orientation," C-SPAN, December 10, 1994, www.c-span.org/video/?62105-1/republican-freshmen-orientation.

36. Kornacki, *Red and the Blue*, 105.

37. Killian, *The Freshmen*, 14; "Republican Freshman Orientation," C-SPAN; Jim Finnegan, "Ralph the Tentmaker. Reply to Critics. Ross Should Reconsider," *Manchester Union-Leader*, December 7, 1992.

38. Gillon, *The Pact*, 117; "School Prayer Tactics," *New York Times*, November 27, 1994, E10.

39. Richard E. Cohen and Graeme Browning, "Team Gingrich," *National Journal*, January 14, 1995, 66; Catherine S. Manegold, "In Loud Political Week, Talk Radio Makes Itself Heard," *New York Times*, January 30, 1995, A13.

40. Thomas F. Schaller, *The Stronghold: How Republicans Captured Congress but Surrendered the White House* (New Haven, CT: Yale University Press, 2015), 100.

CHAPTER 6: ANGRY WHITE MEN—AND WOMEN

1. Belew, *Bring the War Home*, 196–200.

2. Adam Winkler, *Gunfight: The Battle Over the Right to Bear Arms in America* (New York: Norton, 2011), 84.

3. Timothy Egan, "Idaho Freshman Embodies G.O.P.'s Hope and Fear in '96," *New York Times*, January 15, 1996, A1.

4. "Fire Breathers," *American Enterprise*, January 1996, 43–47; Elinor Burkett, *The Right Women: A Journey Through the Heart of Conservative America* (New York: Scribner, 1998), 179.

5. Egan, "Idaho Freshman Embodies G.O.P.'s Hope and Fear in '96."

6. Betsy Z. Russell, "Chenoweth Weighs in on Diversity," *Spokesman-Review* (Spokane, WA), May 10, 1997, A1.

7. Craig Welch, "Chenoweth Unwavering in Her Views Despite Financing Scandals, National Ridicule, She Won't Swerve from Her Conservative Course," *Spokesman-Review* (Spokane, WA), October 20, 1996, A1.

8. Welch, "Chenoweth Unwavering in Her Views."

9. Quoted in James R. Skillen, *This Land Is My Land: Rebellion in the West* (New York: Oxford University Press, 2020), 64.

10. On the "War on the West," see Skillen, *This Land Is My Land,* chap. 6.

11. Burkett, *The Right Women,* 179–180.

12. Burkett, *The Right Women,* 16.

13. Burkett, *The Right Women,* 179; Sidney Blumenthal, "Her Own Private Idaho," *New Yorker,* July 10, 1995, 27–33.

14. Jeanne Brokaw, "The Hand That Rocks the Cradle," *Mother Jones* (September–October 1996): 56; Hanna Rosin, "Invasion of the Church Ladies," *New Republic,* April 24, 1995, 20; Bob Baker, "What's the Rush?," *Los Angeles Times,* January 20, 1991.

15. Rosin, "Invasion of the Church Ladies," 20; Welch, "Chenoweth Unwavering in Her Views."

16. Burkett, *The Right Women,* 181–182.

17. Winkler, *Gunfight,* 71.

18. On the transformation of the NRA, see Winkler, *Gunfight*; Frank Smyth, *The NRA: The Unauthorized History* (New York: Flatiron Books, 2020); Jill Lepore, "Battleground America," *New Yorker,* April 16, 2021, 38–47.

19. Winkler, *Gunfight,* 25; Michele Gorman, "What President Ronald Reagan Told the NRA in 1983," *Newsweek,* April 27, 2017, www.newsweek.com/president-ronald-reagan-nra-speech-1983-590529.

20. Ronald Reagan, "Why I'm for the Brady Bill," *New York Times,* March 29, 1991, A23; William J. Eaton and Karen Tumulty, "Senate Called Back as GOP Keeps Blocking Brady Bill," *Los Angeles Times,* November 24, 1993, A1; Sarah Brady, "What Is Congress Afraid Of?," *Washington Post,* May 9, 1993, C7.

21. Winkler, *Gunfight,* 82.

22. John J. Fialka, "NRA Support for House GOP Freshmen Pays Off but Lawmakers Worry About Reformer Image," *Wall Street Journal,* June 20, 1995, A20.

23. Fialka, "NRA Support for House GOP Freshmen Pays Off."

24. Ronald G. Shafer, "The Wall Street Journal/NBC News Poll," *Wall Street Journal,* June 9, 1995, A1.

25. Mary Lynn F. Jones, "Looking for Slack on Gun Control," *National Journal,* July 19, 1997; Tony Semerad, "Utah Women for Gun Control? Not This Group," *Salt Lake Tribune,* September 5, 1994, A1; Rebecca Walsh, "A Rally for Right to Bear Arms," *Salt Lake Tribune,* January 28, 1996, B3.

26. Rosin, "Invasion of the Church Ladies."

27. James Ridgeway, "The Posse Goes to Washington," *Village Voice*, May 23, 1995, 17; Timothy Egan, "Trying to Explain Contacts with Paramilitary Groups," *New York Times*, May 2, 1995, A19.

28. Blumenthal, "Her Own Private Idaho." 28.

29. Blumenthal, "Her Own Private Idaho," 28; Egan, "Idaho Freshman Embodies G.O.P.'s Hope and Fear in '96."

30. Blumenthal, "Her Own Private Idaho," 32; Kim Murphy, "GOP's Hard Right Flank Under Attack in Idaho House Race," *Los Angeles Times*, November 1, 1996, A5; John Warrick, "Muddying the Waters," *Washington Post*, July 3, 1997, A17.

31. "Republican Candidate Won't Back Off 'White Males' Remark," *Spokesman-Review* (Spokane, WA), September 7, 1994, 14; Eric Sorensen, "Chenoweth Repudiates Racist Paper That Praised Her," *Spokesman-Review* (Spokane, WA), February 28, 1995, 17.

32. Egan, "Idaho Freshman Embodies G.O.P.'s Hope and Fear in '96."

33. Ridgeway, "The Posse Goes to Washington."

34. "NRA Defends Vitriol Toward Federal Agents," *Spokesman-Review* (Spokane, WA), May 1, 1995; "N.R.A. Official Regrets Wording in Letter," *New York Times*, May 18, 1995, A16; John Mintz, "NRA Rejects Links to Militias While Vowing to Defeat Clinton," *Washington Post*, May 21, 1995, A3.

35. Todd S. Purdum, "Shifting Debate to the Political Climate, Clinton Condemns 'Promoters of Paranoia,'" *New York Times*, April 25, 1995, A19.

36. Eleanor Randolph, "Rush and GOP Elite: Getting Too Cozy?," *Los Angeles Times*, December 29, 1995, 1.

37. Randolph, "Rush and GOP Elite."

38. Dale Russakoff, "Fax Networks Link Outposts of Anger," *Washington Post*, August 20, 1995, A1.

39. John Harwood, "Equal Hostility: Women Are Angry at Government, Too," *Wall Street Journal*, May 12, 1995, A1.

40. Russakoff, "Fax Networks Link Outposts of Anger."

CHAPTER 7: RACE SELLS

1. Peter Brimelow, "Time to Rethink Immigration?," *National Review*, June 22, 1992, 30–46.

2. Peter Brimelow, *Alien Nation: Common Sense About American Immigration Reform* (New York: Random House, 1995), 10.

3. Brimelow, *Alien Nation*, 19.

4. "Booknotes: *Alien Nation*," C-SPAN, May 18, 1995, www.c-span.org /video/?65259-1/alien-nation.

5. Steven J. Roberts, "To Be or Not to Be a Protest Candidate," *New York Times*, January 19, 1987, A12.

6. Jerry Adler with Steven Waldman, "Sweet Land of Liberties," *Newsweek*, July 9, 1995, 18; David Rogers, "Maverick's Message: Buchanan Campaign Rides into Arizona with a Pledge to Defend Frontier," *Wall Street Journal*, February 23, 1996, A14; "Buchanan Calls for Tougher Border Control," *Washington Post*, May 9, 1995, A15.

7. Andrew Wroe, *The Republican Party and Immigration Politics: From Proposition 187 to George W. Bush* (New York: Palgrave Macmillan, 2008), 34.

8. Wroe, *Republican Party and Immigration Politics*, 43.

9. Erika Lee, *America for Americans: A History of Xenophobia in the United States* (New York: Basic Books, 2019), 266–268.

10. Daniel HoSang, *Racial Propositions and the Making of Postwar California* (Berkeley: University of California Press, 2010), chap. 6.

11. Lee, *America for Americans*, 271–272; HoSang, *Racial Propositions*, 172–173.

12. Lee, *America for Americans*, 286.

13. William Bennett and Jack Kemp, "The Fortress Party?," *Wall Street Journal*, October 21, 1994, A14; Dan Balz, Bill McAllister, and Edward Walsh, "2 Conservatives Call Anti-immigration Measure 'Bad Policy,'" *Washington Post*, October 20, 1994, A24.

14. Gebe Martinez, "Kemp Defends His Criticism of Immigration Initiative," *Los Angeles Times*, October 20, 1994, 1; Greg Krikorian and Dave Lesher, "Huffington Declares Support for Prop. 187," *Los Angeles Times*, October 21, 1994, 1.

15. Richard Herrnstein and Charles Murray, *The Bell Curve: Intelligence and Class Structure in American Life* (New York: Simon & Schuster, 1994).

16. Richard Herrnstein, *I.Q. in the Meritocracy* (Boston: Little, Brown, 1973); John Aloysius Farrell, "Files Reveal Buchanan's Views in the '70s," *Boston Globe*, January 4, 1992, 1, 8.

17. Tim Naftali, "Ronald Reagan's Long-Hidden Racist Conversation with Richard Nixon," *The Atlantic*, July 30, 2019, www.theatlantic.com/ideas /archive/2019/07/ronald-reagans-racist-conversation-richard-nixon /595102; John Hoberman and Tim Naftali, "What Daniel Patrick Moyni-

han Actually Thought About Race," *The Atlantic*, September 9, 2019, www
.theatlantic.com/letters/archive/2019/09/daniel-patrick-moynihans-real
-views-race/595861.

18. Charles A. Murray, *Losing Ground: American Social Policy, 1950–1980* (New York: Basic Books, 1984).

19. Dinesh D'Souza, *The End of Racism: Principles for a Multiracial Society* (New York: Free Press, 1995), 431–476.

20. D'Souza, *The End of Racism*, 97.

21. D'Souza, *The End of Racism*, 16–17, 245–288.

22. Arthur M. Schlesinger Jr., *The Disuniting of America: Reflections on a Multicultural Society* (Knoxville, TN: Whittle Books, 1991); Hartman, *A War for the Soul of America*, 263–265.

23. Dinesh D'Souza, *Illiberal Education: The Politics of Race and Sex on Campus* (New York: Free Press, 1991).

24. D'Souza, *The End of Racism*, viii.

25. Jason DeParle, "Daring Research or 'Social Science Pornography'?," *New York Times Magazine*, October 9, 1994, 48–53, 62, 70–71, 74, 78–79.

26. Quoted in DeParle, "Daring Research or 'Social Science Pornography'?," 49.

27. DeParle, "Daring Research or 'Social Science Pornography'?," 48–53, 62, 70–71, 74, 78–79.

28. Charles Lane, "The Tainted Sources of 'The Bell Curve,'" *New York Review of Books*, December 1, 1994, 14–17.

29. "Race & I.Q.," *New Republic*, October 31, 1994; "The Issue," *New Republic*, October 31, 1994, 9.

30. "The Issue," *New Republic*.

31. William Raspberry, "The Story of 'Black Is Boring,'" *Washington Post*, June 14, 1982, A17; Dudley Clendinen, "Dartmouth Review: Right-Wing Voice in Liberal Wilderness," *Chicago Tribune*, October 21, 1981, C1; Sidney Blumenthal, "Conservatives Debate Style, Tactics After Dartmouth Incident," *Washington Post*, February 6, 1986, A3.

32. Associated Press, "Dartmouth Group in Privacy Battle," *New York Times*, July 16, 1984, A21.

33. James Panero and Stefan Beck, eds., *The Dartmouth Review Pleads Innocent: Twenty-Five Years of Being Threatened, Impugned, Vandalized, Sued, Suspended, and Bitten at the Ivy League's Most Controversial Conservative Newspaper* (Wilmington, DE: ISI Books, 2006), 30–31.

34. Keeney Jones, "Dis Sho' Ain't No Jive, Bro," *Dartmouth Review*, March 15, 1982.

35. Michael Birkner, "Much Ado About the Review," *Boston Globe*, October 16, 1983, 14.

36. Dinesh D'Souza, "Shanty Raids at Dartmouth," *Policy Review* (spring 1986): 28–34; Panero and Beck, *Dartmouth Review Pleads Innocent*, 325–326.

37. William Raspberry, "A De Facto Defense of Racism," *Washington Post*, September 18, 1995, A19.

38. Deborah Toler, "The Right's 'Race Desk,'" *Fairness & Accuracy in Reporting*, March 1, 1999, https://fair.org/extra/the-right8217s-race-desk.

CHAPTER 8: POLITICALLY INCORRECT

1. James Atlas, "Counterculture," *New York Times Magazine*, February 12, 1995, 32; Paul M. Barrett, "A New Wave of Counterfeminists Is Providing Conservatism with a Sophisticated Female Face," *Wall Street Journal*, October 13, 1995, A16.

2. Paul Farhi, "House Approves Cable TV Measure," *Washington Post*, July 24, 1992, F1.

3. Associated Press, "Dartmouth Group in Privacy Battle," *New York Times*, July 16, 1984, A21; Laura Ingraham, "Test of Devotion," *Washington Post*, February 23, 1997, C1.

4. Ingraham, "Test of Devotion."

5. Though rumored to be engaged, a detail mentioned in a 1991 *Washington Post* piece, both later denied it. Charles Truehart, "Big Man Off Campus," *Washington Post*, April 16, 1991, B1; Stu Bykofsky, "Laura Ingraham, Right on the Radio," *Philadelphia Inquirer*, September 20, 2007, 6; Bill Powell, "How Fox News' Laura Ingraham Used Trump to Become a Conservative Rockstar," *Newsweek*, November 24, 2017.

6. Barbara Ruth Spindel, "'Human Beings First, Women Second': Antifeminism and the Independent Women's Forum" (PhD diss., University of Minnesota, 2004), 67.

7. Spindel, "'Human Beings First, Women Second,'" 130.

8. Jennifer Gonneman, "Angry White Women: A Right-Wing Women's Group Sets Out to Crush Feminism," *Village Voice*, July 11, 1995, 17; Sam Tanenhaus, "Damsels in Dissent," *Vanity Fair*, November 1999, 152;

"Independent Women," *60 Minutes*, August 11, 1996; "New Breed of GOP Women Difficult to Stereotype," *All Things Considered*, June 19, 1996.

9. Spindel, "'Human Beings First, Women Second,'" 160; Marjorie Williams, "Laura, Get Your Gun," *Vanity Fair*, January 1997, 44–46.

10. Laura Ingraham, "How the 'Gender Gap' Is Driving Dole Girl Crazy," *Washington Post*, August 4, 1996, C1.

11. Laura Ingraham, "Enter, Women," *New York Times*, April 19, 1995, A23.

12. Laura Ingraham, "Why Feminists Should Be Trigger Happy," *Wall Street Journal*, May 13, 1996, A20.

13. Ronald J. Hansen, "Skeet Shooters Target Law on Abuse," *Washington Times*, September 14, 1997, 9; Hanna Rosin, "Radical Chicks," *New Republic*, October 13, 1997, 16–18.

14. Spindel, "'Human Beings First, Women Second,'" 169.

15. Tanenhaus, "Damsels in Dissent."

16. David Daley, "Ann Coulter: Light's All Shining on Her," *Hartford Courant*, June 25, 1999, F1; Eric Alterman, "Media Circus," *Salon*, October 21, 1997.

17. Tad Friend, "It's About, You Know, Opinions and Stuff," *New York Times Magazine*, June 15, 1997, 34.

18. Jeffrey Preiss Jones, "Talking Politics in Post-network Television: The Case of Politically Incorrect" (PhD diss., University of Texas, Austin, 1999), 146.

19. Bill Carter, "Lots of Political Humor, and No Morton Kondrake," *New York Times*, February 27, 1994, H33.

20. Rick Du Brow, "Politics and Punch Lines," *Los Angeles Times*, July 6, 1992, B8.

21. Carter, "Lots of Political Humor."

22. Carter, "Lots of Political Humor."

23. Quoted in Jones, "Talking Politics in Post-network Television," 192.

24. Jones, "Talking Politics in Post-network Television," 192; Lawrie Mifflin, "Mix Comedy and Politics with Strange Bedfellows, Then Hope for Sparks," *New York Times*, February 4, 1997, C11.

25. Hugh Hart, "Bill Maher Makes Pitch for More Substance on TV," *Chicago Tribune*, August 10, 1995, F4.

26. Caryn James, "Giggles Intact, Political Satire Is Back on TV," *New York Times*, February 22, 1996, C13.

27. Mifflin, "Mix Comedy and Politics with Strange Bedfellows."

28. Aaron Barnhart, "Filling the 'Politically Incorrect' Gap," *New York Times*, November 11, 1996, D9.

29. Lewis Beale, "Balancing Its Ticket," *New York Daily News*, July 25, 1993, 31.

30. Gabriel Sherman, *The Loudest Voice in the Room: How the Brilliant, Bombastic Roger Ailes Built Fox News—and Divided a Country* (New York: Random House, 2014), 149–151; Cheryl Lavin, "'Go Do It!': Columnist E. Jean Carroll Takes Her Advice to Heart," *Chicago Tribune*, March 14, 1996, E1.

31. Sherman, *Loudest Voice*, 141–157.

32. Jon Meacham, "Surfing on Newt's Network," *Newsweek*, January 29, 1995, 36.

33. Tom Kuntz, "You Want Your Newt TV? Whether You Do or You Don't, It's Here," *New York Times*, January 8, 1995, E7; Marc Fisher, "Babes in the Pundits' Chairs," *Washington Post*, December 9, 1994, D1.

34. Steve Erickson, "Onward Christian Soldiers," *Rolling Stone*, March 7, 1995, 40–45.

35. Lawrence Morahan, "Conservative Icon Weyrich Warns 'Moral Minority' Still Dwindling," CNSNews.com, January 14, 2002.

36. Sherman, *Loudest Voice*, 206–208.

37. Sherman, *Loudest Voice*, 167–170.

38. Friend, "It's About, You Know, Opinions and Stuff."

39. Friend, "It's About, You Know, Opinions and Stuff."

40. Peter Johnson, "MSNBC Hasn't Plugged into Big Audience Yet," *USA Today*, June 4, 1997, D3; Friend, "It's About, You Know, Opinions and Stuff."

41. Ponce de Leon, *That's the Way It Is*, 186–189.

42. Sherman, *Loudest Voice*, 175.

43. Sherman, *Loudest Voice*, 207–209.

44. Sherman, *Loudest Voice*, 182–183, 223–225.

CHAPTER 9: PITCHFORK PAT

1. Richard L. Berke, "A New Quest by Buchanan for President," *New York Times*, March 21, 1995, A16.

2. On Bill Clinton's conservative politics, see Kornacki, *Red and the Blue*, and Gillon, *The Pact*.

3. James P. Pinkerton, "Powell In, Buchanan Out of the GOP?," *Los Angeles Times*, November 3, 1994, B13; Lloyd Grove, "The GOP's General Session," *Washington Post*, October 25, 1995, B1; Francis X. Clines, "Variation on a War Game: How Powell Arrived at No," *New York Times*, November 12, 1995, 1.

4. James M. Perry, "Phil Gramm's Appeal with Conservative Voters Is Sometimes Undercut by Image of Abrasiveness," *Wall Street Journal*, December 14, 1995, A16; Sam Howe Verhovek, "Phil Gramm's Offbeat Charm as a Persistent Conservative," *New York Times*, December 27, 1995.

5. Michael A. Hiltzik and Sam Fulwood III, "Dole Gets Gramm Backing in Bid for Conservative Vote," *Los Angeles Times*, February 19, 1996, A18.

6. Pat Buchanan, "What Will America Be in 2050?," *Los Angeles Times*, October 28, 1994, 15.

7. David Corn, "A Potent Trinity—God, Country and Me," *The Nation*, June 26, 1995, 913–916; Maureen Dowd, "Buchanan's Alternative: Not Kinder or Gentler," *New York Times*, January 15, 1992, A1.

8. David S. Broder, "Taking Buchanan Seriously," *Washington Post*, August 20, 1995, C7.

9. David S. Broder, "Don't Forget Buchanan," *Washington Post*, February 11, 1996, C7; Eleanor Randolph, "Buchanan Is the Press' Favorite Son—and Its Whipping Boy," *Los Angeles Times*, February 28, 1996, 5.

10. Thomas B. Edsall, "Buchanan Hoping to Be GOP's Right Knight," *Washington Post*, July 9, 1995, A4.

11. Edsall, "Buchanan Hoping to be GOP's Right Knight."

12. Dan Balz, "Buchanan and Forbes: Odd Couple of the GOP Field," *Washington Post*, January 9, 1996, A1.

13. Robert Shogan, "Buchanan Attack Upstages Dole at Perot Conference," *Los Angeles Times*, August 13, 1995, A1.

14. "Buchanan Calls for Tougher Border Control," *Washington Post*, May 9, 1995, A15.

15. On Tillman, see Stephen David Kantrowitz, *Ben Tillman and the Reconstruction of White Supremacy* (Chapel Hill: University of North Carolina Press, 2000).

16. Shogan, "Buchanan Attack Upstages Dole at Perot Conference"; Sue Anne Pressley, "Arizona Hails Dual Message of Buchanan," *Washington Post*, February 24, 1996, A10.

17. Rogers Worthington, "Far Right Populists Like Buchanan," *Chicago Tribune*, September 18, 1995, 11; Jonathan Freedland, "Buchanan Aide Forced Out over Racism Charge," *Guardian*, February 16, 1996, 2; "Mr. Buchanan Stumbles," *New York Times*, February 17, 1996, 22.

18. Richard A. Serrano, "Militias See Buchanan as Their Candidate," *Los Angeles Times*, February 22, 1996, A11.

19. Dave Lesher and Sam Fulwood III, "Anti-Buchanan Rhetoric Sets Off Tremors in GOP," *Los Angeles Times*, February 23, 1996, A1.

20. Lloyd Grove, "Buchanan's Two-Pats System," *Washington Post*, March 1, 1996, D1.

21. Elizabeth Shogren, "Buchanan Offers Variations on a Theme," *Los Angeles Times*, March 9, 1996, A16.

22. Lisa Anderson, "Buchanan Declares Cease-Fire—for the Time Being," *Chicago Tribune*, August 12, 1996, 14.

23. Reed's early life is detailed in Nina J. Easton, *Gang of Five: Leaders at the Center of the Conservative Crusade* (New York: Simon & Schuster, 2000).

24. Easton, *Gang of Five*, 150–151.

25. Thomas Edsall, "Christian Political Soldier Helps Revive Movement," *Washington Post*, September 10, 1993, A4.

26. Easton, *Gang of Five*, 207–208.

27. Foege, *Empire God Built*, 125–131.

28. Edsall, "Christian Political Soldier Helps Revive Movement."

29. Ralph E. Reed, "Casting a Wider Net," *Policy Review* (summer 1993): 31–35.

30. Thomas W. Waldron, "Christian Coalition Unveils Social 'Contract with the American Family,'" *Baltimore Sun*, May 18, 1995, 13A.

31. Richard L. Berke, "Some Republicans Hoping for a Way to Stop Buchanan," *New York Times*, February 22, 1996, A1.

32. Elizabeth Drew, *Showdown: The Struggle Between the Gingrich Congress and the Clinton White House* (New York: Simon & Schuster, 1996), 93.

33. Maria L. La Ganga, "Dole Backs Prop. 187 Limits in Valley Stop," *Los Angeles Times*, June 20, 1996, A1; Patrick J. McDonnell, "California's Immigration Hot Button Awaits GOP Candidates," *Los Angeles Times*, March 2, 1996, A10.

34. Pat Buchanan, "Homosexuals and Retribution," *New York Post*, May 24, 1983, 38.

35. Adam Nagourney, "Christian Coalition Pushes for Showdown on Same-Sex Marriage," *New York Times*, May 30, 1996, A19.

36. Drew, *Showdown*, 105–106.

37. Drew, *Showdown*, 23.

38. Katharine Q. Seelye, "Dole Is Imploring Voters to 'Rise Up' Against the Press," *New York Times*, October 26, 1996, 1.

39. Dave Lesher, "Huffington, Alleging Fraud, May Take Case to Senate," *Los Angeles Times*, November 29, 1994, A1.

CHAPTER 10: HIGH CRIMES

1. Gillon, *The Pact*, chaps. 12 and 13.

2. Gillon, *The Pact*, 189.

3. David Brock, "My Scandalmongering Problem—and Ours," *Weekly Standard*, January 27, 1997, 23–26.

4. David Brock, "Confessions of a Right-Wing Hit Man," *Esquire*, July 1, 1997, 53–55, 106–107.

5. Phil Kuntz, "Citizen Scaife: Heir Turned Publisher Uses Financial Largess to Fuel Conservatism," *Wall Street Journal*, October 12, 1995, A1.

6. David Brock, *Blinded by the Right: The Conscience of an Ex-Conservative* (New York: Crown, 2002).

7. David Brock, "The Real Anita Hill," *American Spectator* (March 1992): 18–30; Brock, *Blinded by the Right*, 105.

8. Brock, *Blinded by the Right*, 117; Jane Mayer and Jill Abramson, *Strange Justice: The Selling of Clarence Thomas* (Boston: Houghton Mifflin, 1994).

9. Ed Vulliamy, "The Right Goes Gunning for Clinton," *Observer* (London), May 15, 1994, 13.

10. Brock, "Living with the Clintons," *American Spectator* (January 1994): 18–30; Laura Blumenfeld, "Bill Clinton's Worst Friend," *Washington Post*, December 30, 1993, C1.

11. Brock, "Living with the Clintons," 18–24.

12. Lloyd Grove, "It Isn't Easy Being Right," *Washington Post*, February 14, 1994.

13. Sidney Blumenthal, "The Friends of Paula Jones," *New Yorker*, June 20, 1994, 38–43; Foege, *Empire God Built*, 155–162.

14. Jeff Gerth, "Clintons Joined S. & L. Operator in an Ozark Real-Estate Venture," *New York Times*, March 8, 1992, A1; Gwen Ifill, "Hillary Clinton Takes Questions on Whitewater," *New York Times*, April 23, 1994, 1.

15. Peter Baker, "One Death Altered Path of Presidency," *Washington Post*, July 20, 1998, A1.

16. Joe Conason, *The Hunting of the President: The Ten-Year Campaign to Destroy Bill and Hillary Clinton* (New York: St. Martin's Press, 2000), 83; John Aloysius Farrell, "White House Cleared in Death of Aide," *Boston Globe*, July 1, 1994, 1; Rosenwald, *Talk Radio's America*, 87.

17. Robert O'Harrow Jr. and Michael Kranish, "After Investigating a President, Kavanaugh Reversed," *Washington Post*, August 3, 2018, A1.

18. Philip Wise, "Clinton Crazy," *New York Times Magazine*, February 23, 1997, 34–41, 59–63; Stephen Labaton, "A Report on His Suicide Portrays a Deeply Troubled Vince Foster," *New York Times*, October 11, 1997, A1; Ellen Joan Pollock, "Vince Foster's Death Is a Lively Business for Conspiracy Buffs," *Wall Street Journal*, March 23, 1995, A1; Christopher Ruddy, *The Strange Death of Vince Foster: An Investigation* (New York: Free Press, 1997), 239.

19. Ann Devroy, "Clinton Foes Voice Their Disdain, Loud and Clear," *Washington Post*, May 22, 1994, A1; Wise, "Clinton Crazy."

20. Susan Estrich, "Can It Be Possible? Attack Videos Prove Politics Can Indeed Get Dirtier," *Los Angeles Times*, July 3, 1994, 2; Wise, "Clinton Crazy."

21. Patrick Matrisciana, dir., *The Clinton Chronicles* (Citizens' Video Press, 1994).

22. Wise, "Clinton Crazy"; Pollock, "Vince Foster's Death Is a Lively Business for Conspiracy Buffs."

23. Larry Margasak, "As Committee Chairman, Veteran Republican Seeks to Change Profile," *Associated Press*, December 8, 1996.

24. Howard Kurtz, "The Blonde Flinging Bombshells at Bill Clinton," *Washington Post*, October 16, 1998, D1.

25. Kurtz, "The Blonde Flinging Bombshells at Bill Clinton."

26. Michael Isikoff, *Uncovering Clinton: A Reporter's Story* (New York: Crown, 1999), 182–185; Daley, "Ann Coulter"; Brock, *Blinded by the Right*, 182.

27. Gillon, *The Pact*, 226–238.

28. Laura Ingraham, "The Folly of Impeachment Chic," *Washington Post*, October 26, 1997, C1.

29. Gillon, *The Pact*, 232; Tom Squitieri, "Clinton Troubles Ripe for Republican Attack," *USA Today*, November 7, 1996, 7; Mark Sherman, "Gingrich Keeps Safe Distance from Barr Impeachment Bill," *Atlanta Constitution*, November 6, 1997, A14.

30. Ingraham, "The Folly of Impeachment Chic."

31. Gillon, *The Pact*, 232–233.

32. Lloyd Grove, "Clinton's Public Enemy," *Washington Post*, February 10, 1998, E1; Gillon, *The Pact*, 236.

33. Gillon, *The Pact*, 258.

34. Kennedy, "Big Story—Dumb Plot," *New York Daily News*, September 12, 1998, 6.

35. Gillon, *The Pact*, 256.

36. "The Speaker Steps Down; Excerpts from Phone Call About Gingrich's Future," *New York Times*, November 8, 1998, A24.

37. William Neikirk and Mike Dorning, "Speaker-Elect Admits Illicit Sexual Affairs," *Chicago Tribune*, December 18, 1998.

38. Kate O'Beirne, "Moderate Ambitions," *National Review*, December 31, 1998, 28–29.

39. Rosenwald, *Talk Radio's America*, 105; Emmett Tyrrell, *The Impeachment of William Jefferson Clinton: A Political Docu-drama* (Washington, DC: Regnery, 1997).

40. Brock, *Blinded by the Right*, 275–279.

41. Matthew Lysiak, *The Drudge Revolution: The Untold Story of How Talk Radio, Fox News, and a Gift Shop Clerk with an Internet Connection Took Down the Mainstream Media* (Dallas, TX: BenBella Books, 2020), chap. 13; Brock, *Blinded by the Right*, 281–283; Sherman, *Loudest Voice*, 228.

42. Mark Jurkowitz and Don Aucoin, "Questions Still Shadow Scandal's Impact," *Boston Globe*, February 14, 1999, A27; Lisa de Moraes, "In the Ratings, One Crisis Leads to Others," *Washington Post*, December 23, 1998, C7; "All-News TV Loses Viewers After Trial," *New York Times*, February 26, 1999, A14; David Usborne, "Bedroom Chill: Hillary Ready to Leave Bill?," *Hamilton Spectator*, March 12, 1999, C1.

43. Daley, "Ann Coulter"; *Politically Incorrect*, episode dated March 31, 1998.

CHAPTER 11: THE LAST REAGANITE

1. "George W. Reagan," *New York Post*, November 23, 1999, 38; Eric Pooley, "Meet George W. Reagan," *Time*, June 28, 1999, 39; Joseph Weber, "Just Call Him George W. Reagan," *Business Week*, January 28, 2003; Bill Keller, "Reagan's Son," *New York Times Magazine*, January 26, 2003, 26–31, 42–44, 62.

2. Frank Bruni, "Bush Softens View of G.O.P. After Outcry by Conservatives," *New York Times,* October 7, 1999, 28.

3. Lou Cannon and Carl Cannon, *Reagan's Disciple: George W. Bush's Troubled Quest for a Presidential Legacy* (New York: PublicAffairs, 2008).

4. Paul West and Ellen Gamerman, "Buchanan Leaps to Reform with Jabs at Major Parties," *Baltimore Sun,* October 26, 1999, 1A.

5. Stanley, *The Crusader,* 323; "Road to the White House 2000: Iowa Republican Straw Poll," C-SPAN, August 14, 1999, www.c-span.org/video /?151527-1/iowa-republican-straw-poll.

6. Stanley, *The Crusader,* 334–335.

7. Pat Buchanan, *A Republic, Not an Empire: Reclaiming America's Destiny* (Washington, DC: Regnery, 1999).

8. Francis X. Clines, "Trump Quits Grand Old Party for New," *New York Times,* October 25, 1999, A28; Francis X. Clines, "Buchanan's Views on Hitler Create a Reform Party Stir," *New York Times,* September 21, 1999, A22.

9. On the 2000 recount, see Jeffrey Toobin, *Too Close to Call: The Thirty-Six-Day Battle to Decide the 2000 Election* (New York: Random House, 2001).

10. Paul D. Colford, "No Plans, Yet, for Return to Media," *New York Daily News,* November 21, 2000, 38.

11. Pat Buchanan, "U.S. Pays the High Price of Empire," *Los Angeles Times,* September 18, 2001, B9.

12. Quoted in Spindel, "'Human Beings First, Women Second,'" 172–173.

13. Spindel, "'Human Beings First, Women Second,'" 173–174.

14. *Politically Incorrect,* episode dated September 17, 2001.

15. "Press Briefing by Ari Fleischer," The White House: President George W. Bush, September 26, 2001, https://georgewbush-whitehouse .archives.gov/news/releases/2001/09/text/20010926-5.html.

16. William Bunch, *The Backlash: Right-Wing Radicals, Hi-Def Hucksters, and Paranoid Politics in the Age of Obama* (New York: Harper, 2010), 57; Howard Kurtz, "National Review Cans Columnist Ann Coulter," *Washington Post,* October 2, 2001; Jonah Goldberg, "L'Affaire Coulter," *National Review Online,* October 2, 2001, www.nationalreview.com/2001/10 /laffaire-coulter-jonah-goldberg.

17. Pat Buchanan, *The Death of the West: How Dying Populations and Immigrant Invasions Imperil Our Country and Civilization* (New York: Thomas Dunne Books, 2002), 225.

18. David Carr, "For Buchanan, a New Pulpit and Target," *New York Times*, September 9, 2002, C1; Jim Rutenberg, "Cable's War Coverage Suggests a New 'Fox Effect' on Television Journalism," *New York Times*, April 16, 2003, B9.

19. "Fox News Channel's Talk Show Host Sean Hannity Signs Long-Term Contract with ABC Radio Networks," U.S. Newswire, August 29, 2001, 1; Peter Johnson, "Fox News Surges Past CNN in Total Ratings," *USA Today*, January 30, 2002, D3; Jim Rutenberg, "Fox Portrays a War of Good and Evil, and Many Applaud," *New York Times*, December 3, 2001, C1; Sherman, *Loudest Voice*, 251–252, 267.

20. Sean Hannity, *Let Freedom Ring: Winning the War of Liberty over Liberalism* (New York: Regan Books, 2002); Sean Hannity, *Deliver Us from Evil: Defeating Terrorism, Despotism, and Liberalism* (New York: Regan Books, 2004); Laura Ingraham, *Shut Up and Sing: How Elites from Hollywood, Politics, and the UN Are Subverting America* (Washington, DC: Regnery Publishing, 2003); Ann Coulter, *Treason: Liberal Treachery from the Cold War to the War on Terrorism* (New York: Crown Forum, 2003); Michael Savage, *The Enemy Within: Saving America from the Liberal Assault on Our Schools, Faith, and Military* (New York: Thomas Nelson, 2004); Michelle Malkin, *Unhinged: Exposing Liberals Gone Wild* (Washington, DC: Regnery, 2005).

21. Dinesh D'Souza, *The Enemy at Home: The Cultural Left and Its Responsibility for 9/11* (New York: Doubleday, 2007), 26.

22. Alan Wolfe, "None (but Me) Dare Call It Treason," *New York Times*, January 21, 2007; NR Symposium, "The Enemy D'Souza Knows," *National Review*, March 16, 2007, www.nationalreview.com/2007/03/enemy-dsouza-knows-nro-symposium; Dinesh D'Souza, "The Closing of the Conservative Mind," *National Review*, March 12, 2007, www.nationalreview.com/2007/03/closing-conservative-mind-part-i-dinesh-dsouza.

23. Lloyd Grove and Hudson Morgan, "'Hardball' or 'Slimeball'?," *New York Daily News*, August 24, 2004, 37.

24. Howard Kurtz, "A Hard Right Punch," *Washington Post*, February 16, 2007, C1.

25. Cathy Young, "The Achilles' Heel of Conservatism," *Newsday*, December 3, 2019, 22.

26. George W. Bush, "Remarks Prior to Discussions with President Megawati Sukarnoputri of Indonesia and an Exchange with Reporters," American Presidency Project, September 19, 2001, www.presidency.ucsb

.edu/documents/remarks-prior-discussions-with-president-megawati -sukarnoputri-indonesia-and-exchange-with. On the War on Terror, see Jane Mayer, *The Dark Side: The Inside Story of How the War on Terror Turned into a War on American Ideals* (New York: Doubleday, 2008).

27. Michael Brice-Saddler and Eli Rosenberg, "Fox News Host Tucker Carlson Uses Racist, Homophobic Language in Second Set of Recordings," *Washington Post*, March 11, 2019, www.washingtonpost.com/arts -entertainment/2019/03/12/new-tucker-carlson-audio-released-this-time -using-racist-homophobic-language.

28. Reed Irvine and Cliff Kincaid, "Immigration as a National Security Issue," *Human Events*, November 11, 2002, 21.

29. Laurence McQuillan and Mimi Hall, "Fox Urges Bush to Speed Immigration Reform," *USA Today*, September 6, 2001, A4.

30. "Good Beginning: The McCain-Kolbe-Flake Border Act Could Launch a Humane Immigration Policy," *Arizona Republic*, July 29, 2003, B8; Rachel L. Swarns, "Republicans Put Immigration Laws Back on Political Agenda," *New York Times*, August 4, 2003, A9.

31. Joseph A. D'Agostino, "Immigration Hawks: McCain-Flake Bill Is Amnesty in Disguise," *Human Events*, September 1, 2003, 5; Daniel Gonzalez, "Ariz. Immigration Fight Divides GOP, Pits State Group vs. U.S. Lawmakers," *Arizona Republic*, September 2, 2003, B1; Eduardo Porter, "A Republican Divide Widens," *Wall Street Journal*, December 12, 2003, A4.

32. "Rep. Tom Tancredo's Mass Immigration Reduction Act of 2001 Recognizes Impact of Immigration on Nation Says FAIR," U.S. Newswire, August 3, 2001; Julia Malone, "Immigration Gadfly at Odds with Bush GOP," *Atlanta Journal*, June 21, 2002, B1; Tamar Jacoby, "For the GOP, Immigration Carries a Lot of Baggage," *Washington Post*, December 21, 2003, B2.

33. Kwan Yuk Pan, "Immigration Campaigner Sees 'Tower of Babel' Threat to U.S. Identity," *Financial Times*, February 8, 2006; Michael Roberts, "The Flag-Bearer," *Westword*, July 3, 2003.

34. Ingraham, *Shut Up and Sing*, 217.

35. Jim Rutenberg, "As Talk Radio Wavers, Bush Moves to Firm Up Support," *New York Times*, October 17, 2006, A16.

36. Greg Giroux, "Democrats Retake House on Strength of Bush's Unpopularity and GOP Scandals," *New York Times*, November 8, 2006, https:// archive.nytimes.com/www.nytimes.com/cq/2006/11/08/cq_1923.html.

37. McKay Coppins, "The Bow-Tied Bard of Populism," *The Atlantic*, February 23, 2017, www.theatlantic.com/politics/archive/2017/02/tucker -carlson-interview/516231; Laura Ingraham, *Billionaire at the Barricades: What I Saw at the Populist Revolt* (New York: All Points Books, 2017), 103–106.

38. Daniel Casse, "Is Bush a Conservative?," *Commentary*, February 2004, 19–26; Rutenberg, "As Talk Radio Wavers."

39. Rosenwald, *Talk Radio's America*, 146–148.

40. Peter Hamby, "Conservative Bloggers in Full Revolt over Immigration," *CNN*, June 15, 2007. http://edition.cnn.com/2007/POLITICS/06 /15/bloggers.bush.

41. Jim Rutenberg, "Bush Calls Attacks on Immigration Bill 'Empty Political Rhetoric,'" *New York Times*, May 30, 2007, A16.

42. Hamby, "Conservative Bloggers in Full Revolt over Immigration."

43. Andrew Ross Sorkin, *Too Big to Fail: The Inside Story of How Wall Street and Washington Fought to Save the Financial System—and Themselves* (New York: Viking, 2009).

44. Tim Alberta, *American Carnage: On the Front Lines of the Republican Civil War and the Rise of President Trump* (New York: HarperCollins, 2019), 25–34.

CHAPTER 12: THE TRIUMPH OF PITCHFORK POLITICS

1. Frank Newport, "Limbaugh, Gingrich, Cheney Seen as Speaking for GOP," Gallup, June 10, 2009, https://news.gallup.com/poll/120806 /limbaugh-gingrich-cheney-seen-speaking-gop.aspx.

2. Brian Stelter, "A Lucrative Deal for Rush Limbaugh," *New York Times*, July 3, 2008, www.nytimes.com/2008/07/03/business/media/03radio.html; Adam Nagourney, "After Tussle on G.O.P. Title, an Apology to Limbaugh," *New York Times*, March 3, 2009, A17.

3. "Limbaugh: I Hope Obama Fails," *The Rush Limbaugh Show*, January 16, 2009, www.rushlimbaugh.com/daily/2009/01/16/limbaugh_i_hope _obama_fails.

4. David Sirota, "Pinstriped Populist," *New York Times*, November 12, 2006.

5. Ken Auletta, "Mad as Hell," *New Yorker*, November 26, 2006, F15.

6. Ponce de Leon, *That's the Way It Is*, 274–275.

7. Peter Dreier and Christopher R. Martin, "How ACORN Was Framed: Political Controversy and Media Agenda Setting," *Perspectives on Politics* 8, no. 3 (September 2010): 761–792.

8. For a study of media coverage around ACORN from 2007 to 2008 and the backlash to it in right-wing media, see Peter Dreier and Christopher R. Martin, "The News Media, the Conservative Echo Chamber, and the Battle over Acorn: How Two Academics Fought in the Framing Wars," *Humanity & Society* 35 (February–May 2011): 4–30.

9. Max Blumenthal, "Queen of the Birthers," *Daily Beast,* July 20, 2009, www.thedailybeast.com/queen-of-the-birthers; Michael Calderone, "'Birther' Coverage Hits Fever Pitch," *Politico,* August 10, 2009, www.politico.com/story/2009/08/birther-coverage-hits-fever-pitch-025933.

10. James P. Pinkerton, "Time to Recognize the Delegates from Cyberspace," *Newsday,* November 3, 1998, 30, 32; "Rally Supporting Clinton Investigation," C-SPAN, October 31, 1998, www.c-span.org/video/?114519-1/rally-supporting-clinton-investigation.

11. Peter Wallsten, "In 'Birther' Movement, a Natural-Born Salesman," *South Florida Sun-Sentinel,* January 31, 2010, A21.

12. Matea Gold, "CNN Chief Addresses Obama Birth Controversy," *Los Angeles Times,* July 25, 2009.

13. James Rainey, "A Natural-Born Canard About Obama," *Los Angeles Times,* July 22, 2009, 1.

14. David A. Kaplan, "Will the Real Lou Dobbs Please Stand Up?," *Fortune,* January 4, 2010.

15. Laura Stampler, "At Tea Party Convention, Lou Dobbs Avoids Immigration Issues," *The Nation,* October 11, 2010, www.thenation.com/article/archive/tea-party-convention-lou-dobbs-avoids-immigration-issues.

16. David Weigel, "Virginia Tea Party Patriots Convention: Lou Dobbs and the Next Tea Party Convention," *Slate,* October 8, 2010, https://slate.com/news-and-politics/2010/10/virginia-tea-party-patriots-convention-lou-dobbs-and-the-next-tea-party-convention.html.

17. Alexander Burns, "Dobbs Mulls White House Bid," *Politico,* November 24, 2009, www.politico.com/story/2009/11/dobbs-mulls-white-house-bid-029861.

18. Isabel Macdonald, "Lou Dobbs, American Hypocrite," *The Nation,* October 25, 2010, 11–15; *The Charlie Rose Show,* episode dated December 12, 2006.

19. Jeanne Marie Laskas, "¿Qué Pasa, Lou?," *GQ,* April 14, 2010.

20. Eric Etheridge, "Rick Santelli: Tea Party Time," *New York Times*, February 20, 2009, https://opinionator.blogs.nytimes.com/2009/02/20/rick -santelli-tea-party-time.

21. On the tea party, see Theda Skocpol and Vanessa Williamson, *The Tea Party and the Remaking of Republican Conservatism* (New York: Oxford University Press, 2012); Rachel M. Blum, *How the Tea Party Captured the GOP: Insurgent Factions in American Politics* (Chicago: University of Chicago Press, 2020); Khadijah Costley White, *The Branding of Right-Wing Activism: The News Media and the Tea Party* (New York: Oxford University Press, 2018).

22. Joseph Farah, *None of the Above: Why 2008 Is the Year to Cast the Ultimate Protest Vote* (Los Angeles: WND Books), 77.

23. Kevin Bohn, "Gun Sales Surge After Obama's Election," *CNN*, November 11, 2008, www.cnn.com/2008/CRIME/11/11/obama.gun.sales; Andy Green, "The Militia Movement's Frightening Comeback," *Baltimore Sun*, March 31, 2010, www.baltimoresun.com/bs-mtblog-2010-03-the _militia_movements_frighten-story.html.

24. Robert Costa, "Gingrich: Obama's 'Kenyan, Anti-colonial' Worldview," *National Review Online*, September 11, 2010, www.nationalreview .com/corner/gingrich-obamas-kenyan-anti-colonial-worldview-robert-costa.

25. Dinesh D'Souza, "How Obama Thinks," *Forbes*, September 9, 2010, www.nationalreview.com/corner/246302/gingrich-obama-s-kenyan-anti -colonial-worldview-robert-costa; Daniel Larison, "Obama, Anticolonial Hegemonist?," *American Conservative*, September 9, 2010, www.theamerican conservative.com/larison/obama-anticolonial-hegemonist.

26. Dylan Byers, "The Influence of Dinesh D'Souza," *Politico*, July 25, 2014, www.politico.com/blogs/media/2014/07/the-influence-of-dinesh -dsouza-192867.

27. Doug Robinson, "Making a Better Glenn Beck," *Deseret News*, December 2, 2007, A1; "Glenn Beck," *CNN Transcripts*, September 22, 2008, https://transcripts.cnn.com/show/gb/date/2008-09-22/segment/01.

28. Alexander Zaitchick, *Common Nonsense: Glenn Beck and the Triumph of Ignorance* (Hoboken, NJ: Wiley, 2010), 130, 137.

29. Zaitchick, *Common Nonsense*, chap. 13.

30. Michael Grunwald, "The Party of No: New Details on the GOP Plot to Obstruct Obama," *Time*, August 23, 2012, https://swampland .time.com/2012/08/23/the-party-of-no-new-details-on-the-gop-plot-to -obstruct-obama.

31. On Republican obstruction, see Alberta, *American Carnage*; Michael Grunwald, *The New New Deal: The Hidden Story of Change in the Obama Era* (New York: Simon & Schuster, 2012).

32. Neil King Jr., "In Delaware, Tea Party Gains Newest Star," *Wall Street Journal*, September 15, 2010; Andy Barr and Tim Grieve, "Meet Christine O'Donnell," *Politico*, September 15, 2010.

33. Meghan Daum, "Christine O'Donnell's Real Roots," *Los Angeles Times*, September 23, 2010, A27.

34. Andy Barr, "The GOP's No-Compromise Pledge," *Politico*, October 28, 2010, www.politico.com/story/2010/10/the-gops-no-compromise-pledge-044311.

35. Kevin Sack, "Romney on Healthcare: A Particular Spin," *New York Times*, April 10, 2010, A12.

36. Nicole Hemmer, "The Boys Who Cried Fox," *New York Times*, April 19, 2012, https://campaignstops.blogs.nytimes.com/2012/04/19/the-boys-who-cried-fox.

37. Republican primary debate, Reagan Presidential Library, September 16, 2015, http://edition.cnn.com/TRANSCRIPTS/1509/20/sotu.01.html.

38. Paul Bond, "Leslie Moonves on Donald Trump: 'It May Not Be Good for America, but It's Damn Good for CBS,'" *Hollywood Reporter*, February 29, 2016, www.hollywoodreporter.com/news/general-news/leslie-moonves-donald-trump-may-871464.

39. "Trump Resonates Because Millions of People Are Sick of Political Correctness, Phony Outrage and Phony Apologies," *The Rush Limbaugh Show*, August 10, 2015, www.rushlimbaugh.com/daily/2015/08/10/trump_resonates_because_millions_of_people_are_sick_of_political_correctness_phony_outrage_and_phony_apologies.

40. Chris Cillizza, "Pat Buchanan Says Donald Trump Is the Future of the Republican Party," *Washington Post*, January 12, 2016, www.washingtonpost.com/news/the-fix/wp/2016/01/12/pat-buchanan-believes-donald-trump-is-the-future-of-the-republican-party.

Index

JANELLE GONZALES

NICOLE HEMMER is a political historian and founding director of the Carolyn T. and Robert M. Rogers Center for the Study of the Presidency at Vanderbilt University. The cofounder of Made by History, the historical analysis section of the *Washington Post*, she writes regularly for the *New York Times*, CNN, *Vox*, and *Politico*. She lives in Nashville.